Charles Isaac Elton

The Career of Columbus

Charles Isaac Elton

The Career of Columbus

ISBN/EAN: 9783743324374

Manufactured in Europe, USA, Canada, Australia, Japa

Cover: Foto ©ninafisch / pixelio.de

Manufactured and distributed by brebook publishing software (www.brebook.com)

Charles Isaac Elton

The Career of Columbus

THE
CAREER OF COLUMBUS

BY

CHARLES ISAAC ELTON, M. P.

NEW YORK
CASSELL PUBLISHING COMPANY
104 & 106 FOURTH AVENUE

COPYRIGHT, 1892, BY
CASSELL PUBLISHING COMPANY.

All rights reserved.

THE MERSHON COMPANY PRESS,
RAHWAY, N. J.

THE CAREER OF COLUMBUS.

CHAPTER I.

> "Here and there on sandy beaches
> A milky-belled amaryllis blew.
> How young Columbus seemed to rove
> Yet present in his natal grove,
> Now watching high on mountain cornice,
> And steering now from a purple cove."

"CHRISTOPHER COLUMBUS of famous memory," when he began to acquaint the world with his plans, "was not only derided and generally mocked, even here in England, but afterward became a laughing-stock to the Spaniards themselves." So ran the report of Sir Humphrey Gilbert, that valiant and worthy gentleman, when new discoveries were being planned; and he added that the whole scheme of Columbus was accounted "a fantastical imagination and a drowsie dreame."

Moreover, while the admiral was attending the king and queen in Castile, in how many ways was he not put to shame. "Some scorned the wildness of his garments, some took occasion to jest at his simple looks, others asked 'if this were he that louts so low, that took upon him to bring men into a country that aboundeth with gold, pearle, and precious stones?' 'Nay!' they said, 'but if he were such a man, he would look somewhat loftier, and carry another kind of countenance.' Thus some judged him by his garments, and others by his look and countenance; but none entered into the consideration of the inward man."

A sudden turn of fortune brought wealth and honor to the poor exile who had been jeered at as one of the "vain and deceitful Ligurians," hardly endured by the cold-tempered king, a boaster tolerated only by the queen's kindness. When the cross was raised over Granada, and the King Chiquito was bewailing his fate to his Moorish ladies, the patient inventor had his share of luck with the rest. Genoa had refused his gifts, and Portugal had endeavored to rob him; France and England were hesitating and faint in their offers. The victory of the Catholic kings disposed them to make a slight effort toward a greater success. There was a seaport in Spain which lay at the mercy of the crown for defaults in dues and services; and many of its inhabitants were either convicted of crime or were held liable to exemplary punishment. The penalty was laid upon them of finding ships and men for the new voyage to Cathay, to sail into death and chaos, as their neighbors thought, and to expend themselves in a wicked and desperate adventure; to sail beyond the sunset, as Columbus hoped, to the great city of Cambalu and its golden mountains, to the rivers that flowed from Paradise and the riches of the land of Havilah.

Nothing could be more unjust than the attacks which had been made upon Columbus. Writing to Ferdinand and Isabella in 1501 he said, "It is now forty years that I have been sailing to all the countries at present frequented." He had conversed with scholars from all parts, "Latins, Greeks, Indians, and Moors." He had been very skillful in navigation, "knowing enough in astronomy," and well versed in geometry and mathematics. "During all this time I have seen, or endeavored to see, all books of cosmography, history, philosophy, and other sciences; so that our Lord has sensibly opened my understanding, to the end that I might sail from here to the Indies, and made me most willing to put it into execution. Filled with this desire I came to your highnesses. All that heard of my undertaking rejected it with contempt and scorn. In your highnesses alone faith and constancy held their seat." He had, in fact, a strong sense of personal dignity. Pride kept him on a level with the kings who were discussing or patronizing his plans, and he would never abate a jot of the honors to which he conceived himself to be entitled. It was his natural courtesy and sweetness of temper that had been mistaken for servility.

After his great success he seems to have been reticent about his early life, though he would explain a doubt or difficulty by referring to his stores of experience. Even to his son Don Ferdinand, who afterward wrote his life, he spoke very briefly about their family affairs. "I and mine," he would say, "were always traders by sea"; and on another occasion he wrote, "I was not the first admiral in our family." "Of his voyages to the east and west," says the biographer, "and many other things about his early days, I have no perfect knowledge, because he died when I was confined by my filial duty, and had not the boldness to ask him to give me an account of them, or (to speak the truth), being but young, I was at that time far from being troubled with such thoughts." It happened for these reasons that the first part of the biography was somewhat blurred and indistinct; we have to infer from a casual remark, or a formality in a legal document; how Columbus passed his youth and early manhood, how he traded and fought and explored in the Levant, or among the Atlantic Islands; how he came to the Torrid Zone at "St. George of the Gold Mine" in Guinea, or sailed within the Arctic Circle "a hundred leagues beyond Thule."

It was of importance at one time to discover the exact place of his birth and the social standing of his family, although his son very sensibly remarked that he was personally indifferent whether the admiral's father was a merchant, or a man of quality that kept his hawks and hounds; "and certainly there have been a thousand such in all parts, whose memory has been utterly lost in a very short time among their neighbors and kindred." He thought, however, that his father's merits should have saved him from being classed among mechanics. It must have been generally known that the admiral's father was a tradesman, a Genoese weaver; at one time, perhaps, the owner of a trading vessel, at another keeping an inn at Savona. But when Giustiniani said that Columbus was of a "poor and humble stock," in his note upon the nineteenth Psalm, Don Ferdinand was ready at once with a fierce contradiction. The facts might be true, he argued, but the implication was false. The admiral belonged to no humble tribe or class of handicraftsmen. One ought to say rather that the Columbi were of the best blood, a caste of soldiers and statesmen, reduced, no doubt, in the civil wars and by the peevishness of fortune into somewhat humble circumstances. How indelicate was the style of this base scribe, quite unacquainted, evidently, with the courtesies of literature. He might have said, as authors generally do in such cases, that the admiral's relations were poor and his surroundings lowly, without bringing in such blunt and injurious phrases. It is not easy to follow all the arguments which were adduced to support the admiral's dignity. One can understand the minute patriotism which seeks to connect a particular town with the life of the discoverer of America, but it is strange that a man's reputation should have fallen or risen according to the merits of his birthplace. Yet we are assured that those were most respected who were born in places of importance, and this as a matter of genuine sentiment, and not merely because it is useful to be "the citizen of no mean city."

"It happens," said Don Ferdinand, "that some who wish to cast a cloud on his fame will say, 'He was of Nervi,' and others, 'He was of Cogoletto,' or 'of Bogliasco,' which are all little places near Genoa, and upon the adjoining coast. Others again say, by way of exalting him, 'He was of Savona,' or 'a citizen of Genoa.' Some have soared higher still, and have made him out to belong to Piacenza, where there are indeed some honorable persons of his family, and tombs with the arms and inscriptions of the Columbi." So again we read in the Eulogies of Paolo Giovio, with reference to the Como portrait: "How one must wonder that a man of such fine presence and such commanding intellect should have been born in a rude hamlet like Albisola!" If it is asked whether the true birthplace is known, or whether all these places are like the cities which strove in vain for Homer, the answer must be that Columbus probably knew the facts, and that he claimed to have been born in Genoa. Twice in his last will he makes the assertion; he calls himself "nacido in Genova," and charged his estate with the maintenance in that city of some member of his family, to represent his memory there, and to take footing and root as a native, "because thence I came and there was I born." Columbus was born in 1445, or in the following year. His parents had a residence about that time in Quinto, but there is reason to believe that they had a house in Genoa, which they visited from time to time before they took up their permanent abode, about the year 1451, in the weavers' quarter near St. Andrew's Gate.

Modern inquiry has cleared up the controversies about the original home of the family. A vast inheritance and splendid dignities lay vacant when the admiral's direct male issue came to an end in the fourth generation. A host of competitors, of course, appeared before the Spanish tribunals, provided for the most part with false pedigrees and sham traditions, desiring to prove heirship by showing that they came from places where the family had been established. The pleadings in the great lawsuit, which are still preserved, show that several of the claimants went so far as to trace their titles to persons with the same name as the admiral's father; alleged, moreover, in each case to have had sons with names exactly answering to those of the admiral and his brothers. The mere similarity of a family surname would not have carried them far. The name "Colombo," with slight local variations, was common in France and Italy. It occurred in Spain and in Corsica, and was not unknown in England. It may easily have been derived independently in different places from some common word like "Colonus."

The claim of Cugureo, now called Cogoletto, to be the true home of the family was long accepted as genuine. This, no doubt, was owing to the local traditions about an old house in the village, shown as one of the numerous residences ascribed to Columbus. The evidence in reality goes all the other way. Don Ferdinand tells us that he visited the place in the hope of getting information about his father. "As I passed through Cugureo I tried to learn something from two brothers there who were of the family of the Colombi; they were among the richest people in those parts, and were said to be related to the admiral, but the younger of the two was over a hundred years old, and so they could give me no account of the matter." While the lawsuit was pending, in 1583, a poor peasant named Bernardo Colombo came from Cogoletto to put in a claim to the title. His title rested upon a supposed relationship to a certain Domenico Colombo of that town, alleged to have been the admiral's father; but, though he was strongly supported by the republic of Genoa, his claim was rejected for want of proof. Baldassare Colombo, of Cuccaro, claimed through another Domenico, lord of a castle at that place, who was also set up as "the father of Christopher Columbus." But, though the names in his pedigree were correct, it came out that this ancestor had died in 1456, nearly thirty years before the admiral's father, Domenico Colombo the weaver, was known to have died. The rejection of these claims disposed of the assertions that the family had come to Cogoletto or Cuccaro from Piacenza, or had moved down in more ancient times from Montferrat. There was, however, another title set up for the Columbi of Piacenza. Some of them had been established in Genoa as early as the thirteenth century; and it was said that an important document, dated in 1481, distinctly stated that Domenico Colombo of Piacenza had two sons, Christopher and Bartholomew, who had migrated to Genoa about ten years before that time, and had sailed away afterward "to islands unknown." This document was never produced, and the claim was rejected for that reason. It was also observed that the arms on the houses and tombs of the Colombi at Piacenza were different to those which were used by Columbus himself. It had been suggested that the admiral could have inherited no coat-of-arms, because his relations were merely craftsmen; and it is quite true that his family had not, and perhaps could not legally have had, any place on the roll of the nobles of Genoa. But, after all, we must attach importance to the assertions of the admiral about his own affairs. The weaver's son may have been entitled to a heraldic coat which he put away while he tended the loom, as the noble in the story takes his sword from under the counter and untucks it when he has made his fortune. The arms of the family at Piacenza were of the emblematic or "speaking" kind, the surname being symbolized by three doves. When Columbus returned from his first voyage he was told to meet the Spanish kings-at-arms, that they might prepare the proper augmentations for the arms which he usually bore. The well known shield was blazoned under his personal direction, with the royal quarterings of the Lion of Leon, and the Tower of Castile, the symbolical anchors, and the islands and continent of the Indies; but he took care to retain his ancestral bearings, which duly appear as "a shield *or*, with a band *azure*, and the chef *gules*."

Don Ferdinand was sometimes rebuked for not making out a better pedigree. Friends asked why his father should not have been shown to come straight from "Junius Colonus" (or "Junius Cilo" as they should have said), who conquered the kingdom of Pontus, and brought Mithridates in bonds to Rome? Why not, again, prove a connection with "the two illustrious Coloni, his predecessors, who gained a mighty victory over the Venetians"? This refers, of course, to the sea fight off Cape St. Vincent in 1485, more fully mentioned in a later chapter.

It is enough to say here that the description of the battle cited by Don Ferdinand is wrong in several particulars. "There was," he says, "a famous man called Columbus, of the admiral's name and family, renowned upon the sea on account of the fleet which he commanded against the Infidels, as well as for the country to which he belonged, insomuch that they used his name to frighten the children in their cradles." He was known as "Columbus the younger," to distinguish him from another who was a great sailor before him. The last words refer to Guillaume Coulon, who created the French navy under Louis the Eleventh. This man had a famous son, well known as "the pirate Columbus," under whom the admiral served for several years. This "younger Columbus" of the biography seems to have been a Genoese subject; and from this some have taken him to be the same person as "Colombo of Oneglia," who was hanged at Genoa in 1492 for acts of piracy against the French. We shall deal with their adventures later on. At present it is only necessary to observe that Don Ferdinand made many excuses about the alleged relationship. He gloried indeed in the victory over Venice, which he ascribed to a Genoese corsair. But the admiral, he said, wanted no connection with courts and great men; he was, on the contrary, like the sailors and fishermen who had been chosen as apostles. He ought to be blamed or praised on his own merits. The "Admiral of the Ocean" required no shield or emblematic doves; he was himself the "Columbus" or messenger of hope, the "Christophorus" who bore the banner of the faith. By his own wish, moreover, he was known as "Colon," rather than as one of the family of the "Colombi"; and it might be for some good reason that he had thus severed his direct line from those collateral branches.

CHAPTER II.

> "Often I think of the beautiful town
>   That is seated by the sea,
> Often in thought go up and down
> The pleasant streets of that dear old town,
>   And my youth comes back to me.
>
> "I remember the black wharves and the slips,
>   And the sea-tide tossing free,
> And Spanish sailors with bearded lips,
> And the beauty and mystery of the ships,
>   And the magic of the sea."

THE father of Columbus was Domenico of Terra-Rossa, a weaver by trade, who lived in the suburbs of Genoa, or in one of the neighboring towns, as his business from time to time required. His mother was Susanna, daughter of Giacomo of Fontana-Rossa, a silk weaver working in the same neighborhood. They were married about 1445, either at Domenico's place up in the hills, or at Quinto, where his father had a house by the seaside, and a felucca, as we suppose, for his trading ventures to Alexandria or the Islands. Both families had been long established in the valleys of the Apennines. Terra-Rossa is a hamlet in the

Vale of Fontanabuona, lying above the Lavagna River, a few miles inland from Porto Fino. Fontana-Rossa is a village in the same large valley, set at the very foot of the mountain behind Chiavari. Both families had been drawn closer and closer to Genoa by the attractions of its busy commerce. The weaving trade offered a comfortable subsistence without any need to live within the crowded walls; the spice trade gave a free outlet to all the young men who were ready for adventures at sea. Columbus was born in 1445, or about the beginning of 1446, and at that time his mother's family were settled at Quezzi, a beautiful hamlet in the immediate neighborhood of the city. His own parents lived in the new suburb just outside one of the ancient gates; or, if they changed their abode now and then, went no farther than the seaside at Quinto.

If anyone wishes to see a picture in his mind, showing the places where Columbus spent his youth, he must endeavor to recall the great view from the heights behind Genoa. The gulf curves between the horns of Porto Fino and the "olive-hoary cape" on the Western Riviera. Below the Ligurian Alps are the places connected in truth or by tradition with his memory. At Cogoletto, "in a narrow street and dim," they show the old house where he may have lived, and a picture revered as his portrait. Albisola has grown from a rough hamlet into an expanse of villas and flower gardens. Savona lies beyond, with its port under St. George's Rock, once nearly destroyed by the Genoese, but very flourishing when Columbus sailed in from time to time. Here was the shop where his father made and sold "good cloth of Savona," and the tavern where Susanna looked after the sailor customers; and close to the town lay Valcalda in Legino, where two vineyards were purchased, which involved the whole family in a dreary lawsuit. Looking seaward, the mountains of Corsica recall the fancy that Columbus was a native of the island. Toward the west the view is blocked by the great cape. At San Remo another Columbus, supposed to have been the admiral's kinsman, was born, and made his home; and just behind the promontory is the creek of Oneglia, where the freebooter rested in his lair and divided the spoil with Doria.

We must turn back to Genoa, where Columbus was born and passed a great part of his youth. His parents lived mostly at Quinto until he was four years old; and here his sister Biancinetta and his brothers Giovanni-Pelegrino and Bartholomew were born. The family then came back to live near St. Andrew's Gate, and here was born Giacomo, who was afterward known as "Don Diego."

The course of the old walls, the gate by which Columbus lived, the street on which the shop faced, and its long green lawn in the city moat, are marked by the line of the modern boulevards and public gardens.

We may think of him as visiting the Duomo and the Doria's church, the porch of San Stefano, where the weavers held meetings, and their craft hall in the neighborhood of the Abbey. Down in the port, where he talked with the sailors on the wharves, on one side is the old Mole, where the magistrates hanged Columbus the Rover on a tower, with his friend Bernardo of Sestri; and close to it stands the Bank of St. George, the "Dogana" of our days, with its tiers of statues,

> White and cold,
> Those nichèd shapes of noble mold,
> A princely people's awful princes,
> The grave, severe, Genovese of old.

From the old Mole stretched away the port, filled with ships of all kinds. There were galleys, armed with petronels, three-masters with huge square sails, crowded with a rabble of galley slaves and cross-bowmen to keep them down. One might see galleons arriving from the Levant, or making ready for the Flanders voyage; and long, raking caraccas, better suited for corsair's work than for voyages of commerce and business; and nimble "caravels" from Spain and Portugal, English barks, and pinnacles and trading boats of all kinds. The port was like the harbor of Tyre in the ancient days, and not very different in its actual merchandise.

The principal change was in the places where the commodities were produced. The blocks and bars of tin, the lead and vessels of pewter, came from galleys trading with Southampton, and no longer in the ships of Tarshish. The lawns and camlets of Cyprus had replaced the fine linen and embroideries of Syria. There were raw and spun cottons from Malta as well as from Egypt and India. But the strong wine of Tyre, "the wine of Helbon," was still imported from Palestine in the ships that brought the choice Malmseys from Candia. The "white wools of Damascus" still remained to compete with the "Frankish wools" from London and

Norwich, and the raw wool from the warehouses at Calais; but the best classes of stuffs came from England, such as "Suffolks" and "village medleys," kerseys of all colors, friezes white and unshorn, or "of a looser texture for night wear," and fustians and cloth from Essex and Guildford. The spice trade was a staple industry at Genoa. Her shipmen, like the merchants of Tyre, dealt in myrrh and cassia, the true aloes from Socotra, galbanum and the sweet storax, the scented calamus and the Eastern cinnamon. Here, as in ancient times, one might see the Caspian merchants, who had come with Indian silks, and rhubarb and spices from Persia, up the broad river to Tiflis, and down the gorge to Poti and the waves beating on the sandy bar. Here were "Indians, Moors, and Greeks," like those with whom Columbus held discourse, and the merchants of the East and West, from the "Levante," as they called the parts below Corfu, and from the "Ponente," which included Sicily and all the lands beyond.

Genoa runs out on the southeast as far as the Bisagno Torrent. In the lifetime of Columbus the ancient city walls were still standing, and formed an interior zone of fortifications along the line now occupied in part by the park and the public gardens. The space intervening between the old walls and the newer ambit of the city was occupied by the Borgo di San Stefano, still known as the "Weavers' Quarter." The weavers were protected and encouraged in every way by the Signoria, whose chief aim, as at Venice, was "to provide that all the poor might live and maintain themselves," and to help the wool trade in particular, "because when this manufacture fails the supply of food fails also." In this quarter the cloth weavers and blanket makers, combers and carders, silk throwers and velvet men, lived in a town of comfortable houses and gardens held on ground rents under the Abbey of San Stefano. In a street outside the Olive Gate was the house where Domenico was working, with an apprentice under him, as early as 1439, and here it is believed that his son Christopher was born. St. Andrew's Gate lay nearer to the sea. A street ran from it, turning upward to Porticello, leaving a considerable space between the roadway and the city wall. Here was the house where Columbus passed most of his boyhood. The place is described in the documents collected by Mr. Harrisse. The shop was in front, a yard with a well behind, and the long garden reached back to the foot of the old wall. Something is added about the neighbors. The next house on the left belonged to the weaver Bondi, and afterward to a shoemaker named Tomaso Carbone; beyond him lived another shoemaker, Antonio Pelegro of Plazio, for whom Domenico Colombo on one occasion witnessed a deed; on the right hand, or south side, was "La Pallavania," so called from its owner's name. A little farther off, toward the Piazza di Porticello, was the shop of the cheesemonger Bavarello, whose son afterward married the sister of Columbus.

Beyond the stream of Bisagno we cross the ridge of a hill and look down on the seaside towns, Quarto and Quinto, the sites of stations on the Roman road, and Nervi, and the village of Bogliasco beyond. On one side of the ridge, farther inland, lived the family of Fontana-Rossa at Quezzi; on the other lies Ginestreto, where Domenico Colombo had a little estate. The hill is covered with vineyards and villas, with groves of fruit trees. Four centuries ago the place was already like a garden, but was clothed in most parts with a different vegetation. Lemons and oranges were still unknown; no mulberry trees were required where there was no manufactory of the native silk; but there were already vineyards and olive orchards, and much of the land was covered with a growth of chestnuts and fig trees. Assiduous industry and experiment, aided by a change of weather as the forests disappeared, have converted a rough Alpine district into a fertlie region of the South. We see that this must be so when we look back at the oldest descriptions of Liguria. The natives under the early Empire drank beer because the little wine produced in their country "was harsh and tasted of pitch." They were always at work in the forest getting timber for ship building; some of the trees, we are told, were of a vast height, and as much as eight feet in diameter, and the wood was often well-veined, and "as good as cedar for cabinet work." They seem to have grown no olive trees, for we learn that they brought their timber to the mart of Genoa, with honey and ox hides and the various produce of their flocks and herds, "in order to get in exchange the oil and wines of Italy." It seems that the weaving trade flourished even in those early times, for we are told that there was a ready market in Italy for "the Ligurian cloaks and tunics."

The history of the family of Columbus appears in a series of documents preserved among the archives of Genoa and Savona, which were for the most part collected before 1586 by Giovanni Battista Ferreri of Savona, and published in 1602 by Giulio Salineri in his "Annotations upon Tacitus." After long disputes and investigations the authenticity of all these documents has been established, the originals of those which had been for a long time missing having been recovered through the labors of Mr. Harrisse. Old Giovanni of Terra-Rossa, the admiral's grandfather, was living at Quinto about the year 1445, and he appears to have died there, before 1448, leaving two sons, Domenico and Antonio, and a daughter Battestina. Giovanni seems to have owned a considerable amount of property. The estate at Terra-Rossa may have gone to his son Antonio, but Domenico used the territorial surname while living at Quinto; his son Christopher often signed his name as "Columbus de Terrarubea," and Bartholomew signed in the same way on the map which he presented to Henry the Seventh. There was also property at Quinto and Ginestreto, besides the two houses at Genoa. We hear also of ground rents at Pradello, near

Piacenza, which fell to the share of Domenico, and were inherited from him by his sons Christopher and Bartholomew.

Among the documents preserved at Genoa is a settlement made in 1448 on the marriage of Battestina, then living with her brothers at Quinto, with Giovanni di Fritalo, of the same place. The brothers bind themselves to pay her dowry of sixty gold lire by twelve installments, and each of them further agrees to hand over to her trustee within three years three silver spoons of due weight, "according to the custom of the town of Quinto."

Domenico was evidently of an eager and sanguine temperament, often buying and selling, and too ready to secure a tempting property by mortgaging his future work. In 1445 he sold certain lands at "le Fassiole" in Quinto, described as lying between the two highways, and as being partly in grass, and partly planted with chestnuts and underwood. Six years later he bought some land at Quarto, in a place called "le Toppore," planted with figs and other trees, at the price of fifty gold *lire*, mostly to be paid in cloth of "Genoese medley." Domenico was by this time living in Genoa, and the purchase was effected at the shop of Master Andrea di Clavaro the barber, in the street by St. Andrew's Gate.

In 1470 he sold the property at Ginestreto, and in the following spring his wife released it from her jointure with the assent of such of her male relations as had rights of pre-emption under the law of Genoa. The document by which this transaction was completed contains very minute information about the relations of Columbus on his mother's side. Among those present were his uncle Gioagnino of Fontana-Rossa, Guglielmo from the same village, who was his first cousin once removed, and Antonio de Amico, his second cousin. Among those who were summoned, but did not attend, were five more relations called "de Fontanarubea," and members of the Pitto and Boverio families.

A good many documents have been found from time to time among the archives at Savona which serve in one way to illustrate the life of Columbus. Of these, some relate to the houses at Genoa, where he was born and bred; others show the status of his associates at Savona, his efforts to help his father in trade affairs, and the troubles which came on the old weaver when his sons were gone to the Indies.

One of these documents, dated in 1472, was the will of his friend, Nicola di Monleone, a trader of repute at Savona, living in a shop near the law courts. Among the witnesses' names we find those of Fazio, a cloth shearer; Vigna, and two other tailors by trade; Geronimo, a shoemaker, and "Christoforo di Colombo, of Genoa, weaver."

About this time we find his father engaging vigorously in business. He makes repeated purchases of "wool of Saffi," in bales worth about eighteen gold lire apiece, at eighteen rolls to the bale. The price was usually to be paid in kind, with six months' credit or more, the purchasers contracting to deliver so many pieces of white Savona stuff, each piece in sixteen lengths, and weighing twenty pounds Genoese. In June, 1472, Domenico bought sixty-four rolls of wool on this system. In the August following he bought seven bales more at twenty gold lire the bale, his son Christopher being required to join as security. The terms were cash in a year, or so much Savona cloth within six months. The notarial registers for 1473–74 contain several entries relating to deliveries of cloth by installments under these contracts.

A deed of August, 1473, relates to the old house near the Olive Gate at Genoa. A certain cloth worker had offered to purchase it for a price to be paid in kind. Susanna joins in the deed to release her rights of jointure, and her sons Christopher and Giovanni-Pelegrino confirm the transaction as her nearest male relations. This deed was executed "in the shop belonging to the dwelling house of the said Domenico and Susanna."

In August, 1474, Domenico made an unfortunate purchase of lands in the suburbs of Savona. The price was never fully paid, and the litigation arising out of the contract seems to have dragged on until Don Diego Columbus, about the year 1514, inquired about the affair, and sent an authority from Hispaniola to settle it, long after all the original parties had passed away.

The vendor was one Corrado di Cuneo; the purchaser is described as Domenico di Colombo, of Quinto, a weaver of Genoa, at that time residing at Savona. The price was fixed at two hundred and fifty gold lire of Savona, to be paid by delivery of parcels of cloth in regular installments. The property consisted of two pieces of land on the Valcalda Road, partly under vines and part in grass, with plantations of fruit trees and underwood. One piece was freehold. Among the fixtures were certain wine vats, which may have had a special value to a purchaser who kept a tavern. The other was held on a renewable lease from one of the Canons of Savona at a rent of a few pence. On the confirmation of the purchase by the Cathedral Chapter, this rent was increased to twelve soldi, and it was agreed that the lease should be renewable every ninth year forever.

Domenico Colombo died about the year 1498, his wife having died about four years previously. His estate was insufficient to meet the claims still outstanding under the contract of purchase, and after some preliminary proceedings an action was duly instituted against Christopher, Bartholomew, and Giacomo, as the heirs of Domenico Colombo. They were, of course, living at that time beyond the jurisdiction of the Court, residing, in the words of the legal formula, "beyond the limits of Pisa and Nice in Provence," and were, indeed, according to common repute, in some part of the dominions of Spain. The next neighbors were accordingly summoned in their place, under a provision of the Savano Code, and judgment was given against them.

Before passing away from the subject of the family property we must inquire what became of the house and shop by St. Andrew's Gate in Genoa. Domenico returned to the city when he was past work, and was living on the allowance received from the admiral. The old house, however, had passed from his possession some years since. There had been a mortgage in 1477, made in consideration of an annuity secured in the books of the Bank of St. George; and in 1489 the property was charged with a large sum of money, found to be due to Giacomo Bavarello the cheesemonger, in respect of Biancinetta's unpaid dowry. In 1490 Domenico was still in possession, and gave a receipt for rent to a shoemaker who was occupying the shop. But about two years afterward Bavarello realized his security, and obtained a perpetual lease of the premises from the Abbey of San Stefano. His wife was dead at that time, having left an only son, Pantaleone, then about twenty-seven years of age. He and his wife Mariola released their rights in consideration of certain annuities, and Giacomo Bavarello thus became absolutely entitled to the property.

CHAPTER III.

> " In his drowsy Paradise
> The day's adventures for the day suffice;
> Its constant tribute of perceptions strange,
> With sleep and stir in healthy interchange,
> Suffice, and leave him for the next at ease—
> Like the great palmer-worm that strips the trees,
> Eats the life out of every luscious plant,
> And when September finds them sere or scant,
> Puts forth two wondrous winglets, alters quite,
> And hies him after unforseen delight."

THERE is no reason for doubting the biographer's statement that Columbus was sent to school at Pavia. The great University was then at the height of its fame. Its chief renown was in the school of law, where the jurists kept alive the learning of Bartolo and Baldo. It was celebrated, moreover, for the attention paid to discipline and morals, the careful teaching of theology, and the painful study of the philosophy of that day. Pavia has always been celebrated in the faculty of medicine. Natural science was studied, as far as the restrictions on knowledge would admit, in the departments of botany and anatomy, of the knowledge of the earth and of the celestial sphere. We must remember that the real "order of the universe" was only just beginning to be known. It was still a heresy, and a folly besides, to believe in the Antipodes, with the rain shooting upward and men walking head downward. It was a dangerous error to think of a diurnal movement of all things:

> The Sun flies forward to his brother Sun,
> The dark Earth follows wheeled in her ellipse.

But the age was already excited with the great African discoveries, and looking eagerly for fresh wonders of science. The importance of cosmography, of geometry, and especially of nautical astronomy, was recognized on all sides. The professors at Pavia included the new subjects in their course of instruction. Columbus was sent there to study geography in its widest sense. His mind seems to have run upon this subject from his early childhood. He entered into all the departments of knowledge, without which he could not become one of the cosmographers. Latin and arithmetic were among the preliminary rudiments. He advanced toward the sciences of the measurement of the earth and the apparent movements of the stars, and that knowledge of their appositions and occultations which he afterward himself compared to "a prophet's vision." We are told that he also learned painting "in order to depict the regions of the world, and to represent solid and lineal figures." Don Ferdinand adds as another reason that the greatest of geographers had said, "No one can be a good cosmographer unless he is a painter too." The quotation from Ptolemy is incorrect, perhaps taken from a conversation with the admiral without referring to the book. The ancient writer drew a distinction between the science of geography and the art of "chorography," or description of places. The science, he said, dealt mainly with quantities, and the inferior art with qualities. The former is a mathematical description of the proportions existing in nature, and requires only signs and symbols. The other deals with outward and physical appearances, "and no one," he adds, "will ever do this well unless he is able to paint." We are not considering the correctness of his view, or the fallacy of confusing the atlas with the panorama. It is easy to see why Columbus attached great importance to the practical knowledge of map-making. He was, we are told, so excellent a draughtsman, and such a "penman," that he could have maintained himself as a master of calligraphy. He was, we know, so skilled in the preparation of charts, "sea cocks," and sailors' cards, that he was able to keep his family out of the profits when he lived at Lisbon and in the Atlantic islands. Something of this kind we may learn from his own letter to the Catholic king, where he describes his intended journal; he promises to set down at night all that happened by day, and every day the navigation of the night before: "and I purpose to make a chart and to set down therein the lands and waters of the Ocean Sea, with all their positions and bearings, and to compose it into a book, and to illustrate the whole with paintings, showing, as we go, the latitude from the Equator, and also the western longitude."

It has been said that Columbus was too young in 1460 to be sent to a distant university, and that there was, in fact, no time for study at Pavia if he not only began to go to sea when he was about fourteen years old, but also had to serve an apprenticeship in the weaver's trade. There is no doubt that he was so apprenticed, probably to his own father, and we know from the family records the exact nature of the contract. At some time after he was ten years old he was bound to work at weaving for a term of years, to obey all lawful orders, to remain in Genoa except when the plague was raging, and in return to get board and lodging, a blue gaberdine and a good pair of shoes, and so forth. But his father could of course relax or suspend the obligation, and, inasmuch as Genoa began in 1459 to be the center of warlike preparations for the great expedition against Naples, it seems more than probable that an opportunity would be found for removing the boy to more peaceful quarters. The same remark applies to the suggestion that sufficient schooling in maritime affairs could have been found at home without going to lectures in an inland city. It should be remembered also that the expense of living at Pavia would be very slight, if we may judge by the records of our English universities during the same period; and that it was the fashion of the time for boys to attend the professor's lectures at an age when, in our own state of society, they would be entering a public school.

Looking back to the time when Columbus was being educated there, one would see a very different place from the Pavia of our day. Some features, of course, remain unchanged. The town stands in the circuit of the ancient walls within a network of confluent streams. The covered bridge is still as favorite a resort as when Sforza set the roof on its hundred pillars. But at that time the building of the great castle behind the linen market had only just begun; scores of private fortresses preserved the memory of the feudal age and suggested an appropriate name for the "City of Towers." No great cathedral church was erected as yet, but there were many old Lombard churches, "carved like a feverish dream," most of which have long since been destroyed. Some of their monuments, still preserved in the University's courtyards, show the figures of the ancient professors, Baldo and Alciati and the rest, lecturing in the midst of a circle of scholars old and young. Some change for the worse has come over the place. It is dismal and (as some say) unwholesome. But, according to its historians, this was a delightful region in the time of which we are speaking. There were green plains around, and hanging woods, with thickets of box and tamarisk. On the meadows round the city the boys played and raced in the winter sunshine; in summer, to quote Sacci's description, the time came for walks and dozing in the shade. The air is full of singing and fluttering birds. No venomous creatures are here; the whining cicada is still, and even the flies are kept off by the cool Alpine breeze. We read in old eulogies of the University how broad were the streets and piazzas full of bustling scholars, how bright the gardens laden "with the odor and color of flowers." We can learn something even of the sports and games. The boys raced and played at bowls, or fell into groups for games of catching; and Pavia was especially famous for "balloon-ball," or a kind of rude tennis, for which Sforza had built courts about the time when he restored the schools.

One would wish to know somewhat more about the scholars themselves, their lessons, and ways of living. A few figures, chiefly those of professors and lawyers, may still be disengaged from obscurity. Filippo Decio, the unconquered disputant, was a few years younger than Columbus; he came as a boy to learn law at Pavia, and long afterward had a house demolished there by the army of Pope Julius the Second. Giasone

Maino, "the glory of the civilians," was born in 1435. He may, therefore, have been at Pavia with the young Columbus. We hear something of a reckless youth, a torn gown, and a vellum Code left at the pawn shop; afterward, we are told, he "pulled himself together," and became the most illustrious of the professors. An eye-witness reports a scene of the year 1507, when Genoa had been taken by the French. Louis the Twelfth went on to Pavia to hear a lecture from "the solid doctor," as Maino was at that time called. The old classroom was crowded with cardinals and nobles; the professor wore a gold-laced gown, and was knighted; and there was even some hope of a cardinal's hat. Paolo Giovio, who tells the story, describes the college life as he saw it, the competition in lectures, the fine addresses of Torriano on new discoveries in anatomy and medical botany, and the degree day when Paolo himself received the ring and laurel wreath as a Master in Arts and Medicine.

A letter written by one of the professors during the lifetime of Columbus shows us the effect produced at Pavia by the new discoveries. It was sent to Ludovico Sforza by one Nicolo Scillacio, a lecturer in philosophy, who kept up a correspondence with Spain. It is valuable as containing an independent account of the events of the second voyage; but its chief interest lies in what is disclosed as to the state of geographical learning. Columbus thought that he had arrived at the neighborhood of China and Japan. By the general opinion of Pavia the new islands were at the back of Africa, near the spice country and the Arabian shore; they were, in fact, the goal of the Carthaginian commerce, the market of King Solomon's navies, and had been described by many of the great writers of antiquity. Scillacio labored at this point when describing the natives of Hispaniola. "It is ascertained," he says, "that these are the Sabæans of the spice country, noted in foreign chronicles, and over and over again described in our books at home." It should be observed that he came from Sicily himself, and makes a constant use of the collections of Diodorus the Sicilian. "Everyone has been repeating, 'The kings shall come from Sheba, bringing gold and incense'; and with those kings the island teems copiously and in bounteous abundance. For the Sabæans are most wealthy in the fragrance and fertility of their forests, and in gold mines, and well watered meadows, and good store of honey and wax."

Scillacio was, of course, referring to the brilliant description of Arabia by Diodorus. "On the coasts grow balm and cassia; in the heart of the land are shady woods and forests, graced and beautified with stately trees of myrrh and frankincense, palms, and calamus, and cinnamon." Of the Sabæans in their chief city, he said that they lived in a flood of gold and silver; their cups and vats were of the precious metals, their beds and chairs had silver feet. "The porticoes of their houses and temples are some of them overlaid with gold, and silver statues are placed upon the chapiters of the temples."

The professor next shows, still with constant references to the ancient historian, how the King of Spain, like another Hercules, had passed the bounds of Ethiopia and found the lost islands of the Indian Sea. One point is made that was afterward taken up by Columbus: The geographers, he says, and even the great Ambrosio Rosato, must have been rather careless in their inquiries about the Southern Ocean. "They have always insisted that this vast tract of water was shut in on all sides by a continent; but in our time, under the good auspices of the Spanish kings we have seen this ring sailed through." Columbus speaks of the same thing in the account of his mystical vision. The voice said, "He gave thee the keys of those barriers of the Ocean Sea which were closed with such mighty chains, and thou wast obeyed through many lands." It is plain that there is also a reference here to one of those sayings in Esdras on which the admiral was fond of basing his predictions. "The sea is set in a wide place that it might be deep and great. But put the case the entrance were narrow like a river; who then could go into the sea to look upon it and to rule it? If he went not through the narrow how could he come into the broad?"

Let it suffice, said Scillacio, that in this voyage the islands have been found; something has been learned of the climate, and some of the ports have become known. "When they go back again, and are able to traverse the coasts and to explore the country inland, I shall take pains to complete the descriptions of the classical writers; I shall add all that old tradition reports about the savage manners and customs of the nations of monsters, which Augustine, Bishop of Hippo, an African himself, a pillar of the faith, saw with his own eyes in the ends of Lybia, and collected them in the book entitled 'Sermons to the Eremites.'" St. Augustine never wrote the book in question, though he was credited with having seen the one-eyed folk and people with heads beneath their shoulders. St. Jerome, in the same way, was believed to be the authority for half the absurdities which were collected in the "Cosmography of Æthicus," and afterward in the pretended travels of Mandeville. All the travelers' gossip of the Greeks and the stories of the Eastern bazaars had been foisted into general belief under the pretended authority of Aristotle. It was one of the chief impediments of learning in the time of Columbus that the very sources of knowledge were polluted in this fashion. The classical works of Pliny and Mela, on which the student had to depend, were full of scraps of romance, taken from some Syrian story about Thule, or some imaginary voyage out of the Caspian Strait toward the cannibals beyond China and the islands of gold and silver. Cosmas the Voyager was supposed to have demolished the theory that the earth was a sphere. Little was to be gained, beyond a list of names, from the Geographer of Ravenna and his collection of the learning of the Ostrogoths. The most popular treatise on the subject was a mere travesty of an ancient novel about the wanderings of Apollonius.

It is not surprising, therefore, that men of science relied on authorities of little value, and altered their opinions on evidence which seems very slight in our eyes. Even the description of America, as we have seen, had been found in the pages of Pliny and Diodorus. Columbus himself easily gave up the notion that the earth was round, though the experiments of Ptolemy had proved it by eclipses and other observations. On equally light evidence he concluded that he had found in Veragua a savage nation described by Herodotus, as well as the golden Chersonese depicted in the histories of Josephus. In framing his theory of the distribution of land and sea, he appears to have based his reasonings on the dark questions of Uriel and the responses of Esdras: "How great dwellings are in the midst of the sea, or which are the outgoings of Paradise?" He argues that, of the world's seven parts six are in the domain of Behemoth, wherein are a thousand ills; "unto Leviathan Thou gavest the seventh part, namely the moist, and hast kept him to be devoured of whom Thou wilt and when." It must have been from a few vague sayings of the Fathers, and certain fables of the Ravenna Geographer, that he learned to look near India for the site of the Garden of Eden and the outfalls of its fourfold river. We have no means of ascertaining the exact details of his studies, though his biographer and Peter Martyr agree in the statement that he attended classes in astronomy and the use of the celestial sphere, and made some practical acquaintance with the astrolabe and other instruments of the art of navigation. The archives of the University have been minutely searched for anything that could illustrate the great man's career, and some of the professors have been identified as having given lectures which he most probably attended. The list begins in the year 1460, about the time of his return to Genoa. We learn by its help that Stefano di Faventia and Antonio di Bernadigio were at that time lecturing on astrology, which, according to the ideas of that time, would include geometry and a knowledge of astronomy proper, as well as the art of interpreting the signs of future events. Francesco Pellacano and Alberto di Crispi were lecturing about the same time on natural philosophy; and we may suppose that it was in their classes that Columbus acquired his first instruction in Ptolemaic geography and the physical science of Aristotle.

CHAPTER IV.

> "Ship to ship, cannon to cannon, man
> To man, were grappled in the embrace of war,
> Inextricable but by death or victory;
> The tempest of the raging fight convulsed
> To its crystalline depths that stainless sea."

COLUMBUS left Pavia when he was about fourteen years old. For a few months he was employed as an apprentice at home, working at the wool-carding and helping his father at the loom. He looked forward, like most of the boys in Genoa, to a life of adventure at sea. He cherished his private hope of probing the deep secrets of nature in every part of the earth "from Thule to the girdle of the world."

There was, however, at that time, a sudden outburst of war, which kept him cooped up within the walls. Early in the year 1461 Genoa had thrown off the yoke of France. The foreign garrison was driven into the Castle and besieged by the civic militia. King Réné, whom Genoa had often befriended, came over the sea from Provence and blockaded the port with a fleet of privateers. But as the summer advanced the citizens gained strength and ventured on a decisive battle, in which the foreigners were driven away beyond Savona. Columbus, "still in his tender youth," was free to begin his career, and was soon going about in the trading boats to Sicily and Aleppo and up and down among the islands. When he wrote long afterward his description of the mastic trees of Hispaniola he told the Spanish king that he had seen the lentiscus shrubs growing in Scio, while the island still belonged to Genoa, and had noticed how the white gum was got from the plants by incisions made just as they began to flower. When he speaks of his discussions with learned Indians we may suppose that he had passed the Golden Horn, and visited the Black Sea factories, where the Genoese conducted their Crimean trade and collected at Poti the Indian goods which the merchants brought down through Georgia.

It was not until 1470 that he set up his home in Lisbon. It was at the end of 1484 that he fled into Spain, and he said in a letter to King Ferdinand that he had then been negotiating with the Court of Portugal for fourteen years. We cannot account for all his employments from his first going to sea until he was wrecked on the coast of Portugal. We know from his own statements that he was seldom away from the water for any length of time; and we may suppose that he was often at Genoa and Savona. But it seems clear that during the latter part of the period he gave up trade and engaged in privateering under the command of the younger Colombo, one of the two "admirals" whose fleets were the terror of the West.

There has always been a great confusion of ideas about the lives and exploits of these men. They were closely connected in many ways. It seems probable that they were father and son. They sailed under the same flag and were engaged in the same undertakings; each of them was described in official documents as a vice-admiral of France, and each was known as "the Pirate Columbus" to the merchants whose ships they captured.

The elder Columbus makes a figure in French history under the title of "the Admiral Coulon." He belonged to the family of Coulon, or "De Columbo," long established in the neighborhood of Bayonne, and was the owner of an estate in Gascony called Casenove or Caseneuve. In some of his family documents we find him officially styled "Guillaume Casenove, dit Coulomp." This man was one of the most useful tools of Louis the Eleventh. He had been the king's friend before he came to the throne, and during the whole length of the reign he was loaded with gifts and privileges. He was appointed vice admiral of Normandy before the year 1465, and he held the office till his death in 1483. Besides this, he was Controller of Forests and Waters for Normandy and Picardy; he was one of the royal equerries; he had privileges in some of the southern forests, and fees and pensions charged on various ports and havens in the North. More than all this, he was permitted to marry a great heiress, Guillemette le Sec, who brought with her estates at Varelme, Charleval, and Mesnil-Paviot, and the mansion at Gaillart-Bois, near Rouen, where Louis used to stay with the old admiral and weave plans for the destruction of their enemies. Knowing the king's superstitious character, it is interesting to hear that "the bold Coulon" kept an astrologer in the house, one Maître Robert de Cazel, who knew the secrets of navigation, and made such good calculations "that the admiral did more in his time than any seaman since Messire Bertrand du Guesclin, and was more feared than any living man on the sea by the Norman coasts." Wherever Louis had work to be done, there the old sea-wolf was found. He captured English ships returning from their voyages to the Levant. He swept the Dutch and Flemish traders from the sea in the face of the navy of Charles the Bold. In 1474 he took two galleons belonging to the King of Naples at Viverro on the north coast of Spain; and two years afterward he entered Brest Harbor, and took four Spanish vessels, putting all his prisoners to death "by the edge of the sword." A little later we find him convoying the defeated King of Portugal with a great navy under the French flag. Soon afterward he is in the North again, and in 1479 he revenged the invasion of France by Maximilian and the defeat of Louis at Guinegatte by capturing eighty Dutch ships coming from the Baltic with cargoes of rye, while other *écumeurs de mer* acting with him captured the boats returning from the herring fishery, a blow which struck the whole population of the Low Countries and led at once to the peace concluded at Tours.

The other "Admiral," called for distinction

"Colombo il Zovene," or "filius Columbi," was more of an adventurer, we might say more of a corsair, than Coulon de Casenove. We do not know, nor is it of much importance to know, whether he was the natural son of the French vice admiral. He was certainly not the son of Guillemette le Sec, whose heir, Jean de Casenove, succeeded her in possession of the estates; nor was he connected, so far as is known, with the other Jean de Casenove, who was employed in the French navy after the vice admiral's death. His real name was Nicolo Griego, or Nicholas the Greek; and that this was not a mere by-name is shown by the mention of Giovanni Griego and Zorzi Griego, who fought under his command in 1485, and took part in the negotiations for restoring the ships which he had captured to the Republic of Venice. Some time afterward there was another Nicolo Griego, who was killed by the Turks at Constantinople; and it seems likely that there was a family of the name driven away from their country upon the fall of the Eastern Empire, and established either at Genoa or somewhere in that neighborhood. It was said of this Nicolo Griego, or "Nicolo Columbo," that no one could actually say that he came from Genoa, but that he was believed to be a citizen of Savona, within the territories of the Republic.

There are many stories about this Griego, under whose flag Columbus served so long. We have seen that he began by equipping at his own expense a fleet against the Infidels. We can sympathize under the circumstances with the desire to smite the Turks hip and thigh. But his main object seems to have been to damage the Venetians, partly as being the hereditary rivals of his adopted country, and partly, no doubt, because the French king secretly encouraged everyone who would attack the friends of his enemies.

The true explanation is afforded by the correspondence which passed in 1474 and the year following with respect to the ships captured at Viverro. As soon as Ferdinand of Sicily heard of Coulon's action, he at once sent to Louis and demanded full compensation. In a letter of the 9th of December, 1474, he expresses the astonishment with which he had heard, "that one Columbus, in command of certain ships, being a French subject, should have taken two great galleys, which last year went by our orders to trade with England and Flanders," turning out the crews and the merchants, and carrying off the galleys to Normandy. It had been reported, while the ships were still at Southampton, that this Columbus was fitting out a squadron; but absolute reliance had been placed on the good feeling of the King of France, and now that the galleys were within his jurisdiction the writer felt confident that they would be duly restored with all their contents. "The whole world," he added, "will judge between the parties to this cause. Wherefore we have thought fit to send Arminius, our king-at-arms, to carry this letter to your Majesty, and to bring back the answer which your Majesty may think fit to deliver to him." Louis was delighted with his admiral's prowess, and was still more pleased, in this instance, at being able to gain an ally on cheap terms.

The answer was written on New Year's Day. Louis remarked, after many compliments, that he had never had any injury from his friend, except, indeed, when he allowed his soldiers to attack the French expedition for the recovery of Roussillon. As to the capture of the galleys, it was done without the king's knowledge and against his wish, and as soon as he heard of it, orders were given to impound all the spoil that could be found. It was true that a good deal of merchandise had been stolen or concealed by the captain or by some of those who were with him; nevertheless, the king would, on receiving proper schedules and declarations, account for all the freight, besides giving the crews some wages, and sending back the galleys properly victualed and fitted out. "But," said Louis, "when we come to inquire of Columbus and his men what led them to make this capture, against our wish, and without any orders, what is their reply? Why, they answer at once that it was because your Majesty's people attacked our forces in Roussillon; because, moreover, these galleys were at that very time returning out of the jurisdiction of the English, the inveterate enemies of our crown, and because the origin of their voyage had been in the territory held by Charles of Burgundy, one of our disobedient subjects. These galleys had begun their voyage as carriers of goods for the comfort and assistance of our enemies, and were returning with stores intended to be used to our loss. Moreover, this Columbus urges that by the laws of war, as always used and acknowledged in these western seas, any ship, galley, or bark may be lawfully captured which is coming from an enemy's country, especially if carrying goods whereby he may be enriched or strengthened. Now those galleys certainly carried a quantity of goods belonging to our enemies and to rebels against us; and they had no license or permit such as the French galleys have always had when they have visited your Majesty's dominions." Such, said the French king, were the reasons which might be properly adduced in favor of the capture; but in spite of all this he intended to restore the ships as before mentioned. As to the enemy's goods on board, the ordinary rule would be followed, that such goods may be seized, even under a friendly flag, on making good the freight, as the king was now ready to do.

The services of Nicolo Colombo were at one time engaged by Réné of Provence. The titular King of Sicily claimed a right to attack the ships of the reigning sovereign. News had been brought to Marseilles that a great vessel, called *La Ferdinandina* of Naples, was lying off the African coast near Tunis. She was a "galeass," which has been defined as a large galley with three masts and two lateen or triangular sails, with an armed crew and heavy catapults set between the benches of the oarsmen. Colombo's squadron was lying in the port, and Christopher Columbus was chosen to go across in command of a "cutting-out" expedition. He has told the story himself in a letter written in January, 1495, from Hispaniola. "It happened to me that King Réné, whom God has taken to himself, sent me to Tunis to take the galeass, and when I got near the island of San Pietro off Sardinia, I heard that she had two ships and a long caracca in her company. This discomposed my men, and they resolved to go no further, but to return to Marseilles for another ship and more men. I saw that there was no going against their will without some contrivance, and seemed to give way; but then I turned the needle of the compass right round, and set sail when it was getting late; and the next day at sunrise we found ourselves off Cape Certegna (in Africa), though all the crew had thought for certain that we were making homeward to Marseilles." We do not know the result of the engagement. Columbus was only referring to the matter as an illustration of his knowledge of nautical science. But we may conjecture that it began in the same way as Colombo's fight in 1475, when he attacked the Venetian squadron off Cyprus. "We came upon Colombo," says the report to the Duke of Milan, "with ships and galleys, and we were strongly minded to let him pass; but they raised a shout of 'Viva San Giorgio,' and would not move, and so the fight began."

We have fuller information about the attack on the Venetian galleys returning from England in 1470, and generally about the danger to which these ships were exposed in their annual voyage. It should be remembered that the successful attack of 1485, in which Christopher Columbus was not engaged, was made on the galleys soon after they had left Cadiz, and had got to Cape St. Vincent on their outward course. The whole trade was a development of an earlier intercourse between Venice and Flanders. Towards the end of the fourteenth century it was found that there was sufficient demand to justify the loading of cargoes for London and Southampton, as well as for the ports in Flanders. Two additional vessels were usually detailed for this purpose. The whole trading squadron, still known officially as the Flanders galleys, arrived every summer in the Downs, and there separated for the ports on either side of the Channel. For the return voyage in the autumn they all assembled again at Southampton.

They brought us the produce of the East, and all kinds of goods from the Mediterranean ports. The nature of the commerce appears from the schedules of rates and prices current. The English market required wine, dried currants, Sicilian sugars, and raw silks and cottons for the home manufacturers. From Venice itself came damasks, velvets, and worked silks of all kinds. Of Genoese goods we took the gum mastic and fine "terebinths," or resins, from Scio; from Sicily, among the less bulky goods, were sweets and preserved fruits, coral beads and gall nuts, and lambskin "astrachans" brought over to Palermo from Apulia. Among the spices we required, of course, all that were commonly used in cookery, including saffron, which had not yet become an English crop and was largely imported from Italy; of other spices and drugs we may note the aloes and dragon's blood from Socotra, scammony from Aleppo, camphor and red sandalwood, cloves and clove stems, cinnamon and reed cassia, ambergris from the Southern Ocean, and the dried Indian fruits called "myrobolans," which were used in medicine as astringents. The cargoes for the Flemish cities consisted of much the same kind of goods; but there were special demands at Bruges for tabbies and silk yarns from Syria, cardamums, woad and indigo, the hepatic aloes, Barbary wax, and unworked ostrich feathers; the Antwerp merchants demanded in addition Sicilian sulphur, ivory for combs, diamonds, rubies, and manufactured jewelry.

There was a brisk demand for English woolen cloths, and for cups, platters, and other articles of wrought pewter. But the bulk of the cargoes for the return voyage consisted of raw materials. Of the five staple commodities that might be purchased by the Venetians either in London or at Middelburg in Zealand, by far the most important were the wools and wool-fells, which are described in the Great Ordinance of the Staple as "the sovereign merchandise and jewel of our realm." Next in importance were lead and tin in sheets, rods, and blocks. Leather was in demand, if the quality were good. Large Flemish dressed oxhides sold well "at all the scales," especially at Pisa and Palermo; and there was a demand for calfskins, "if they were very large and heavy." Copper, unworked amber, and a few other articles of occasional demand appear from time to time in the lists. There seems to have been a special trade with Barbary, under rules enforced with great severity. One of the returning galleys was allowed to call at the Moorish ports with "fine English cloths" and certain manufactured articles; but no tin or copper, or article containing either of those metals, might be landed without incurring ruinous forfeitures and penalties.

There are many entries in the Venetian archives showing the dangers with which the trade was surrounded. In one year the captain reports that it would be dangerous to go near Sandwich "by reason of a powerful English armada"; on another occasion a ship is only licensed to proceed "if it be known that she can pass Sandwich in safety." We hear continually of attacks apprehended from "those who wish to live at their neighbors' cost."

In the spring of 1468 the danger seemed to be increasing. There were rumors in the Rialto that *La Justiniana* was lying in the Port of London, short of sailors and "in manifest peril." She ought to have had nearly forty more crossbowmen, besides her complement of rough Slavonian rowers. The Senate met on May the 5th, and the Doge was instructed to write to Ser Luca Moro, commanding the fleet. The letter still remains enrolled among the "Sea Decrees" at Venice. Moro is directed to raise the crew to the full strength without delay. Should he not have left Bruges, he may raise twenty-five or thirty men in Flanders, and take them across to Southampton. Then he might put them on board the galley lying there, and take a corresponding number of picked men from Southampton across the country to London. Should he be in England, he was to transfer enough men from his other ships to man the *Justiniana*. In any case, he must engage enough sailors, and he was to take care that they belonged to as many different nationalities as possible. "He is to take the money required for manning the London galley on a bill of exchange, if the master will not disburse it, on the security of the freight, as well as on the primage and freights from Sicily and Barbary."

In the following month the Milanese ambassador reports a suspicious circumstance to his master. The English and the Spaniards were in the habit of capturing each other's ships in a never-ending series of reprisals. But something had recently happened which looked as if there was an understanding between the two governments to fit out a combined fleet against France. "The Admiral of France," meaning the Vice Admiral Coulon, had captured two English ships, with cargoes of spices and other merchandise, returning from the Levant. As he was going home with his prizes he was himself captured by a Spanish man-of-war. The Frenchman protested, on the ground that his country was at peace with Spain, and demanded immediate release. "You need not think of such a thing," said the Spanish captain; "you would do as much to me, and worse too, if you had the chance"; and he reminded Coulon of the letters of mark and reprisal under which so much property of Spanish subjects had been seized.

The imprisonment of Coulon relieved to a great extent the anxieties of the Venetian merchants. It seems, however, as if they did not know the real nature of their danger. We can see that Louis the Eleventh never lost an opportunity of setting their enemies upon them, and yet was unwilling to take part in any open hostilities. He has explained the matter himself in a letter written to Francesco Sforza on the 27th of

December, 1469. He informs the Duke of Milan of the arrival of an envoy from Venice, asking that the republic may have security on the open sea and within the French dominions. Louis does not care much about the matter; he only denies the request because the Venetians are hostile to Sforza, and therefore enemies of France. He would be glad to know what ought to be done. He therefore asks Sforza to dispatch a special envoy, and to send word what the Venetians had done about resisting the French clauses in the treaty lately concluded at Rome. It may be mentioned here that the safe conduct was not actually granted to the Venetians until 1478. This appears by a dispatch sent by the Signoria in that year to Giovanni Candida, Secretary to the Duke and Duchess of Burgundy, in which it was stated that "of late years the King of France had taken several Venetian ships, and had repeatedly waylaid the Flanders galleys." Finally Domenico Gradenigo had been sent as an ambassador, and the ships and galleys had been guaranteed "without any detrimental conditions."

In the month of July, 1469, letters were received at Venice from the English consul, Marco de Ca, and from merchants in the factories of

London and Bruges, which stated that "the pirate Columbus," evidently meaning Nicolo Colombo, was in the Channel with eight ships and barges. "There he awaits the Venetian galleys with intent to damage them, and if the ships come singly the mischief might not be limited to mere damage." The Senate was convened, and a decree passed in haste, directing the consuls in London and Bruges to order all Venetian captains to put themselves under the orders of Ser Zuane Capello, commanding the galleys, and to remain in his company until he should be out of danger from the corsair. "Should it behove the ships to await the galleys, let an average be made to defray the costs of demurrage, payable thus: one-third by the goods, freight, and tonnage of the ships, according to the proper rate, and two-thirds by the merchants and freights of the galleys."

In the early part of the year 1470 there were more serious alarms about the trading fleet. The galleys had arrived at the Downs in the spring, under the command of Ser Gabriele Trevisano. By the middle of May they had not yet finished loading for the homeward voyage, but were expected in a short time to assemble at

Southampton as their place of rendezvous. The Venetian ambassador in France reported that fresh preparations for attack were being made by the "pirate Colombo." Moreover, the seas at that time were in a very unsafe state. We hear incidentally of English corsairs in the Bay of Biscay, and of "Easterling pirates" off the coast of Flanders; the Venetians themselves were in trouble with the English about the capture of a vessel belonging to one William Cooper off the Island of Scio. There seemed also to be some likelihood of a war between England and France. Edward the Fourth was for the moment in full agreement with the king-maker Warwick, who in the world of politics was "the mover of both wind and tide," and it was suspected that they were arming for a descent upon Normandy. Should such an invasion take place, attacks would doubtless be made by Louis upon any neutrals trading with England or carrying her goods to the Mediterranean. There was danger besides, in any case, from the fact that they were "comforting and assisting" Charles the Bold by trading with his ports in Flanders. On May the 17th the matter was debated in the Senate, and it was decreed that the ships *La Malipiera* and

La Squarcia should be ordered "instantly to join the captain of the Flanders galleys, and to convoy him until he be out of danger from the pirate." Should the galleys not have finished loading, the ships were to wait for them, and to be allowed payment of demurrage from the date of their arrival at the Isle of Wight; and it was ordered that the insurances on the ships were not to be impugned on account of anything arising out of this special service.

All calculations were upset by the strange course of events in England. The Wars of the Roses were a wild confusion of alternate victory and ruin, of tragedy and farce. "One piece of news," men said, "is never like the last; they are always as unlike as day is to night." Continual treachery was helped by the universal carelessness. The Italians had a proverb that you should not let go the man whom you ought never to have caught; but the king-maker pushed his puppets up and down, unmindful of their chances of revenge. Edward the Fourth was one day a prisoner, and the next day was hunting with Warwick; in a little while the king-maker is overthrown, and Edward is entering London in triumph. An outburst of the

Lancastrians was luckily suppressed at Stamford, and it forthwith appeared that the army was all for the White Rose; Warwick fled across the sea, and with him his newly chosen son-in-law, "the perjured Clarence," soon to betray him again, and to plot for a share of his inheritance. They crossed with a few ships to Calais, and on being repulsed went to meet the French king at Amboise. Their best refuge seemed to be Dieppe, where they brought a few ships captured in the Channel, belonging to subjects of Charles the Bold, or to his allies in Brittany. The duke demanded instant reparation for the insult; and he pointed out that some of his ships had been taken by the fleet which the King of France, according to his own account, had collected to make war against the English. Louis was ready, of course, to appoint commissioners to inquire into the matter. Meantime the ships under Warwick moved to Grandeville, and afterward to Cherbourg. Charles the Bold showed his impatience of the delay by a letter of May the 29th, addressed to the Archbishop of Narbonne and the Admiral de Bourbon, in which he complained of the proceedings of the French ships, including, as we suppose, the squadron under the "pirate Colombo," and swore by St. George that he would soon find a remedy of his own.

A few days afterward the duke heard that Warwick had captured more of his ships, and that the Frenchman was about to send an incendiary to destroy the rest of his fleet. He at once sent his whole force to the mouth of the Seine, under Admiral La Vire; and here, near Chef-de-Caux, they were soon afterward joined by men-of-war from England and Brittany. The Burgundians were especially strong; the duke had found at Ecluse two galleys from Genoa, besides a good many Spanish and Portuguese ships, and a few German trading boats, which were all impressed for his service.

The Burgundians proceeded to summon the English fleet, giving notice at the same time that they had no quarrel with the French. The Admiral de Bourbon replied that in any case there must be no fighting in French waters. Meantime every vessel that could be spared was being equipped for Warwick's benefit. Réné of Provence was sparing no trouble or expense to aid the cause of his daughter, the exiled Queen Margaret. Louis himself was superintending the business, passing and repassing among the coast towns, under his habitual pretext of a pilgrimage to Mont St. Michel. According to Polydore Vergil, a fairly large fleet and "an army not to be despised" were got together in the course of the summer. In September it was arranged that Warwick and his fleet should shift their quarters to Havre, and slip across to England whenever the chance arrived. On the night of September the 13th a great storm arose. The Burgundians were caught and scattered far and wide, some toward Scotland, some back toward Flanders and Holland. Then the wind veered to the southeast. Some say that a fog came on, which puzzled the English commanders in the blockading squadron; others tell us, with greater probability, of a breeze blowing hard for Devonshire. Warwick at once sailed out, and made for Dartmouth, where he had left the people, a few months before, all well-disposed to the Red Rose and old King Henry. The French fleet sailed with him as a convoy, under orders to run ahead without fighting, unless they were actually attacked. After a run of nearly three hundred miles they passed Torbay and Berry Head, and stood at the entrance to the haven; the great chain was lowered, and they passed in between the castles.

King Edward had been vainly warned of his danger. Even after the landing he wrote to Charles of Burgundy to come and catch the invaders in the trap. But while he was getting his forces together the armies of the West came upon him, sixty thousand strong, and in a few days he was a fugitive, and making for his refuge in Flanders again.

Amid the clash of these great events the trouble about the Venetian galleys was forgotten. We are not told in so many words that Colombo and his ships gave up the pursuit for a time; but it is obvious, from what the historians have recorded, that the squadron must have joined the main French force, and must have been blockaded with the rest at the mouth of the Seine. It is difficult to suppose that they took no part in the expedition to Dartmouth.

Under the orders of Louis, or of Réné, or as the habitual associates of Coulon, one must suppose that the younger Colombo and his men were made to carry part of Warwick's forces, or to help in convoying his fleet. If this be so, it is nearly certain that Christopher Columbus must have seen the south coast of Devonshire and entered the port of Dartmouth. We know, from his own words to Ferdinand, that he was in the service of Colombo, and fought for him off Cape St. Vincent; and it is expressly stated in his letters that he had been in England and had seen the harbors there, "though he never saw any harbors as good as those which he found in the Indies."

When the galleys were going home in the autumn with the ships detailed for their protection, they found the enemy awaiting them off the coast of Portugal. Creeping past Vigo Bay and the broad estuary of the Tagus, they came in sight of the bar of Odemira, where Columbus afterward saw land at the end of his second voyage; and the place is memorable for the reason that he had used what seemed to be a prophetical power, and had guessed the longitude by the variations of the needle, when all the pilots were at fault. Further on there stretched into the sea the great wedge-shaped form of Cape St. Vincent, the "Sacred Promontory" of the ancient geographers, who believed it to be the western extremity of the world. Behind the Cape was the favorite lurking-place of the "French pirates." Here in February, 1477, while Christopher Columbus was in the North Sea, his old commander waited for the galleys and a crowd of merchantmen from Cadiz. Here, too, on the 21st of August, 1485, the four galleys, sailing this time from Cadiz without protection, "fell in with Colombo, that is to say, Nicolo Griego, captain of seven armed ships under the flag of King Charles of France," or, according to a fuller description in a letter from King Ferdinand to Henry the Seventh, "met Columbus, the vice admiral of the French seas and commander of the navy of the most Christian king." At daybreak they came to blows, and the battle, which ended in the capture of all the galleys, lasted as we are told "from the first hour of the day till the twentieth." The Venetians threatened reprisals, but the matter soon subsided in a long negotiation. A few years afterward, the admiral himself had to change his course on his third voyage across the Atlantic, in order to avoid an attack from the French ships hovering off the cape. Some time afterward the "French pirates" had a great success in capturing a Portuguese trader passing near the cape with a cargo of gold, ivory, and African merchandise from the Gold Coast. The King of Portugal was not so peaceful as the Venetians had shown themselves.

He threatened instant war, unless both ship and cargo were restored; and when everything was given up, except one gray parrot, he again threatened war until the French king gave back the parrot at last, and so averted a catastrophe.

The picturesque and fervid account of the action of 1470, in which Christopher Columbus took part, must have come, one would think, from the admiral's own lips, in the very words reported by Don Ferdinand. The narrative is no way injured by the error which the biographer made in thinking that the later battle, described by the Venetian writers, was that in which his father had been engaged. After speaking of Colombo the Younger, he proceeds as follows: "I say that while the admiral sailed with the aforesaid Colombo el Mozo, which was a long time, it fell out that, hearing of the galleys coming from Flanders, they went out to look for them, and found them near Cape St. Vincent. Then falling to blows, they fought furiously, and grappled and beat one another from ship to ship with rage and fury, with their pikes and hand grenades and other fiery artillery; and so after they had fought from matins to vespers, and many had been killed, the fire seized on my father's ship and also on one of the great galleons. Now they were grappled together, with iron hooks and chains such as sailors use, and neither of them could get free because of the confusion and fear of the fire; and the fire soon grew so great that the only hope was for all who could to leap into the water, and to die quick rather than face the torment of the flames. But the admiral being an excellent swimmer, and seeing himself about two leagues from land, laid hold of an oar which Fortune offered him, and sometimes resting on it and sometimes swimming, it pleased God, who was preserving him for greater ends, to give him strength to get to land, but so tired and spent with the water that he had much ado to recover himself."

The story now concludes: "It was not far from Lisbon, where he knew that there were many Genoese, and he went there as fast as he could; and being recognized by his friends, he was so courteously received and entertained that he set up house and married a wife in that city."

CHAPTER V.

> "Sanguine he was. But a less vivid hue
> Than of that islet in the chestnut bloom
> Flamed in his cheek; and eager eyes, that still
> Took joyful note of all things joyful, beamed
> Beneath a mane-like mass of rolling gold."

COLUMBUS was about twenty-four years old when he settled at Lisbon. Some rumors of the world's admiration of his fine appearance and vigorous mind have come down to our times. He was gifted with the physical strength, the subtle intelligence, and the instinctive love of the sea which antiquity attributed to the Ligurians. He had little other resemblance to their dark and slender race. He bore the signs of descent from a Teutonic stock, being light-haired and fair, like one of the Lombard warriors on the frescoes in the Palace of Theodolind. Both his sons, as well as the historian Herrera who was in possession of many of his documents, have said that he was of a comely presence. He was tall and large of limb. His face was long, with an aquiline nose; the cheeks rather full, "neither large nor lean," according to Don Ferdinand; he had a very clear complexion, with a ruddy glow and bright patches of red; his eyes were of a bluish gray; his hair and beard were red in his youth, but they lost their color and became gray before he was thirty years old.

There are many portraits of Columbus, but none which have been absolutely accepted as genuine; and we have probably no means of recovering the outline of any original from which subsequent copies may be taken to have descended. According to an ancient tradition in Spain, the admiral's portrait was taken at Seville, after his return from the second voyage. Navarete has shown that, if this were so, the artist must have been Antonio del Rincon, who was at that time attached to the court of King Ferdinand; but the fact that he was painted still remains to be proved. There are two portraits in Spain to which a high antiquity is attributed, the one now in the Arsenal at Carthagena, and the other belonging to the admiral's descendants. The latter is very like the ancient bust of Columbus at Madrid, and may possibly have been taken from it. A copy of it was prefixed to Navarete's work as being that which the family have considered to be nearest to the truth. The portrait in the National Library at Madrid has been so much repainted that it is difficult to guess at its original appearance; but there is some reason to think that it may have been copied from an Italian version.

A peculiar interest attaches to a set of portraits derived from an original which once belonged to Paolo Giovio and was exhibited in his museum at Como. The learned Bishop of Nocera made the first great collection of portraits. His method is explained in his own delightful descriptions of the gallery. In dealing with the great men of antiquity, he had recourse to likenesses on coins and to old statues; in the case of famous Italians, he copied the figures on tombs and monuments. Sometimes, as when dealing with the leading jurists, he found a set of portraits ready to his hand in one of the small local collections. Other pictures were copied for him at Rome, Florence, and Milan. Sometimes he was able to secure the work of the great masters themselves. His "Solyman the Magnificent" was a *replica* of the picture painted by Gentile Bellini, in fear and trembling, at Constantinople. His "Matthias Corvinus" was by Andrea Mantegna. Giulio Romano had delivered over to the museum the heads from Bramantino's frescoes, which Raffaelle himself had copied in the Vatican. We find him writing to Aretino for another portrait, this time to be taken by Titian. He usually tells us the source from which he obtained his treasures. The set of Turkish Sultans, for instance, was a present to the King of France from the pirate Barbarossa; the likeness of the last Sultan of Egypt was copied from the picture taken at the storming of Cairo; the lineaments of "Scanderbeg" had been compared with the face of his descendant as he lay dead on the battlefield at Ravenna.

The bishop himself had seen Tristan d'Acunha at Rome, and could vouch for the excellence of his likeness, as well as for the truth to nature of the figures of Tristan's elephant and rhinoceros, which were depicted in the entrance hall.

The museum itself stood on a promontory opposite to a little island, just beyond the entrance to the harbor of Como. The island has been reclaimed, and the whole site is now taken into the town. From the terrace on the northern front the visitor came into a spacious hall with open porticoes, and rooms on all sides filled with statues or pictures. The upper gallery was used for the historical portraits, and here, in the series of heroes and warriors, was hung the fine picture of Columbus of which mention has already been made. It was set in a frame carved with emblems of maritime discovery, and containing the figures of an Ethiopian king and of an Indian in a garment of parrots' feathers. Attached to it was a parchment scroll containing the eulogy on the admiral, together with a somewhat inaccurate account of the celebrated voyages, from which a few sentences may be taken. "Here is that Christopher Columbus, the discoverer of a wonderful world unknown to any age before; whom we may believe to have been born under the benign influence of fortunate stars, to be an incomparable honor to Liguria, a choice adornment of Italy, a flaming light of our age, and that he might outshine the fame of the heroes of old. Columbus from his first youth was given up, like all his countrymen, to navigation, and traveled to all the marts and islands and shores of the Mediterranean Sea; and, as one vehemently given to geography, he turned all the strength of his deep-searching mind to the contemplation of all matters and regions in the terrestrial sphere, and that with such spirit and force as to learn from astronomy the measures of the tropics and equator and the various zones, as well as the exact use of the compass and the whole chart of the sea; and he predicted, with no vain conjecture, that quite new lands lay under the western sun, whereof, indeed, Plato himself and Seneca, and other Greeks and Romans, had left certain arguments to be weighed and considered by the cosmographers." The inscription ended by recommending the Genoese to set up a statue of the discoverer of a world, though in that day they had the character of admiring the present and rather underrating the past.

Paolo Giovio was a contemporary of Columbus, having been born in 1483. But he can hardly have begun making his collection till after 1527, the year of the sack of Rome, in which he lost all his possessions. It is said that he closed his historical series in 1544, when his dying brother Benedetto was gratified by being added to the persons there commemorated. Paolo himself died in 1552. The portraits were hurriedly copied by Cristofano dell' Altissimo and others working under him; and the copies are still to be seen in the Uffizi Gallery at Florence. Almost all the portraits appear in the woodcuts to the volumes of "Elogia," published by Peter Pera at Basle in 1575 and 1577, and reprinted in 1578 after a closer examination of the original. Roscoe states, in his "Life of Pope Leo," that the collections as made by Paolo Giovio were long preserved in the College of the Holy Rosary at Venice, the seal of the college being affixed to the back of every picture. We learn that on their dispersal he acquired many of them for his own collection; but nothing is stated by him as to the fate of the admiral's portrait. A discovery has lately been made at Como which may throw some light on the question. A portrait of Columbus in his old age has been found among the heirlooms of the Giovio family by Dr. De Orchi, its present representative. It differs considerably from the Florentine picture, but might perhaps have been the original from which Perna's woodcut was derived. Paolo Giovio may very well have had two portraits of his favorite hero; but it is important to observe, in any case, that he refrains from saying where he procured the painting to which the text of his biographical narrative was attached.

Returning to Columbus at Lisbon, we must

now notice a curious mistake that has crept into some of the biographies, to the effect that his brother Bartholomew was already established there, and was celebrated as a famous geographer; and that Christopher Columbus thereupon proceeded to learn map-making from him and all the science and information which led to the discovery of America.

It was one of the thirteen lies, to use Don Ferdinand's rough phrase, which Giustiniani crammed on to a sheet of paper when he set about illustrating the Psalter, that the admiral went to Lisbon to learn cosmography from his brother: "which was quite the contrary, because the admiral lived in that city first, and afterward taught the brother everything he knew."

Giustiniani had taken the story from Antonio Gallo of Genoa, who wrote an account of the discovery during the admiral's lifetime, after reading the letters in which the voyages were originally described. As a matter of fact, Bartholomew was not in Portugal in the year 1470, nor for more than ten years afterward. How then, it may be asked, did the mistake arise? The matter is interesting, as showing the kind of ignorance among educated men with which Columbus had so often to contend, when he discussed his projects and theories, again and again, in fruitless conference.

Gallo was all the time confusing Don Bartholomew with Ptolemy, or "Tolomeo," the ancient geographer of Alexandria. He thought that Columbus was referring to instruction received from his brother when he was discussing the measurements in maps of the second century, or was declaring his preference for the still older views of Marinus of Tyre. One example will serve to illustrate the point. It has reference to the position of the ancient city of Cattigara, on the eastern confines of India. Marinus had placed it in a certain position of eastern longitude, and in the same latitude as the mouths of the Indus. This fixed point of Marinus had been altered by Ptolemy, who thought that he had corrected his master's measurement by bringing it thirty degrees nearer to Africa.

When Columbus saw the eclipse at Evangelista near Cuba, as mentioned in his Jamaica letter, he thought that he had reached the fixed point indicated by Marinus, and had therefore arrived at India, and had joined the map of his own route to the map of the world as known to the ancients. He was on the 24th parallel of latitude and "in the 9th hour" of western longitude, so that he must be near the city in question. Now Gallo goes into all these details, quoting the words of the admiral's letter, and concludes that Columbus had reached the point indicated by Ptolemy "only two hours east of that place which Bartholomæus called Cattigara, and considered to be the last inhabited region of the East." For such reasons he describes Don Bartholomew as a very celebrated cosmographer, "whose charts showed by just lines and proportions all the seas and ports, and the shores, gulfs, and islands"; and he credits the younger brother with showing to Christopher, as a practical sailor, how he must follow the Portuguese track along the coast of Africa, and then turn to the right, and then, sailing always toward the West, he must arrive at the continent beyond the ocean.

The biography tells us how courteously Columbus was received by the Italian merchants in Lisbon, and how his reputation was increased when it was found that "he behaved honorably, and did nothing but what was just." There is naturally but little information as to the names of those who assisted him and helped him to set up in business. It has been thought, however, that some indications may be gathered from the death-bed codicil, in which his son Don Diego was told to pay certain legacies to persons whom his father had known in Lisbon, or to the representatives of such of them as were then dead, and make the payment in such a way that no one might know from whom the benefit came. It has been suggested, indeed, that these gifts may have been repayments of outstanding commercial debts, or of debts at least binding in honor; but it seems more probable, from what is known of his character, that they were recognitions of the kindness which he had received during the early part of his career in Portugal.

We find in this list the names of several Genoese merchants who were trading at Lisbon in the year 1482, the date to which the codicil specially refers, and of other Italians, connected with that city, whom the admiral may have known at an earlier period. There is a gift to the heirs of one "Antonio Vazo" of Genoa, whose name should be "Tobazo," according to the researches instituted by Mr. Harrisse. There is also a small legacy of twenty ducats, or their value, to the representatives of Geronimo del Puerto of Genoa, who was the father of Benito del Puerto, afterward Chancellor of the City. A legacy of 30,000 reals, equivalent to about seventy-five dollars, was bequeathed to the heirs of Centurione Scotto Luigi, a member of a family that still flourishes at Genoa. Another gift of a hundred ducats went to the heirs of Paolo de Negro of the same place. Baptista Spinola, belonging to a noble family established near Alessandria, was to receive twenty ducats; and, finally, there was a bequest of eight ounces of silver in favor of the old Jew "who used to live close to the gate of the Jewry in Lisbon."

CHAPTER VI.

> "If I had a friend that loved her,
> I should but teach him how to tell my story,
> And that would woo her. Upon this hint I spake;
> She loved me for the dangers I had passed,
> And I loved her that she did pity them;
> This only is the witchcraft I have used.
> Here comes the lady. Let her witness it."

PHILIPPA MONIZ, the hero's beautiful and courageous wife, came of a race that loved the sea. Her father, Perestrello, was one of the great explorers who had found again the lost islands of the Atlantic. To her family belonged the government of the new colony at Porto Santo. Some of her nearest relations were companions of Vasco da Gama, and took part in the Portuguese expeditions to India and China.

Like Columbus himself she belonged to the fair Lombard race. She was a descendant of Gabriel Pallastrelli, one of the best-born nobles of Piacenza, and through his marriage she claimed alliance with the line of the fighting Bracciforti. Gabriel's son, Philip Pallastrelli, had married a kinswoman of the Visconti reigning at Milan; and he was Philippa's grandfather, after whom she was named. When all the bold adventurers went out to Portugal to take part in the maritime discoveries, Philip followed with the rest, and became naturalized there under the name of Perestrello.

His family seems to have prospered in its new home. Raphael, his elder son, became the head of a branch that still flourishes in Lisbon. Bartholomew, the father of our Donna Philippa, was brought up at the court of Prince Henry and became one of his bravest captains. Philippa's aunt was married to the statesman Pedro de Naranhos, and their son was Archbishop of Lisbon at the time of which we are writing.

When Columbus came to Portugal, Philippa's father had been dead for about twelve years. Her mother had a house at Lisbon, but the young lady held a somewhat independent position. Either through her father's merits, or by the favor of her cousin the Archbishop, she was a "cavaliera," or dame, in one of the knightly orders, with a home, if she pleased, in the rich Convent of All Saints. Here, it is said, she used to sing in the chapel choir. The young Genoese found his way to the same church and became constant in his attendance at the service. She noticed his fine figure and handsome appearance, and soon permitted him to make a closer acquaintance.

> O tre fiate avventurosa figlia
> Di Perestrello ! ti condusse amore
> Ad incontrar l'eroe.

To some of her prosperous relations an alliance between Philippa and an Italian adventurer must have been extremely distasteful. He was clever enough, and able to keep himself with his charts and scrolls; but, after all, he was nothing but a foreign captain who had lost his ship, and had joined the crowd of adventurers full of rich promises and fantastic inventions.

The lady had inherited a strong will. Her father, we know, was dead, and he had left her a plantation in his island of Porto Santo. She admired the brave spirit of Columbus, and shared in his fervid dreams; and "she was so taken with him," says the biographer, "that she soon became his wife."

Columbus found that he was introduced to a host of new friends and relations. Philippa had much to tell him of her father's exploits, and of her young brother serving in Africa, who would soon be taking over his governorship. Her father had been twice married. She had three half-sisters, the children of Donna Beatrix Furtada. These were Kate and Beatrix and Iseult, "Queen Iseult, at Porto Santo," whose husband was Pedro Correa, the governor, or rather, perhaps, the acting-governor, ready to give up the post to young Bartholomew as soon as he was of age to take it. She had sisters of her own. The name of one of them appears in the last will of Don Diego, the second viceroy, who left a good legacy to his "Aunt Brigulaga." We know that one of her sisters was married to a Spanish gentleman named Mulia, residing at Huelva, with whom Columbus took refuge when he fled from Portugal. Her home, by a curious chance, was near the pine woods that enfold the monastery of La Rabida, where the admiral found peace and good counsel; and it looked out over the Port of Palos, across the red bar of Saltes, where he sailed out with his little fleet on the first night of his great adventure.

Philippa's mother was Donna Isabel Moniz, one of the children of Gil Moniz, a man of good family from Algarete, who had raised himself from the position of a secretary to a place of some dignity and importance. Several members of his family are mentioned in the Portuguese records. He had three sons, Diogo, Vasco, and Ruy, and a daughter Guiomar, who was married to Don Diaz de Lemos before Columbus and Philippa became acquainted. Philippa's uncle Diogo was one of the guardians of her brother's estate. The other uncles were very busy about a family lawsuit that began in the year before her engagement. Her grandfather, Gil Moniz, had endowed a private chapel and vault in the Carmelite monastery, and it was clear that no one out of his direct line was intended to use the vault. But the Prior had unjustly allowed a stranger to be buried there; and the family hoped and believed, quite rightly, as the event turned out, that they would obtain a plain decree that the lineage of Gil Moniz alone had the right of interment. The chapel and all its monuments were long ago swallowed up in the pit of the great earthquake; but the family tradition remains that Donna Isabel was buried there, and that Philippa's body rested for a time in the vault before her son, the heir of Columbus, removed them to the famous tomb in the cathedral church of San Domingo,

Philippa could tell many a story of the lonely rock of Porto Santo where her childhood had been spent. When Perestrello died in 1457, Donna Isabel was glad to take her children home, and to leave her son-in-law Correa to look after the plantations and to keep up the dignity of a court and colony in miniature. The children, we suppose, would be as tired as herself of the long white bay and the huddled crowd of sand hills, with here and there a peak of basalt, or a cliff with staring expanses of lava. There was nothing to be seen on the island, except the new sugar mills and the vineyards where the vines were pegged down a few inches from the ground. You might see rabbits in multitudes among the sand hills, and there were armies of rats and lizards to feed upon the grapes. The former pest, indeed, had nearly destroyed the colony when it was first established. Perestrello himself had turned out a litter of tame rabbits, and the rash experiment had resulted in a total destruction of the crops. Nothing seemed to thrive there except dragon trees, and even these had become scarce. It was said that there had been thousands of them when the island was first discovered; and Philippa's father had hoped to become rich by selling the gum, which some people called "cinnabar" from its red color, and others "dragon's blood"; and there was a story about an Eastern gum of the same nature being drawn from the blood of an Indian serpent. The fruit was used in fattening pigs; it looked like a yellow cherry, but was rather bitter in taste. Only a few of the trees were left. There had been some with trunks large enough to make a boat for six or seven men; but they had been cut down for all kinds of uses, whenever a man wanted "wood for a shield, or a bushel for his corn."

When the marriage took place the young couple went to live with Donna Isabel. Columbus set to work in earnest at map-making, and his wife soon found that she was able to do a great deal in assisting her husband. Her mother became a close ally, and encouraged her son-in-law to persevere in the path which his courage had marked out. The widowed lady was fond of talking about her husband as "a great seafaring man," and she knew all about the compact of the three captains that had led to the settlement of Madeira. Everyone had heard of Tristram Vaz, who ruled the province of Machico, and of old Zarco, called "Camara dos Lobos," who till within a few months past had been carried out every morning at Funchal into the sunshine, "to hear complaints and to administer justice."

Madeira was said to rank next to Britain as "a princess of the islands in the ocean." Whatever can be known about its ancient history is of some importance still, because the finding of each stepping-stone in the Atlantic had a bearing upon the discovery of America. Madeira and her twin colony are thought to have been the "purple islands" described by King Juba, the country where the great Sertorius had longed to dwell, "far from the noise of war and free from the troubles of government." Here was the land where the Spaniards in old times had placed the fabled gardens of Alcinous, where the fruit never fades nor perishes, "but pear upon pear waxes old, and apple upon apple." It might be worth while to go back to one ancient authority, and to investigate the obscure question whether Madeira was not the subject of one of the enigmatical descriptions in the cosmography of Æthicus. The matter would, at any rate, have a bearing on Humboldt's strange theory that the dragon trees in the Atlantic islands were introduced by merchants from India. This cosmography, as the work now stands, professes to be the abstract, by a priest named Hieronymus, of a philosopher's travels between Thule and the Earthly Paradise. It is based in fact on the romantic "Life of Apollonius," compiled in the reign of Nero; but it is plain that its later editor intended to assume the name and authority of St. Jerome. The aid of Æthicus was commonly invoked when the marvels of geography ran short. Roger Bacon was blamed for drawing from this source; and its influence may be easily traced in the book of Mandeville and the writings of Olaus Magnus. The philosopher is represented as coming from the East to an island in the temperate zone, the last place reached before he arrived at Cadiz. He was wrecked upon an uninhabited island; and some parts of its description are appropriate to Madeira. We read of an abundance of tamarisks, and of trees with bark and fruit as bitter as aloes. On the shore, the traveler found shoals of little creatures "quilled like porcupines"; and he met with a "multitude of sirens." He seems to have been referring to the sea-urchins that are seen in great numbers on some parts of the coast of Madeira; and his "sirens" remind us strongly of the monk seals, or sea wolves, afterward found in the same neighborhood, near the cave called the "Camara dos Lobos." When the Portuguese explorers first came to this spot, they reached a recess where a troop of these seals ran down into the sea. Zarco himself took a title from the adventure, and became Count Camara dos Lobos, with a new coat of arms and two sea wolves for its supporters. The description by Æthicus concluded with his account of the ascent of a great mountain by steps and galleries, "along the southern side of a chasm with terrible shelves and crags"; and this might almost be taken as a reminiscence of the precipices of the Grand Coural.

Coming now to the mediæval period, it should be noted that explorers from Normandy, from Catalonia, and from Genoa had, in fact, long preceded the Portuguese in many of their African discoveries. Madeira itself, under a name of equivalent meaning, and Porto Santo, under the name which it still bears, and even the desert rocks in that neighborhood, had been inscribed about the year 1351 in the Italian and Catalan maps. The expedition of Bethencourt, with a fleet from Normandy, to take possession of the Canaries, made it certain that the two islands to the northward would soon become generally known. Long lost, and then found for a time and lost again, they were finally added to the civilized world by Perestrello and his two companions.

According to his widow's simple story, he had set out to discover new countries with his comrades Joam Zarco and Tristram Vaz, and they had agreed among themselves to cast lots for the first choice of all that they might find. On reaching the islands, which, in Donna Isabel's opinion, had never before been discovered, they divided the larger country into the provinces of Machico and Funchal, which fell to her husband's comrades. "Porto Santo," she said, "was Perestrello's share, and he held the government till he died."

The discovery was in reality a result of the attempts to pass Cape Bojador and to reach the rich coast of Senegambia. Prince Henry the Navigator had for many years been trying to open a new passage to the East. He knew all the ancient traditions of Phœnicians sailing round Lybia, and of the fleets of Carthage pushing into the torrid zone, and how Eudoxus had sailed for India from Cadiz "with doctors and workmen and dancing girls." But the Portuguese sailors were discouraged by constant failure, and feared to pass a barrier from which there might be no returning.

A determined attempt was made in 1419 by Zarco, then a young follower of Prince Henry, who had already distinguished himself at the siege of Ceuta. He failed to pass Cape Bojador, and was tossed about for many days in a storm, until at last he saw the basaltic peaks of Porto Santo, and anchored in its long sandy bay.

Next year an expedition was sent to look out for the island and to explore the seas in its neighborhood. This seems to be the joint undertaking described by Donna Isabel to Columbus as that in which her husband was engaged. Their old pilot, who had been a captive among the Moors, had heard something about Madeira from certain English galley-slaves. These men had, according to their own story, been driven there in 1347, when the unfortunate Robert Machin fled from England with the rich Anne d'Urfey, and they had been obliged to leave the lovers to die on the shore of the Gulf of Cedars. The old tradition was confirmed by the appearance on the horizon of a black cloud that never changed its outline. But the sailors were reluctant to cross the stretch of open water. Some feared that the cloud was the covering of a pit of fire. Others admitted that it might be Cipango, or the long-lost Land of the Seven Cities. The pilot, on the other hand, maintained that what they saw was a rain cloud attracted by the forests in a range of mountains. The opposition to his argument reminds us of the difficulties encountered by Columbus. "This pilot," they said, "is a foreigner from Castile, and he is only too anxious to injure us Portuguese"; and they thought it quite enough to be prepared to fight with men, without entering on a contest with the forces of nature. Zarco, as one of the crew remarked, "had enough courage for all," and he set out one morning to find the shadow on the sea. A thick fog came on, and there was a terrible noise of breakers; as they passed the Desertas, where a tall rock loomed like a ship, the sailors cried out that an armed giant was rising from the waves. When they got near Madeira the cloud began to roll up, and they saw red cliffs and the low black promontory of San Lorenzo, and a broad forest with trees crowding to the water's edge and filling the glens and ravines.

No regular attempt was made to erect a colony at Porto Santo till the year 1425, and even then it had to be abandoned for a time owing to the destruction caused by the rabbits. The colony was finally established in 1446, when it had been determined to use Madeira and Porto Santo as sugar islands.

"The admiral," says his son, "was much delighted to hear such voyages and relations," and was particularly interested in learning about the later discoveries in Senegambia and the seas beyond Cape Verde. Donna Isabel brought out from her family treasures her husband's box of papers, with all his old sea charts and memoranda, and a description of what he found at Porto Santo; and we are told that by this "the admiral was still more inflamed." We know something of the contents of these papers from Cadamosto's account of a visit paid by him to Perestrello about the year 1445. The most valauble production of the island at that time was the lichen called the "archil," or orchilla weed. Of this there were two kinds, the darker and better sort being found inland, and the lighter kind on rocks by the sea. The plant is thought to have been the source of the "Gætulian purple" of the ancients. It produces a lilac dye, but it is generally used as a mordant for brightening other colors. It it said that, when the Canaries were first occupied, this orchilla weed was collected as eagerly as the American gold was afterward gathered by the Spaniards. Porto Santo has a good soil for corn in the calcareous strata which rise above the sand drifts; but a great part of the island remained useless until the new industries of wine-making and sugar-boiling were introduced by Prince Henry. He brought a stock of canes from Sicily, and plants of the Malmsey vine from Candia; and the trade thus started almost at once attained to a surprising prosperity. Madeira became a special center of the sugar trade. As soon as this took place the sugars of Sicily and the Levant fell to a very low price; and, according to the Venetian archives, it was not long before "there arrived annually at Venice five or six ships freighted with Madeira sugar," with a cargo in some cases of five hundred butts at a time. Sugar was also produced to a large extent in the Canary Islands. Scillacio mentions the supplies of sugar which Columbus purchased at the Grand Canary on starting for the second voyage. It was of excellent quality: "This is the sugar that used to come from Arabia and India, taken like gum from the canes; it is very white and brittle, and some people say that it is the Indian salt of the physicians." Columbus mentions the subject in his Memoranda of 1494, where he remarks: "It will be very useful to get from Madeira fifty pipes of molasses, which is the best and wholesomest food in the world; a pipe usually costs two ducats, besides the cost of the butt, and if their Highnesses would order one of the caravels to return by way of Madeira she might buy the molasses, and also take in ten butts of sugar, of which we are in great need."

There are other passages in the admiral's journal that seem to refer to the papers which he studied with his wife and her mother at Lisbon. He remarks, for instance, in his journal for December, 1492, that he knew how the Portuguese had owed their discoveries to observing the flight of birds; and this was his reason for his memorable turn toward the southwest, so as to follow the birds returning home at sunset. Everyone knows the picturesque notices throughout the first voyage on the flight of the sea swallows, the boobies, and the tropic birds, and the supposed distances at which each species might be found away from land. He seems to have had a great store of notes upon the habits of animals. When they met with a sperm whale on the same voyage, the admiral said that these creatures always stayed near land; and the little swimming crab found upon the gulf weed could not, it was thought, be more than "thirty leagues from home." The approach to San Salvador itself was heralded by the appearance of a great green fish, "of the sort that goes not far from the rocks." Soon after starting for home the admiral announced the neighborhood of new islands on seeing a fish swim round the ship and suddenly dart toward the southwest; and only a few hours before that, he had said, of a passing shoal of tunnies, that they appeared to be making straight for a certain nobleman's fishery in Spain.

We do not suppose that Columbus attached undue importance to the calculations and memoranda, the scraps of navigation and weather wisdom, which Perestrello's widow had preserved. But, as Don Ferdinand said, "however it was, as one thing leads to another, he began to think that, as the Portuguese traveled so far to the south, it were no less proper to sail away to the west"; and for greater certainty he took to looking over the cosmographers again, and to seek for astronomical reasons in support of his view. His own papers show that he now proceeded to collect all available information, especially from the reports of sailors, to justify the conclusion that there were many lands west of the Canaries, and "by such mean arguments to support so vast an undertaking."

By this time Philippa's brother had grown up, and was ready to assume the captaincy of Porto Santo. He had served in an African campaign, and had shown some capacity of government. Accordingly in the month of March, 1473, the temporary appointment of Pedro Correa came to an end, and the young Bartholomew was made head of the colony, with all the profits of salt dues, mill tolls, monopolies and privileges which his father and uncle had enjoyed.

Pedro Correa, with his wife Iseult, who called herself "Hizeu Perestrella," soon afterward returned to Lisbon, and made acquaintance with their new brother-in-law. Correa had much to say about the signs of new land in the west. Porto Santo lies within the influence of that returning current of the Gulf Stream, which sweeps downward past the Azores and brings flotsam from tropical America to the western coasts of Europe. A pilot named Martin Vincente had been more than four hundred leagues out from Cape St. Vincent, and had found a piece of floating wood, curiously carved, but apparently not cut with any tool of metal, "and, the wind having been long in the west, he thought it must have come from some island out that way." This story was fully confirmed by Correa, who declared that he had seen another piece of wood of the same kind brought by westerly winds to Porto Santo. Nay, more, he had found great canes afloat, "and they were so big that every joint would hold a gallon of wine." If this were doubted, the canes might be seen at Lisbon at that very time, for they had been sent to the king as a curiosity. On inquiry being made, the statement was found to be quite true. The king himself showed Columbus the canes, "and there being no place in our parts where such things grow, he looked upon it as certain that the wind had brought them from some island, or perhaps from India."

These things seem to have had a great influence on Columbus. What discoveries might not be made if they were all living at Porto Santo, especially as his young brother-in-law was the new governor, and his wife the owner of a plantation! Why should they not go back to Donna Isabel's old home, set as it were in the busy track of commerce, and on the direct line to the new African conquests? The plan was sensible, and was easily carried out. Columbus and his wife set up their home for some years in the island, and here their son Diego was born. Porto Santo was a place of call for merchants, where maps and charts might easily be sold; and it was a convenient center from which Columbus could start on his yearly voyages, to the Mediterranean or the Azores, or the North Sea, as the case might be, while his wife remained at home to look after their little estate.

CHAPTER VII.

> "And all the place is peopled with sweet airs:
> The light, clear element which the isle wears
> Is heavy with the scent of lemon-flowers,
> Which floats like mist laden with unseen showers,
> And falls upon the eyelids like faint sleep;
> And from the moss violets and jonquils peep."

COLUMBUS was deeply interested in the tales of Tyre and Carthage about the discovery in ancient times of fertile islands in the ocean and half-submerged tracts of ooze and sand. Colored as they were with romance, and distorted into many versions in their long descent, so as hardly to be distinguishable from the fictions of which they became the base, there was still a great vitality in the legends of the Hesperides and of the fruitful country of Antilla. This last, indeed, was marked on all the maps. In Toscanelli's chart there was a space of no more than 225 leagues between Antilla, or the Land of the Seven Cities, and Cipango, off the coast of Cathay, where the palaces were roofed with gold. Columbus observed that the Portuguese had placed this country about two hundred leagues west of the Azores, and that, according to their belief, seven bishops had gone with a crowd of followers, when Spain was conquered by the Moors, and had each of them built a city; and so he hoped that, before he came to India, he should find "some well placed island or continent, from whence he might the better pursue his main design."

The older forms of the tradition were accepted on the authority of the "Book of Wonders," at that time attributed to Aristotle, and of a long and flowery description contained in the collections of Diodorus. It is probable that the whole story arose out of the voyages of Hanno and Himilco "in the flourishing times of Carthage," when one of their two fleets went southward to the neighborhood of Sierra Leone, and the other was blown about in the Atlantic till they came to the region of floating weed, to which Columbus afterward gave the name of the Sargasso Sea. They reached a place "where the waters seemed so shallow that the weeds lay in masses on the waves, and their keels were impeded as if passing through a thicket of underwood"; and the sea beasts, we are told, went up and down upon the banks, and swam round the ships as they slowly drifted along. Here we seem to have the beginnings of the myth of Atlantis and the prototype of Lucian's imaginary voyage "through pines and cypresses growing in the sea"; and perhaps we might attribute to the same source the story in Pliny of a great tree in the Atlantic, with crowds of tunnies feeding like sea hogs on its acorns.

In the collection of stories which was wrongly ascribed to Aristotle, we read of certain banks in the ocean where the sailors of Cadiz got the fish for the markets of Carthage. "Men say that they sail out from the Straits for four days with an east wind, and come on a desert full of rushes and seaweed, and they land and find a great number of tunnies of wonderful size and fatness." Then follows a variation of the story, to the effect that the Carthaginians had sailed out into the Atlantic and discovered a most fruitful island: "Men say that in the sea beyond the Pillars of Hercules the Carthaginians found an uninhabited island, with woods of all kinds, and navigable rivers, and a wonderful abundance of produce; it lay at a distance of several days' sail from land. Many expeditions were made to it, and some of the Carthaginians even settled there; but the Senate made a decree, forbidding any more visits on pain of death, and the settlers were all killed, for fear of their spreading the news, lest a great population might gather there, and by chance get the upper hand and destroy the prosperity of the city."

Yet another account of the matter was preserved by Diodorus Siculus, which does not, however, appear to have been known to Columbus at the time when he was collecting his information. This version is so ornate that it seems to have been taken from some romance. The details about a great population and an abundance of animals of the chase must be due to the imagination of a novelist, who may be supposed to have added such embroidery as might please the fancy of his readers.

Diodorus described the country as being thickly inhabited, and attributed the discovery rather to the Phœnicians of Tyre than to their Carthaginian kindred: "Over against Africa lies a very great island in the vast ocean, of many days' sail from Lybia. The soil here is very fruitful. A great part of it is mountainous, but much likewise is champaign, and this is the most sweet and pleasant part of all, for it is watered with several navigable rivers, beautified with many gardens of pleasure, planted with divers sorts of trees and abundance of orchards, and interlaced with currents of sweet water. The towns are adorned with stately buildings, and banqueting houses up and down, pleasantly situated in their gardens and orchards; and here they recreate themselves in summer time, as in places accommodated for pleasure and delight. The mountainous part of the country is clothed with large oak woods and all manner of fruit trees, and for the greater diversion of people in these mountains they ever and anon open themselves into pleasant vales, watered with fountains and refreshing springs. There you may have game enough in hunting all sorts of wild beasts, of which there is such plenty that in their feasts there is nothing wanting either as to pomp or delight. Now this country," he says, "by reason of its remote situation was at one time altogether unknown, but was afterward discovered in this way; the Phœnicians in ancient times undertook frequent voyages by sea in way of traffic as merchants, so that they planted many colonies both in Africa and in these western parts of Europe. The Phœnicians having found out the coasts beyond the Pillars, and sailing along by the shore of Africa, were driven by a furious storm afar off into the main ocean, and after they had lain under this violent tempest for many days they at length arrived at this island, and so coming to the knowledge of the nature and pleasantness of the isle they were the first that discovered it to others; and therefore the Etrurians (when they were masters at sea) designed to send a colony thither, but the Carthaginians opposed them, fearing lest most of their own citizens should be allured to settle there, and likewise intending to keep it as a place of refuge for themselves, in case of any sudden and unexpected blasts of fortune."

The African voyage of Hanno was of great historical importance. The details were recorded in a tablet suspended in a temple, and were also preserved by chance in a Greek version which survived the destruction of Carthage. His fleet coasted round Morocco, and passed Cape Bojador; and the trading station or mart of Kerne was established either in the Isle of Arguin or, more probably, at the mouth of the Rio del Ouro. From this station two separate expeditions appear to have set out. The first set of

explorers reached the Senegal, which they called
Bambothus, or the River of the Behemoths, from
the abundance of crocodiles and hippopotami;
and they afterward pushed southward along the
flat coast till they reached the green heights of
Cape Verde. The leaders of the second expedition went far beyond the former limit. First
they came to the Bissagos Islands, in front of a
winding gulf. They called this gulf the Horn
of Hesperus, and the islands themselves were
afterward known as the Hesperides. Then they
came to a gigantic cliff, which they named the
Chariot of the Gods; this is the cape which the
Portuguese called Sagres, in memory of Prince
Henry's home by the "sacred promontory" of
Cape St. Vincent. Passing onward by the ridge
of Sierra Leone, where the thunder always roars,
they arrived at the "Southern Horn," which is
now known as the Sherbro River. Here they
landed on a little island full of apes. The interpreters called them "gorillas"; but the Carthaginians took them for negroes. "The men,"
they said, "escaped by climbing the cliffs, and
throwing down stones, but we caught three of
the women; they bit and scratched their keepers, but we killed and flayed them." According

to Pliny and his imitators, these skins were seen by travelers at Carthage, suspended on the walls of the Temple of Ashtaroth.

In the course of time this story took many different forms. When Cape Verde became known to the Romans it received the old name of the Horn of Hesperus which the Carthaginians had given to the Gulf of the Hesperides. The Roman geographers were very vague about the situation of the Fortunate Islands, although the group was the starting-point of their first meridian. Even Ptolemy of Alexandria can be shown to have been in some confusion about Madeira, the Canaries, and the Cape Verde Islands, and to have treated them as if they formed one compact archipelago. Be this as it may, some knowledge was gained in very early times about the Cape Verde Islands, which lie about three hundred miles from the African shore; and these were called the Gorgon Islands, with an evident reference to the "wild women" of the ancient voyage. Here was laid the scene of the Greek legends of Perseus and the Three Gray Sisters; and the Hesperides, of which all exact knowledge had been lost, were moved into a sunny climate far to the southward, where a dragon guarded the golden tree. There was an old romance about wars between the Gorgons and the armies of Hesperus; and some were found to believe in the existence of this shadowy land. Statius Sebosus maintained that the true Hesperides lay forty good days' sail beyond Cape Verde. Pliny considered that all the reports upon this matter were uncertain; Solinus added that these Hesperides were withdrawn into the furthest recesses of the sea. The opinion of Columbus was colored by what he hoped to prove. "These authors say, that from the Gorgon Islands, supposed to be those off Cape Verde, was forty days' sail on the Atlantic to the Hesperides"; and the admiral concluded that these were the West Indies. The Spaniards afterward based another argument on the mythological tradition, contending that the former lord of these isles was Hesperus, the King of Spain, and that his lawful successors must therefore be the owners of the newly found world.

After America had been discovered the controversies about Antilla and the Seven Cities were less hotly debated, and the ancient traditions were localized at Barbadoes and among the ruined cities of Yucatan. But it may still be worth while to touch upon the arguments which passed between Oviedo and Ferdinand Columbus, on a subject which had so deeply affected the admiral's theories and projects. These arguments turned on the exact words of the legend as reported by the Greeks; and it may be here observed that neither disputant was properly equipped for the fray. Neither of them had the original version before him. Don Ferdinand had the Latin text of "Propositions from Aristotle," published by Theophilus de Ferrariis in 1493; and this book professed to contain an exact translation of the passages relating to Antilla, made about the year 1477 by Antonio Becaria, a geographer living at Verona. It was clear that he had inserted several matters differing from the original; "and this will appear," said Don Ferdinand, "to any man that will observe it." Oviedo, on the other hand, had nothing but "a friar's pamphlet," as it was called, consisting of a rough Spanish translation of the text as published by Theophilus.

The result of the controversy was that Oviedo maintained the identity of Antilla with one of the West Indian islands; he gave his readers the choice between Cuba and Hispaniola, and hoped, in either case, to fortify some mythical claim of the Spaniards by diminishing the merits of the discoveries of Columbus. Don Ferdinand criticised somewhat too seriously the minuter details of the story, which he pronounced to be a mere fabrication. "In great travels there are great lies," he said; and if they came to lying, it would be as easy to make out the identity of the island with "Atalanta, that was drowned in the Peloponnesian War," or even with the lost Atlantis of which Plato and the Egyptians had discoursed. But, granting that the fable was based upon the events of a real voyage, it was clear that the merchants would have had no mind to run further than the wind obliged them to go, and that no storm could last so long as to carry a ship from Cadiz to Hispaniola. He derided the idea that the Carthaginians were afraid of settlements being made in the West Indies, "between which and them there lay one-third of the world." Their merchants would never have given up such a fine country. They would rather have fortified the place so as to make their trade secure. "This we know," he adds, "from what they did at another time upon a like occasion; for having found the Cassiterides, now called the Azores, they kept the voyage very private, because of the tin that they procured; and so, granting the truth of what Aristotle wrote, it might be said that he meant to describe the voyages to the Azores; though Oviedo, either for want of better understanding and from the great antiquity of the story, or through that affection by which men are blinded, argued that it should be understood of the Indies which we now possess."

The traditions of these Carthaginian voyages were utilized in very early times for the purposes of descriptive romance. There was a fashion for stories of adventure in unknown lands, and it was a favorite device to describe the finding of tropical islands and a new continent in another hemisphere. "How many writers," said Lucian, "have presented us with their travels, and have told us of wondrous great beasts and savages and new-fangled ways of living!" It was like Odysseus telling the flighty Phæacians about the bags of wind, and the cannibals, and the Cyclops, and a thousand other falsehoods besides; and he proposed to write a traveler's tale himself in which there should not be a single grain of truth. It is interesting to observe how this "True Story" reads in several respects like a parody of the journals of Columbus. Lucian supposes himself to have sailed from Cadiz with fifty comrades, all anxious to explore the Ocean and to discover new nations in the opposite continent. They suffer many strange adventures, being swallowed by a monstrous fish, and being whirled into the circle of the moon. They reach the polar ice, and dig out caverns to protect themselves from the cold; and they find forests growing in the sea, and skim the tree tops in a "woodland voyage." They arrived at last at the Island of the Blessed through a land wind heavy with the scent of roses and the blossom of the vine. The rivers were as clear as crystal and the woods full of singing birds, "and from the whole country arose a mingled noise, such as may be heard at a banquet, where there are minstrels and flute-players, and others dancing to the music of the harp and the flute." Seven other islands lay in sight, and after reaching the most distant of these, as the travelers are told, "you will come to the Great Continent which stretches over against this country, and there shall you meet with many strange fortunes, and pass through many nations and new and barbarous peoples, and so at last come home."

One Iambulus, too, had written a story of the Great Sea, which was thought to be entertaining, though everybody knew that it was untrue. The details may be found in the collection of Diodorus, the Sicilian. The story begins with an expedition from the Red Sea to Ceylon; and the wanderers pass onward to the Seven Islands, four months' journey to the east of India. "Here are exceeding great serpents, which yet do no one any harm; nay, their flesh is good meat, and very sweet; here the people make their clothes of a soft cotton, growing on reeds and canes, and they color it with a shell-fish dye made up in balls and kneaded into the stuff, and so with great pains they prepare their purple garments."

The writer was guessing at the possibility of the task which Columbus performed. The singularity of this anticipation of his ideas occurred at once to the admiral's contemporaries; and when Scillacio was comparing the account of the Second Voyage to the discoveries of Hanno in Africa, he remarked that it was truer indeed than Lucian's tale, though perhaps as full of trifles as the story told by the Sicilian.

CHAPTER VIII.

> "From the destined walls
> Of Cambalu, seat of Cathaian Can,
> And Samarcand by Oxus, Temir's throne. . .
> On Europe thence, and where Rome was to sway
> The world; in spirit perhaps he also saw
> Rich Mexico, the seat of Montezume,
> And Cusco in Peru, the richer seat
> Of Atabalipa, and yet unspoiled
> Guiana, whose great city Geryon's sons
> Call El Dorado."

IT was one of the chief problems of geography to fix the position of Thule. It was agreed that the island was one of the principal points by which the length and breadth of the world might be determined. Thule was regarded as the most northern of all habitable lands, but there had been disputes about its exact situation ever since the first Greek travelers had explored the northern seas. One ancient school of thinkers, eager to enlarge the world's boundaries, had set Thule far up within the Arctic Circle, and had spread out the limits of Asia more and more toward the east. Others, of a more timid kind, had brought

Thule close down to Scotland, and at the same time had reduced the length of the inhabited land area in what they thought to be a due proportion. Thule in the north was balanced by a "world's end" in the south, at a cape not far from the Red Sea's mouth, in the region of cloves and cinnamon; and a line drawn between these latitudes gave the measure of the breadth of the world.

It was believed that, by virtue of some natural law of proportion, the world's length was somewhat more than twice its breadth. Some of the geographers asserted that the inhabited earth was shaped like an open sling, and they meant, apparently, that it was of a long, oval shape, drawn out to a point at each end. India and Spain formed its extremities, and the broader part was made up of the three continents, joined together at certain points, though nearly separated from each other by the gulfs running in from the ocean.

In Ptolemy's system of geography the figure was changed. The world was said to be something like a soldier's cape spread out; and the map has somewhat of that appearance, as if the cloak were cut away for the neck, and were narrow at top and spreading out below, so as to take the breadth of the shoulders. This has always been a favorite method of comparison. We all speak of the boot shape of Italy and compare the Morea to a mulberry leaf. The ancients used to say that Spain was like a bullock's hide with the neck at the Pyrenees. Britain was compared to the long, narrow blade of a battle-ax; Scandinavia was like a cedar leaf floating on the sea; and Columbus followed the same fashion when he compared Hispaniola to the leaf of the chestnut.

When Thule was discovered, an extra breadth of about one thousand miles was added northward, with a corresponding addition of breadth toward the equator. It was therefore necessary, according to the rule already mentioned, to add more than four thousand miles to the length of the world from east to west. Taking a line through Athens and Cadiz, the geographers of Alexandria computed the earth's circumference at about twenty thousand miles. Eratosthenes covered the whole of this unknown space with the Atlantic Ocean; and he drew the bold deduction, on which Columbus acted in a later age, that "if the size of the Atlantic were not of itself an obstacle we might easily cross by sea from Spain to India, keeping always on the same parallel of latitude." Posidonius, on the other hand, divided the globe into four quarters. In one he placed the inhabited portion of the earth as known to the geographers; and he conjectured that there might be another tract of the same kind on the other side of the northern hemisphere. Below the burning zone of the equator there might in the same way be worlds inhabited by the nations of the Antipodes. Some of his followers added that we could not cross over to our neighbors in the temperate zone, "because the Atlantic is not passable by ships, and is haunted by monsters of the deep."

Strabo took a narrow view of the question. He thought that there probably was another continent between Spain and India, though it did not follow that the inhabitants would be like the men of the Old World. There might be regions where life could be supported, as far off as Thule or beyond the equator; but, as a practical geographer, he had only to deal with the countries between the line of the spice countries in the south and the latitude of the northern parts of Ireland, "where the savages could hardly live for the cold."

Columbus adopted the ancient opinion that the Atlantic covered the whole space between the east of Asia and the west of Europe, while claiming the benefit of the suggestion that at least land of some kind would be found by passing the ocean. He cited the authority of Aristotle, on the one hand, for the belief in a continuous tract of waters; and, on the other hand, he laid stress on Seneca's acceptance of the theory of the earlier Stoics. He quoted that passage in Seneca's "Medea," where the chorus sang "how Oceanus will loosen Nature's chains and allow a vast region to appear; the sea goddess will draw aside the veil from another world, and Thule no longer will be the last of lands." He quoted another fine passage from the same writer's "Physical Problems." "This world in which you make your voyages and lay out your kingdoms is but a point in Nature, if you add all the gulfs of ocean that run in on either side. The host marching out under your banners, with all the cavalry scouring ahead or gathered on the flanks, is but an army of ants running to and fro upon the ant hill. But above us are the vast spaces of the firmament into which a man's soul may enter and take possession. Then will he despise the narrowness of his ancient dwelling. For what is the space that lies between the Indies and the furthest shores of Spain? Nothing but a very few days' journey, if the ship were favored by the wind. But in that celestial region there spreads a road whereon for thirty years at a time, never halting, never ceasing, the swiftest star may travel."

The position assumed for Thule in Ptolemy's maps was perhaps due to certain statements of Tacitus. He had described a broad ocean stream in which were set the British and Scandinavian islands. Beyond lay an outer sea, so sluggish as to be nearly without movement; "and this," he says, "men take to be the girdle and frontier of the world, because there the brightness of the setting sun lasts till his rising, so as to make the starlight pale." He tells us that, when the fleet of Claudius subdued the Orkneys, the crews caught a glimpse of Thule, till then encompassed and hidden with driving snow, and that, as they passed on, the waters became sluggish and heavy against the oar, and were not even raised by the wind like the waves in other seas. In his speculations about the source of the tide-washed amber he hazards another theory as to the existence of new lands in the West. The glittering shapes of winged and creeping things, imprisoned in the gum, were an indication that the mass had formerly been liquid; and he supposed that "as in the remote places of the East, where the shrubs bleed balm and frankincense, so in the islands and countries of the West there may be fertile groves, where the gums exude in the rays of the sun, that sets so near to those parts, and so may flow down to the sea close by and be carried off by the waves to the opposite German shores."

Marinus of Tyre, an authority often quoted by Columbus, made an important attempt to resettle the boundaries of the world. He lived about the beginning of the age of the Antonines, not long before Ptolemy of Alexandria. His method was novel, and in some ways even fascinating. He abandoned mathematics as much as possible, and constructed a new map out of narratives of voyages and military expeditions. One of his most important innovations was his placing the first meridian on the line of the Canary Islands instead of near Cape St. Vincent; it is to this change that Columbus referred when he noted that "Marinus began his discoveries from the westward." Marinus also undertook a new description of Africa. Two expeditions of the Roman armies, recorded by him alone, had carried the line of the world's known breadth to a point far beyond the equator. Septimius Flaccus advanced from the oasis behind Tripoli for a three months' journey southward. Julius Maternus started from the same oasis, and went on for four months to a region where the rhinoceros most abounded. On the east coast he described the voyage of Diogenes down to a cape "near the lakes from which the Nile flows out," and the return journey of one Theophilus who got back to Cape Guardafui in twenty days, sailing at the rate of a hundred miles a day.

When we come to his map of Asia we find some very surprising results. There is a carved rock or Stone Tower in the highlands of Pamir, now called King Solomon's Throne; and here the Chinese silk merchants used to meet the traders from Samarcand and Bokhara. An itinerary compiled by one Titianus described the whole route from the Euphrates to the interior of China; and seven months were allowed for the silk merchants to return home from the markets held at the Stone Tower. Marinus considered that no less than a length of 3600 miles should be attributed to this part of the journey. Another estimate of the length of Asia was afforded by the voyage of Nearchus, who had taken four months to sail from the Indus to the Persian Gulf. More modern travelers had given very exaggerated accounts of the distance from the Ganges to the Golden Chersonese. A merchant named Alexander had said that one might go from the Straits of Malacca for twenty days eastward to the city of Zabræ, and then on again for many days to the mart of Cattigara, a place which some have placed in Borneo and others in the neighborhood of Hongkong. But even here, thousands of miles beyond the Ganges, as he thought, Marinus found no limit, and was forced to leave some parts of the Indies still undescribed.

The result was that he doubled the old estimates of the world's length, and made the land area cover about two-thirds of the world's whole circle, or fifteen out of the twenty-four hours, if we adopt the measurement by time. Columbus felt justified, therefore, in believing that the space between the easternmost point known to Marinus and the Cape Verde Islands "could not be more than a third part of the whole circumference of the globe." As Marinus had not come to the end of the east, one might allow for the land stretching out still further; and the more it advanced to the east the nearer it would be to us in the west. If the space between were sea, it might be crossed in a few days; if it were mostly land, it would be all the easier to reach it. There was, besides, the authority of the Greeks quoted by Pliny, who all thought that the Indies covered a third part of the earth; "and if India be so large, it must be near Spain, if we take the western route."

The exaggerations of Marinus were, to some extent, corrected by Ptolemy; but the space left uncovered in the map was still very much too small. For one thing these ancient geographers measured by very small degrees, so that there was a loss of quite one-fifth in the estimate of the earth's circumference. Columbus himself went by the calculations of Alfragan, an Arabian geographer, who took the length of a mean degree of the meridian at fifty-six and two-thirds Italian miles. This still further reduced the estimate of the earth's circuit; and the result in short was this, that if Marinus was right about

India and Alfragan correct in his measurement, there would be no room for any very wide ocean on the route which Columbus was to explore.

Ptolemy placed in the northern limit of the world at "Thule," by which it is clear that he meant the largest of the Shetland Isles. The earlier Greek travelers had found their "world's end" on the verge of the Arctic Circle; they approached the region of the midnight sun, and described the swift passing of the northern night. "In some places," they said, "the night was three hours long, in some only two hours, and at last the sun would rise almost as soon as he had set." The northern parts of Scandinavia were afterward connected with these descriptions. On the death of "Amaricus" the King of the Heruli, his followers sent to Thule for another offspring of the royal line; and the Byzantine historian has recounted the incidents of the long journey, and the strange customs of the "men of Thule."

The mediæval writers were in favor of identifying Thule with Iceland, and this theory had been adopted in many quarters even before the time of Adam of Bremen. The first to start the opinion seems to have been the Monk Dicuil, an Irishman, who in the year 825 wrote a treatise on the measurement of the earth. He said that about thirty years previously certain Irish clerks had told him of their discovery of Iceland, which he took to be the Thule of the ancients, though in his time it was unnamed and uncolonized.

The discoverers were some of the missionaries to the Faroe Islands, who had been expelled by the heathen Northmen. They had first landed on the rocky islets which after took their names from bells and books that were left there by the "Pope's men." Then they had occupied the outlying Westmann Isles, which were named in like manner from this visit of the men who lived west of Norway. Finally they landed in Iceland itself, and reached the north coast about the beginning of February. At this time of year the darkness was almost continuous. At midsummer they had no night at all; "the sun only disappeared for a few minutes at midnight, as if he were passing behind a little hill." They noted that the sea was not frozen near the shore, but that at one day's journey from the north coast they had come upon an icy sea. This may have been the drift ice, or it may have been the sludge and spongy ice like that which the barbarians described to Pytheas on his voyage from Marseilles: "After one day's sail beyond Thule men come to a sluggish sea, where there is no separation of air, land, and water, but only a mixture of elements like the stuff of a jelly fish, through which one can neither walk nor sail."

Columbus was satisfied that the world's northern limit had been discovered. He could calculate the measurements of the globe between the equator and the Arctic Circle. It only remained to find out the length of the circumference from the beginning of India on the east to the end of Africa on the west.

The results of the old theories on this point had been stored in the works of Roger Bacon, and they were again brought to light by Pierre d'Ailly in his essay on the "Image of the World." Something more was to be learned from other mediæval authorities. Capitolinus had been of opinion that "Spain and India are neighbors westward." Marco Polo had been further east than any place of which Marinus had heard. It was clear that in the course of his travels he had touched the further shore of the ocean. It must be possible to find once more the marvelous city of waters, where Kubla Khan had reared his palaces, and the harbors where the Tartar fleets were equipped to attack the rich island of "Cipango," or Japan.

"These and the like authorities," says the biographer, "led the admiral to think that the opinion he had conceived was right." In projecting the actual voyage of discovery he was encouraged by the help and sympathy of another great scholar. Paolo Toscanelli of Florence was a cosmographer of the highest renown. While Columbus was on a visit to Lisbon, about the end of the year 1474, he heard that Toscanelli had lately been in correspondence with Fernando Martinez, a canon of Lisbon, who was inquiring, on behalf of the Portuguese, about "the short way from Lisbon to the Indies." Columbus knew that his friend Girardi was about to return to Italy, and he ventured to send a letter by him to Toscanelli asking for information on his own account, "sending him a small sphere, and acquainting him with the nature of his design." Toscanelli's answer was prompt and favorable. He praised "the noble and earnest desire" which appeared in the request of Columbus, and inclosed a copy of the letter sent to Martinez and of the chart prepared for the King of Portugal. This chart showed India and a multitude of islands, and "a most noble country called Zacton," where every year a hundred large ships were loaded with pepper alone. "This country," it was said, "is mighty populous, and there are many provinces and kingdoms, and innumerable cities under the dominion of a prince called the Great Cham, who resides for the most part in the province of Cathay." More than two centuries had passed since the predecessors of this emperor had endeavored to communicate with Rome. But quite lately, in the pontificate of Eugenius the Fourth, an ambassador had actually arrived, and had told the Pope of the friendship that existed between his master's subjects and the eastern Christians. "I discoursed with him a long while," says Toscanelli, "about the grandeur of their royal buildings, and upon the greatness of their rivers; he told me many wonderful things about the multitude of cities along these rivers, and that there were two hundred cities on one river alone, with marble bridges over it of great length and breadth, adorned with abundance of pillars. This country deserves to be visited as much as any other; and there may be great profit made there, and gold and silver found, with all sorts of precious stones, and spices in abundance, which are not now brought into our parts." The chart was divided into "spaces," each representing a length of 250 miles. A line due west from Lisbon, covering twenty-six of these "spaces," reached the "noble vast city of Quinsay." This was the capital of that part of Southern China in which the Emperor was believed to reside. The island of Antilla was shown on a higher parallel, opposite to the island of "Cipango," or Japan; and between these points there was a distance of no more than ten spaces, or 2500 miles.

Toscanelli soon afterward wrote again to Columbus, in answer apparently to a demand for further explanations: "I received your letter with the things that you sent me, which I take as a great favor. .... I am glad that the chart is well understood, and that the voyage laid down is not only possible, but true, certain, honorable, very advantageous, and most glorious among all Christians." He repeats that the discovery can only be made by having regard to the wise men who have come to Rome from those parts, and from the merchants who have traded in the East. "When the voyage is performed it will be to powerful kingdoms and to most noble cities and provinces, rich in all things of which we stand in need, particularly in all sorts of spice and in a store of jewels." He ends by showing the advantages that will result from opening communications with the learned men of those distant countries; "for which reasons, and many more that might be alleged, I do not at all wonder that you, who have a great heart, and the Portuguese nation, which has always had notable men engaged on its undertakings, are eagerly bent upon bringing this voyage to pass."

CHAPTER IX.

> "Of Iceland to write is litel nede
> Save of stock-fish; yet, forsooth, indeed,
> Out of Bristowe and coastès many a one
> Men have practised by nedle and stone
> Thitherwards within a litel while,
> Within twelve yeres, and without perile
> Gone and come, as men were wont of old
> Of Scarborough unto the coastès cold."

"I WAS sailing in February, 1477, a hundred leagues beyond the Isle of Thule, whereof the south part lies distant from the equator seventy-three degrees, and not sixty-three degrees, as some would have it; and it does not lie within Ptolemy's westernmost meridian, but is much further out to the westward; and to this island, which is as large as England, the English go with their merchandise, especially the men of Bristol. And at the time I went the sea was not frozen, but it rose in some places twenty-six ells high, and then fell again as much."* "Moreover," it is

* "Io navigai l'anno 1477 nel mese di febbraio oltra Tile isola, cento leghe, la cui parte australe è lontana dall' equinoziale settantatrè gradi, e non sessantatrè, come alcuni vogliono; nè giace dentro della linea che include l'occidente di Tolomeo, ma è molto più occidentale.

added, "it is quite true that the Thule mentioned by Ptolemy lies just where he said that it lay; and this is what people of our time have called Frisland.'

The first of these statements is in the words of Columbus himself. The note as to Frisland was added by Don Ferdinand. They were one day reading and discussing an essay on the five zones, in which the younger man sought to prove by the experience of travelers that some part at least of each zone was fit for the habitation of man. "Ay, ay!" said his father, "and I am a good witness to prove it. I have been in the King of Portugal's fortress of St. George of the Gold Mine, and that lies right under the equator, so that it's not so uninhabitable as some would make out." As to living in the Arctic zone, he had been there himself in the middle of winter, a hundred sea leagues beyond Iceland, at four miles to the league. They were far away from the "Thule" of the ordinary maps, but he knew exactly where he was. By his reckoning, as we have seen, there were fifty-six and two-thirds miles to the degree; and seventy-three of these degrees from the equator just brought them to the south of the "Thule" of the ancients; and his ship was far beyond that point, right up in the Arctic Circle.

It has been sometimes said that these remarks of Columbus are full of geographical blunders; but if we read his words carefully, and distinguish what he said from his son's commentary, we shall find that he knew perfectly well what he was talking about. From what he said about the men of Bristol it has been assumed that he went himself to Iceland on board a Bristol ship. We shall see later on that the English traders were not allowed to land in Iceland at the time of which he was speaking. But, even assuming that a Bristol merchant had obtained the necessary licenses from the Kings of England and Denmark, we should still have to explain what they would be doing in Iceland during the winter. The whole voyage would be dreary and unprofitable. At that time of year there was nothing doing in the ports; the Scotch herring fishery was not begun, there was no business to be done at Shetland, no crowd of ships round the Monk Rock off Faroe, and nothing but deserted quays at the shipping center of Thorshavn. If they were going for stock-fish to fulfill an army contract, or to get fine cod and mackerel for the

Italian market, the ship would have arrived too soon. The fishing season only began in February, and lasted for fully three months. The mackerel and the cod and ling had to be dried in the cold winds and stacked like firewood, ready for sale at the summer fair. Nothing could be sold except at the fairs, which few of the unruly English were at that time allowed to attend. There are minute descriptions of these gatherings and of the terrible difficulty of preserving the peace of the fair. "The traders make their preparations as if they were about to engage in battle." The Governor and his officials were there to levy tolls and grant licenses. But it was a wretched sight, says Olaus Magnus, to see how the merchants fought to get the pick of the places. There was a crowd of Hanse merchants, who had for a long time the monopoly of trading between Iceland and Norway; and after them came the English and Scotch, fighting among themselves for the first place; "but however they might injure each other there was always the clerk of the market waiting to take the toll, and to punish the offenders by fine and imprisonment."

Such was the course of business at the regular

fairs, and we have no reason to suppose that any arrangements were made for receiving traders at any other seasons of the year. This of itself would lead to the belief that the visit of Columbus to the North Sea had nothing to do with the intercourse between Bristol and Iceland. It is, of course, an obvious remark that he never said a word about being in Iceland at all. But such eagerness has always been shown to charge him with a furtive knowledge, and a determination to conceal what the Icelanders knew about America, that it is necessary to discuss as arguments a series of suggestions without evidence to support them.

The remark of Columbus about the freedom of the sea from ice is said to be corroborated by the Icelandic records. It is very likely that the drift ice had not come far south in the winter of 1476-77. There is great variation in the extent of the drift. In some years the whole coast is open; in others the sea has been covered with ice all round the island, "so that a man might ride from one cape to another, across all the gulfs and bays." Professor Magnussen quoted the Icelandic Annals, for 1477, as containing a memorandum in the native language that in

March there was no snow upon the ground. Professor Rafn cited the same entry as relating to the months of February and March in the same year. The fact, we are told, "proves, by a singular coincidence of time and place, the veracity of the narrative of Columbus." There might be some slight interest in noting that his statement about the mild weather was incidentally supported in this way; though Columbus was, of course, only commenting on the report mentioned by Pliny that after one day's journey from Thule one came to an impassable sea. But the form and language of the memorandum seem to show that it referred to the Icelandic way of reckoning, and not to the month of March in the Roman calendar. The classical months were not at that time used in Iceland, and are even now regarded "only as book dates to be looked up in the almanac." The Icelanders' year lasted till the beginning of spring. After the Yule-tide came "Thorri," last but one of the winter months, and "Gói" the last month, which began on the 8th of February and ended on the 8th of March, when the "First Month" of the new year began. Any event taking place in the last three weeks in February would be counted as part of the old year. When an Icelander talked of the close of the year 1477 he was referring to a time which we should call the spring of 1478. It seems probable, therefore, that the remark as to the absence of snow was intended for the beginning of the year 1478, nearly a twelvemonth after the date of the admiral's voyage.

Professor Magnussen considered it "not altogether improbable" that Columbus met the Bishop of Skalholt at the trading-port, and inquired from him what the Icelanders knew of a western continent. The Bishop was head of a monastery at Helgafell, where there had been a temple in ancient days, and a settlement from which some of the Icelanders were supposed to have started on their western voyages; "and the Bishop, no doubt, was thoroughly acquainted with these narratives, which, indeed, at that period as in later times, were generally known in Iceland."

It is curious to notice how the Professor gradually became more and more certain that Columbus arrived with the English traders and studied the old memorials of Greenland. The English trade, he says, must merit the attention of historians, if it furnished him with the occasion of visiting the island, "there to be informed of the historical evidence." The next step is reached when he remarks that accounts of the ancient voyages "could not have escaped the ardent researches of Columbus," as he was in a land where these discoveries were not forgotten. "If Columbus should have acquired a knowledge of the most important of these accounts, we may the more readily conceive his firm belief in the possibility of rediscovering a western continent and his unwearied zeal in putting his plans into execution." The admiral is supposed to have held conversations in Latin with the Icelandic scholars and perhaps to have learned something of other accounts, of which some may have been destroyed and others have only come in our time to the knowledge of the general public. In the end he concluded that all these suppositions might be accepted as actual facts; "the discovery of America, so momentous in its results, may therefore be regarded as the immediate consequence of its previous discovery by the Scandinavians, which may thus be placed among the most important events of former ages."

We shall deal separately with the story of the voyages from Greenland, and of the total wreck and oblivion which had come upon the distant colony, so that even the place of it was forgotten. But, before leaving the subject of the British trade, it may be useful to note some of the information collected by Professor Magnussen upon the general subject of the intercourse between England and Iceland. When the island first came under the power of Norway, its trade was at once crushed out under the stress of a terrible monopoly. No more English linens, no implements of husbandry, no wax for the church, or honey for the household might be brought to Iceland from the southward. In fact no trade at all was to be carried on without the royal permission. The stock-fish and crates of butter were all to be carried to Bergen for sale at the King's "Staple of Nordberg," as the authorized trading center, and ships were to be sent in return from Norway with a supply of the necessaries of life. There is nothing to show that any other commerce was henceforth carried on until the trade with England was renewed in the beginning of the fifteenth century.

In 1413 an English merchant was allowed to trade under a special license, but soon afterward a great number of merchantmen and fishing smacks came, uninvited, with a letter from the

King of England, "requesting permission for his subjects to trade without molestation." Notwithstanding all protests, within two years there were six of our ships in a single harbor, and it is said that the governor freighted one of them with a return cargo, and made the voyage in person to England. Our parliamentary records show that this led to fresh complaints and to the issue of a proclamation in 1415 prohibiting the men of London, Lynn, Yarmouth, and Boston, from trading to Iceland, or fishing there "in any other way than according to established usage." The matter was of vast importance to this country, because the English armies at that time were always fed on rations of stock-fish. The Icelanders in vain petitioned for leave to trade with the foreigners, as a matter of life and death; and when their reasonable demands were refused, the natural consequence ensued. The Englishmen, forbidden to carry on their business, retaliated by plundering the royal warehouses and carrying on a private war. The trade degenerated into smuggling, and turned afterward into mere freebooting and brigandage. If the natives would not sell their fish, it was taken by force. The revenue officers were "knocked on the head," and the magistrates captured and held to ransom. On one occasion three English crews landed on the north coast, "marching in order of battle, with colors flying and trumpets sounding," and, having insulted the bishop and killed a magistrate, returned to their ships with considerable booty. Another party laid three churches in ashes, "taking away the church plate and priestly robes, besides a great number of horned cattle and sheep, as well as many of the inhabitants." A complaint was forwarded to the English Parliament which summed up these grievances in the following way: "There is an island on the coast of Iceland called Westmann Isle, which is the lawful property of the King of Norway, so that no one but he has the least right to it. This is the best place for fishing on all the coasts, and the English have constantly made it their station ever since their trade commenced. There they build houses, pitch tents, dig up the soil, and make use of everything as if it belonged to them, without obtaining or even seeking for permission from the king's officers. They have, in fact, established themselves there by force, and will not let fish belonging to the king or anyone else be carried away until their own vessels are loaded; in short, they act in every way just as they please." There was a further complaint that these foreigners traded without a license, whereas merchants from Denmark and Norway were bound to have one and even then could only carry their fish to Bergen, "which is the general staple for stock-fish, as Calais is the staple for wool." After a great number of proclamations in London and Copenhagen, a treaty was made in 1450 whereby English subjects were forbidden to trade with Iceland or the northern parts of Norway, with the exception of William Canynge, the Mayor of Bristol, who was allowed, for special reasons, to send two ships to Iceland in each of the two years following.

The illegal traffic appears to have soon revived, and we learn that in 1453 Bjorn Thorleifsson, afterward Governor of Iceland, was ordered to put it down. In 1467 an event occurred which led to a war between England and Denmark. The village of Rif was much frequented by the English from London and Hull. One day, when Bjorn Thorleifsson came to this place, "these traders fell upon him and killed him, together with seven of his followers." His wife, the Lady Olof, escaped with a few companions, but Thorleif Bjornsson, the governor's son, was taken prisoner. The Englishmen seem to have treated the lady with a shocking insolence. When she received the mangled body of her husband, which the English sent to her all in pieces, she would not shed a tear, "but vowed to take good care that Bjorn should not fall unrevenged." When young Thorleif was ransomed, she put on a shirt of mail, and went with him at the head of her followers to attack the English. The foreigners were defeated; the crews of three of the vessels were nearly all killed, and the rest were carried off as prisoners. Olof left Iceland the next year to ask the king for further vengeance, and four ships from London and Bristol were seized by way of reprisals. When peace was made, in 1474, the trade with Iceland was again forbidden, and the prohibition was renewed in the year when Columbus started for the north. Thorleif had been appointed governor soon after his father's murder, and he was holding that office at the date of the admiral's voyage. He was, as will be shown later, the owner of the very valuable manuscript in which the traditions of the Scandinavian explorers were recorded. It can hardly, one would suppose, be argued that a visitor arriving on a Bristol ship would be favorably received by the governor or any of the leading officials, or that the literary treasures of the island would be collected and thrown open for his inspection.

The words of Columbus have shown us that he was sailing within the Arctic Circle. The object of his voyage remains unknown. It is not likely that he had personally anything to do with the fisheries, though he may have been in communication with the fleet engaged upon the winter fishing on the great banks near the Lofoden Islands. By the 8th of February the watchers on the cliffs expected to see rorquals and grampus attacking the moving army of herrings; according to their proverb, "on the last of Thorri and first of Gói, there's whale and herring seen in the sea." They fished for these early shoals with the drift nets, "and one might see in the compass of a mile upward of two or three hundred fishing boats lying on their station for a month together." Further on in the spring the smaller herrings were caught with casting nets, and a net with a large mesh was used for the great cod which followed the herrings. We read also of a longshore fishery with night lines; and there was a deep-sea business besides, carried on far out from the islands "in the sea between Norway and Iceland." The latter was described by Olaus Magnus, who dwelt on the peril from storm and drift ice and the hard life of the sailors in the long winter nights. They caught cod and ling, skates and rays, and were especially successful in taking the large halibuts, one of which would fill a barrel by itself. We are told that the fins and long slices of the meat were salted down and packed for export to the Mediterranean, and that the French, when they began a "turbot fishery" in America, learned how to cut off and cure the fat from the fins and strips from the body of the fish. The old writers are full of the superstitions and terrors of the fishermen. There were dangers from the great squids, enlarged by fancy into serpents and krakens, from the saw fishes "with teeth like a cock's comb," and the swordfish "with a head like an owl and a bill like a sword." Sometimes, in the place of a thornback, they would draw up a cramp fish or torpedo ray; or instead of a large skate would appear a "monk" or angel fish "and when such are taken," says the historian, "if they be not presently let go, there ariseth such a fierce tempest, with a horrid noise of that kind of creatures and other sea monsters there assembled, that a man would think the very heavens were falling and the vaulted roof of the world running to ruin."

These fisheries were conducted under the direction of the merchants at Bergen. No foreigners were allowed to intervene; and the English especially were forbidden to come near the coast, though it may have been impossible to keep them from the deep-sea fishery. Their great opponents were the Hanse merchants, who would have had little scruple in engaging armed assistance in support of their usurped authority. When our traders in 1428 had nearly been successful in restoring their commerce at Bergen the freebooters in the pay of the Hanse League burned and sacked a great part of the city, besides plundering a fleet of vessels from Normandy, "which had come for the summer fishing"; and the Germans soon re-established their oppressive dominion over the whole trade of the port. We may suppose that the governments of England and France would be driven on some occasions to protect their subjects' rights, even though there were laws against fishing or trading on the coast. Might not Columbus, it will be asked, be engaged in some such service under Admiral Coulon or the younger Colombo? But as a Portuguese subject since his marriage, and indeed as "a Portuguese sea captain," he would hardly be free to serve under the flag of France; and as to the freebooter Colombo there is direct documentary evidence that he was spending the winter at Lisbon, and had gone with nine ships early in January to lie in wait for the Flanders galleys on their outward voyage from Cadiz.

It is difficult, as we have seen, to suppose that Columbus was engaged on a voyage under the elder Coulon for the protection of the French king's interest in the Lofoden fisheries. On the other hand, it is almost impossible to believe that he sailed to Iceland on any English ship. His language implies that he was navigating a ship of his own; it also appears from his journals that he had touched at some port in England, which he describes as "the way to the North." On the whole, we are led to suppose that his journey beyond Thule had a direct relation to his projects of oceanic discovery.

He had a favorite scheme of making a Polar expedition. Some reference is made to this scheme in his own account of the Fourth Voyage, when he declared that he would make for Arabia around the Cape or explore the region of the Arctic Pole. "I would undertake," he says, "to go to Arabia Felix as far as Mecca, as I have said in the letter that I sent to their Highnesses by Antonio de Torres, with reference to the division of the sea and land between the Spaniards and the Portuguese; and I would afterward go to the North Pole, as I have said and as I have stated in writing at the Monastery of the Mejoreda." We know that the advisers of John of Portugal were at that time considering how to reach India by a northeastern voyage round Siberia.

Olaus Magnus, who wrote his history toward the end of the sixteenth century, has given an interesting account of the state of the North Sea in his time. He mentions the renewal of the commerce with England under a decree called "Pinning's Judgment," which had been accepted by Henry the Seventh; he then notices the great increase in number of the German traders from the Baltic; and he adds that these northern waters were frequented by the Portuguese, "always on the lookout for new countries," as well as by the Spaniards and Frenchmen, who were always complaining of the natives and never knew a word of their language. The historian also says that the ships from the southern countries were subject to piratical attacks by the natives of Greenland; but as he places the locality in the direction of the White Sea and Spitzbergen, it looks as though he were referring to the Norwegian freebooters, and to premature attempts of the Spaniards and Portuguese to break through the adverse barriers of the icy "Cronian Sea." It seems, therefore, to be a reasonable supposition that Columbus was engaged in the Portuguese service in searching for the route, found only in our own time, to the rich coast of Cathay, "along the imagined way, beyond Petsora eastward."

One more point should be mentioned, in reference to the suggestion that Columbus might have concealed what he had heard about a country to the west of Iceland. As a matter of fact, it was his habit to write down all that he could learn in any quarter which tended to the confirmation of his theory. He would have no particular interest in the traditions of Icelandic discovery. He was aware of the existence of "Tartary," and would certainly have accepted the notion that it might be reached by crossing the Atlantic. His own object was to take advantage of the supposed prolongation of Asia in the regions of China and Japan; but he made careful memoranda about every alleged discovery of the transatlantic world. He tells us, for instance, that about the year 1452 a Portuguese captain came with a story about finding "Antilla," and told Prince Henry about the islanders taking the crew to church, where a regular service was performed; "and it was reported that while the sailors were at mass the ship's boys gathered sand for the cook's caboose, and found that a third part of it was gold." Among the Portuguese who set out to find this island was a gentleman named Diogo de Teive, who had just left his sugar factory at Madeira, and was about to go on business in the Azores. His pilot was one Pedro Velasquez, who lived at Palos in Spain, and who talked over the matter with Columbus when he was staying at the Monastery of La Rabida. According to this pilot they set out from Fayal and sailed for about 150 leagues without finding anything, but in returning they came upon the Isle of Flores, to which they were guided by the flight of land birds, chiefly buzzards, making in that direction. Starting once more, they sailed to the northeast, not far from Cape Clear in Ireland, where they met with stiff westerly winds, and yet the sea was smooth, as if there were some island sheltering it on that side. When Columbus was talking over this matter at the Port of Palos, one of the sailors said that he had made the same voyage; he was on the way to Ireland, and saw the land in question, which he took for part of Tartary; but in Don Ferdinand's opinion "it is likely enough that this was Labrador, or what we call the land of Bacalaos, and that they could not get to it because of the bad weather." If there were any truth in the story, it might have been the Porcupine Bank, or the whole thing may be only a reflection of the Irish legends of a Land of Youth on the blue verge of the Western sea. Columbus never paid any great attention to statements about islands a few score of leagues to the westward; but he told his son that the story exactly agreed with what Pedro de Velasco, the pilot of Galicia, had told him when they met in the city of Murcia, and this was to the effect that in sailing toward Ireland they went out of their course and found this new land; "and what is more," said Columbus, "you may take it to be the same as that which is called the Isle of the Seven Cities, which Fernan d'Ulmo went out from the Azores to discover under the royal letters patent, and perished; and his sons went several times on the same voyage, and perished, one after the other, without being heard of again." "And these things," says Don Ferdinand, "I faithfully set down as I found them in my father's writings, so that it may appear what great matters some people have raised upon a very slight foundation."

CHAPTER X.

> " The old seafaring men
> Came to me now and then,
> With their Sagas of the seas,
> Of Iceland and of Greenland,
>   And the stormy Hebrides,
> And the undiscovered deep.
> I could not eat nor sleep,
>   For thinking of those seas."

MANY attempts have been made to diminish the fame of Columbus by statements that America was well known to the Norsemen, and that he himself was well aware of the fact. The story goes that the Scandinavian explorers had discovered a pleasant region which they knew as Vinland the Fair, where the grass never withered, and no frost was felt at night, but the hill slopes were clad with vines and the valleys with self-sown corn. We shall consider the origin of the story and the various transformations which it underwent from time to time; and it will be seen how unlikely it was that the admiral ever heard of it or would in any case have attached importance to its details.

The romance of Vinland rests partly on a passage in an early chronicle, and partly on two much later Sagas which were brought to light at the end of the sixteenth century, when learning revived in the North. Adam of Bremen, who wrote upon the history of the Baltic countries about the time of our Norman Conquest, was a good scholar himself, and lived among men who were familiar with all parts of Europe from the White Sea to the Golden Horn. His chronicle, however, is chiefly remarkable for the credulity which accepted the fables about monsters, which had been stale even when Pliny collected them. The dog-faced tribes and one-legged men, the Amazons and Cannibals, the Albinos and men with faces on their shoulders, all appear among the nations of the Baltic, as they once had figured in the oldest descriptions of Africa, and as they were destined again to appear on the finding of America; and the chronicler adds that "there are monsters of many other kinds, which the sailors say that they have seen, though we find it hard to believe them."

Norway and Sweden are imagined as lying along the slopes of the Rhipæan Hills, "where the tired world comes to an end." In front of these hills, to the north of Sweden, lies Greenland, far off in the Ocean. It takes from five to seven days to reach it from Norway, or about as long as the ordinary voyage to Iceland. "The natives are blue with the brine, and this gives its name to the country; they live in much the same way as the Icelanders, but they are more ferocious, and they make piratical attacks on voyagers; some say, however, that to them also the Gospel has been carried across the sea." The historian then quotes a conversation held with King Sweyn of Denmark, the nephew of our King Canute. "He said that another island in that ocean had been reached by many men; it was called Vinland, because the vines grow there of themselves and produce most excellent wine; and it is also rich in self-sown crops of corn; and this comes not from any mere tradition, but rests on the actual testimony of the Danes."

It is a fact of some significance that Greenland should have been placed in a line with the range of mountains between Norway and Sweden. Many of the theories of the mediæval geographers can be traced back to legends about the exploits of Alexander the Great. Among these notions was the belief that one might sail down from the north into the Caspian Sea. Leaving the Rhipæan Hills upon the left, one would come first to the land of the Griffins, and then to Albania, the pirates' islands, and the forests and golden plains of the fruitful land of Hyrcania. When we examine the Saga of Eric the Red, from which it has been suggested that Columbus may have gained his information, we shall find that the local color is mostly derived from traditions of this kind. It is possible that Leif the Lucky may have seen maize and fox grapes growing wild in the latitude of Canada; but the rest of the story seems to have been written by a scribe who knew nothing about America.

One of the earliest statements about the matter is contained in the "Life of Olaf Tryggvason." We are told that a mission was sent to Greenland about the year 1006. The ship was driven off her course and wrecked; but the crew were rescued by Leif Ericson. "Leif went to Greenland in the summer; in the sea he saved a crew clinging to a wreck; he also found Vinland the Fair, and arrived about harvest time in Greenland with the priest and the teachers."

The Saga of Eric the Red is preserved in a MS. known as the Flatey Book, belonging to the

National Library at Copenhagen. Mr. Vigfusson described the book as forming a huge encyclopedia of northern history, its pages containing more than half of what is known of the older history of the Orkneys and Faroes, of Greenland and Vinland. It was compiled about the year 1387 for a yeoman living in the east of Iceland, not far from the monastery at Thingore, where no doubt there was "a goodly library," abounding in material for the scribes. The title page gives an interesting list of contents. "This book John Haconsson owns. There are herein, first poems, then how Norway was settled, then the story of Eric the Far-traveled, and next, that of King Olaf Tryggvason with its episodes, and next are the histories of St. Olaf and of the Orkney Earls, etc. The priest, John Thordsson, has written of Eric the Far-traveled, and the histories of the two Olafs; and the priest, Magnus Thorhallsson, has written all before and all after that, and has illuminated the whole."

This book belonged afterward to a rich family in the west of the island, who afterward took it to their house at Flatey on the eastern coast. It has been traced into the possession of Bjorn Einarsson the Pilgrim, who died about the year

1415. From him it descended to "Lady Christian of Waterfirth," and from her to Bjorn, the Governor of Iceland, who was killed by the English sailors in 1467, and whose son was governor in 1477, when Columbus was sailing in the Arctic Circle. It remained in this family as an heirloom until the year 1630, when the following note was made on the title: "This book I, John Finsson, own by gift from my father's father, John Bjornsson, whereof proof can be given, and it was delivered to me and in that way made my own by my lamented father, Fin Johnsson, personally." The book was then given to John Torfason of Flatey, who passed it on in 1647 to Bishop Bryniulf of Skalholt, a great patron of literature. Torfoeus, who wrote the history of Vinland, came to Iceland a few years afterward, "hunting after vellums for the king's new library," and he conveyed the book to Copenhagen as a contribution from the learned bishop.

The story of the finding of Vinland, as it was copied into the Flatey Book, cannot have been older than the middle of the fourteenth century, since it was about that time that the "Skraelings," or Eskimos, first came into contact with the Northmen in Greenland. This period is known to have been marked by a great activity in the collection of local traditions. It has been described as a period of appreciation rather than an age of original production. The Icelanders were collecting the stories connected with their great men or the ancestors of their best known families. When a later generation attempted to create as well as to collect, the exploits of the native heroes were abandoned, and the Icelandic writers gave themselves up, like the rest of the world, to stories of Roland and the Paladins, or Sir Tristram and the dreamer Merlin.

All remembrance of the ancient times seems to have passed away before the beginning of the sixteenth century. Many works, says Mr. Vigfusson, were written during this period, but their subjects were taken from foreign or fictitious romances. The English trade, and the change in the physical circumstances of Iceland, may have had something to do with this "rapid, but complete oblivion of things past." Even the fifteenth century became "a mythical semi-fabulous age" to the Icelanders of the succeeding generation; they had forgotten the death of Bjorn, the sorrows of the Lady Olof, and the war with the English traders. The pedigrees are not carried further back than the beginning of the sixteenth century. It was not even known, says Mr. Vigfusson, that the age of the Sagas was "looming behind." Late in the next century, however, the old records were brought to light again, fresh pedigrees were arranged, and were joined "by false links" to the genealogies of the ancient heroes. The Saga of Eric the Red rises into importance, as containing the notice of the first European born in America; and Snorri, the son of Thorfinn from Vinland, is accepted as the ancestor of Snorri Sturlusson the historian and many other distinguished persons.

The stories with which we are dealing seem to have remained unknown outside Iceland itself until the beginning of the seventeenth century. A taste for the literature of the North revived when the King of Denmark became interested in the exploits of his ancestors. The history known as the "Heimskringla," or "World-ring," containing the lives of the ancient kings of Norway, was translated into Danish in 1594, and a number of literati were set at work to recover such of the historical manuscripts as might still be moldering in the farmhouses of Iceland. Among them was Arngrim Jonsson, commonly known as Arngrim

the Learned, the author of several important
works upon the antiquities of his country. He
brought out in succession a commentary on the
Kings' Lives, on Constitutional History, and a
spirited criticism, or "Dissection" as it was
called, of the libelous account of Iceland published by one Dittmar Blefken. Besides all
these he was the author of a short history of
Greenland, in which he inserted a full and impar-
tial account of the travels of the children of Eric
the Red. The books used by this great scholar
are known by his careful references to authority,
and it is somewhat remarkable that he appears
never to have seen the Flatey Book, though he
had authority from the government to examine
historical records. It is known that he used his
authority freely; and he said himself that on one
occasion he had "no less than twenty-six vellums
in his possession." His benefice lay in the Eastern Province, where he was busily engaged as
coadjutor to the Bishop of Holar, and by that
time the Flatey Book had been moved to another part of the country; but inasmuch as Arngrim's home was in Wididale, where the famous
manuscript had been compiled, and near the site
of the monastery of Thingore, it is not very diffi-

cult to account for his familiarity with the tradition.

The Saga deals with events at the end of the tenth century, when Eric had started with his settlers for Greenland. There was an Icelander called Heriulf, we are told, who used to trade to Norway in partnership with his son Bjorn. As soon as Heriulf heard of the new settlement he determined to sail off at once without waiting for his son, and he arrived in time for an allotment of territory, and set up his home at a place which he called Heriulf's Ness.

When Bjorn came to Norway and heard of his father's departure he started off also for "the strange and remote land," though he had but little information as to the route. For three days he sailed west, and then was driven far to the south by a storm. When the storm was over they sailed on for a day and a night, and came to a flat island, very woody and free from rocks; then, starting again, they sailed to the northwest and arrived in Greenland, passing two more islands in their course.

About the year 1002, Leif, the son of Eric the Red, set out for Heriulf's Ness to look for the countries which had been thus discovered. The first that he found was the island nearest Greenland, where he cast anchor. He saw nothing but flat rocks and ice, and he called it Helluland, or the "land of flagstones." Soon afterward he found the flat wood-covered island, and this he called Markland, or the "land of woods." Then he sailed on for two days and nights with a northeast breeze, and came to a much more fertile coast. They landed on a small island, and afterward sailed westward round a promontory, and ran the ship into a creek. They determined to winter here, as there was plenty of fish, especially a large kind of salmon. "The winter was not very severe; they had not nearly as much frost and snow as in Iceland or Greenland, and they could see the sun for fully six hours on the shortest day. They likewise found vines and grapes, which the Greenlanders had never seen before; but they had with them a man from the South who was no stranger to that sort of fruit, and who said that he was born in a country where the vine grew in abundance. Leif returned to Greenland in the spring, and he called the country Vinland." The compiler of the Saga enters into minute details about the climate. "It was so fine," he says, "that there was no need of hay for stall-feeding the cattle; there was no frost throughout the winter, and the grass was but little withered." According to him the sun rose at 7.30 A. M. on the shortest day, and set at 4.30 P. M.; and this calculation would suit the latitude of Massachusetts; but the statement as to the absence of frost would carry us to the climate of Virginia.

We now come to the voyage of Thorwald, the second son of Eric. He is said to have started from Greenland with a crew of thirty men, and to have wintered in the huts which his brother had built in Vinland. During that winter he reconnoitered toward the west, and in the summer following he surveyed the eastern districts; and in the course of the year after that he started again to explore a number of uninhabited islands to the westward. Toward the end of their stay they came one day upon three small boats of a kind quite unknown to them, "made of skins, with ribs or bones bound together with twigs." There were three men lying by each boat upon the shore, two keeping watch and the third asleep. Of these men they killed eight, and the ninth escaped. Soon afterward a crowd of natives appeared, armed with bows and arrows, who attacked the Greenlanders. Thorwald received a wound in the face, of which he died. He was buried near a cape on the east coast, which they called Crossness. The others stayed on in Vinland for the winter, and in the spring they loaded their ship with vines and the boat with grapes, "and so returned to Greenland in good condition."

Boats of the kind mentioned in this extract, though unknown among the Northmen, were often mentioned by the classical writers. The Iberians of Spain "built their ships with skins, and traversed the seas in their boats of hide"; and their canoes were compared by Lucan with the curraghs used in Britain. There were old Greek stories of the tin fetched from islands in the Atlantic "in wicker boats sewn with hides." But perhaps the nearest approach to the Icelandic story is to be found in a passage of Æthicus about the boats used in the age of Alexander by the pirates of the Hyrcanian Sea. "They are long and narrow, woven thickly with osiers and sewn round with goat skins and bear skins, so as to resist the waves and the wi ds; and they are handy and swift for pillaging the neighboring countries and islands." It may be remembered also in the same connection that Olaus Magnus, on seeing some Eskimo fishing boats hung up in St. Halward's Church at Christiania, thought that they must be some of the diving vessels described in the legends about the Caspian pirates, "with which the sea robbers would claw hold of a passing ship and scuttle her by boring through the planks"; though these diving vessels were not a whit more real than the "ship of glass" in which Alexander the Great was fabled to have explored the depths of the sea.

There are other touches of the same kind which seem to indicate that the compilers of the Saga were drawing upon the common stores of mediæval romance. Next to Vinland, for instance, we hear of "Whiteman's Land," sometimes called Western Albania, or "Ireland over the Sea"; and just in the same way the next country to Hyrcania was the great realm of Albania, which was so called, says the Book of Mandeville, "because the folk ben whiter than in other marches thereabouten." So again, when one of the Greenlanders is killed in fight by a swift-running one-legged monster, we can but think of the old travelers' tale that "in this contree be folk that have but one foot, and thei gon so fast that it is marvaylle." The Saga-writer's story of the honey-dew is evidently imported from the classics. When the Greenlanders landed on the first island the weather was serene and still, "the dew was on the grass, and they touched and tasted it, and thought that nothing had ever been so sweet." According to the traditions about Alexander, the Greeks found certain trees in Hyrcania, of which the leaves were bedewed with honey "engendered in the air." "There is a tree in that country," says Diodorus, "which distills honey from its leaves, and this the natives gather in great plenty." These soft sweet showers, and the unsown corn and vines, appear in every vision of the Islands of the Blessed. We come to a land where "the earth unplowed brings forth her yearly crop, and the vine flourishes untouched by the pruner's hook." If the young Marcellus could only have lived, according to the poet's prayer, the oaks would be distilling their "honey, pure as the dew,"

> Plains will be turned golden and wave with ripening corn,
> Purple grapes shall blush on the tangled wilderness thorn.

We are told that the next voyage was undertaken by Thorstein, the third son of Eric the

Red. He set out with his wife Gudrida, but never found the right way. They were driven about by storms all the summer, and only got home in the first week of winter, when Thorstein died of the plague. Gudrida was married again to an Icelander called Thorfinn Karlsefne. They determined to establish a colony in Vinland, and when they arrived they found plenty of provisions; the crops were fruitful, the fish abounded in the streams, and they were so lucky as to find a stranded "rorqual," or whale of the largest kind.

About the end of the year the natives appeared in great numbers, and traded skins and furs for food. In the course of the next summer they came again, and a chief was killed in trying to take an ax from one of the Greenlanders; and in the following season they came again, prepared this time for war, but were defeated with great loss. These natives are always called "Skraelings," a term which is more regularly confined to the Eskimos; but none of the true Eskimos have ever been found to the south of Labrador. There is nothing in the Saga to identify these natives with the Tuscaroras or any other Red Indian tribe. On the contrary, when anything like a description is given, it is of a kind which might be expected in a romance. Black men, like specters, form a funereal host. They sail up from the South, as if they came from Ethiopia. "They were black, and of fierce looks, with matted hair; their eyes were very large, and their faces broad." They are in fact like the peoples of Gog and Magog whom the Greeks could not subdue, the Caspian tribes and "Turchi with sooty faces and crow-black hair." The Syriac version of the legend of Alexander describes such tribes as living in the Hyrcanian Forest. "In that wood there were trees bearing fruit, and their fruit was very luscious, and within the wood there were wild men, whose faces were like ravens, and they held darts in their hands, and were clothed with skins."

When Thorfinn left Vinland he brought home, so the story ran, a precious cargo of furs and hides, with vines and grapes and specimens of timber. A stranger from Bremen offered to buy a piece of wood like a broomstick, of the kind called "Mausur" or Butcher's broom, which was believed to keep off mice and other vermin from houses. "Thorfinn refused, unless the merchant would pay its weight in gold, and upon these terms it was sold at last." Other versions of the story put the price at four ounces of gold; and in modern times the whole anecdote has been exaggerated until the merchant appears as purchasing a quantity of precious "mazer wood" or a cargo of bird's-eye maple.

Yet one more voyage to Vinland was said to have been made by a child of Eric the Red. His daughter Freydisa had taken part in the voyage when Leif made his first discovery. After Thorfinn's return she determined to go out again, and persuaded her husband to take part in founding a settlement. They provided one ship, and another was furnished by two Icelanders, with a crew of thirty men, five of them accompanied by their wives. Soon after their arrival a bitter quarrel broke out, and in the end all the Icelandic men were killed at the instigation of Freydisa; and, as the women had been spared, she herself took an ax and cut them down. The story, as Mr. Vigfusson pointed out, takes some of its coloring from the "Attila Lay," in which the tale of the Niebelungs was sung with a peculiar "savagery and grimness." In that version the Lady Gudrun appears as a furious Medea, quite unlike "the gentle Andromache" or the

Electra of the German poem: "When the high-born lady saw that the game was a bloody one, she hardened her heart; she threw off her mantle, and took a naked sword in her hand, and fought for the life of her kinsmen."

A wilder version of these traditions, known as the "History of Thorfinn Karlsefne," was preserved by Bjorn of Scardsa, an eminent Icelandic antiquary, who died at a great age in 1656. The main lines of the story may still be discerned in this version, though most of the details are different. Many of the classical references have been omitted, and are replaced by local allusions, showing that the compiler was well acquainted with the habits of the settlers in Greenland. Bjorn of Scardsa was a self-educated yeoman who took to the study of antiquities when he was about fifty years old; and he is described as having a poetical and imaginative turn of mind, and "a force of character and enthusiasm which led to his dicta being eagerly accepted by his countrymen." He wrote a history of Greenland, in which the extinction of the colony was described and the vague reports as to its former site were discussed. Some parts of the work were taken from a MS. called "Hawk's Book," noted as "a very magazine of antiquities," and ascribed to one "Hawk," a well known magistrate, who died in Iceland about 1334, and who, according to his own account, was the ninth in direct descent from Thorfinn.

The legend of Thorfinn was inserted in Bjorn's history of Greenland without any note as to its origin or comparative antiquity. It reads like a travesty of the story in the Flatey Book; but it has a certain literary interest as a storehouse of magic and witchcraft, and it has at any rate preserved that picture of the spae wife in a Hunlandish belt, "in a cap of black lamb's wool and a blue vest spangled with jewels," which is familiar to all who know Gray's version of the Descent of Odin.

Some of the characters in the older Saga reappear in the new story and take part in its strange adventures. Thorfinn and his wife deprive the children of Eric of all the credit of finding and naming the new countries, except that they are accompanied by Thorwald and his fierce sister, Freydisa, with her husband from Iceland. The travelers go first to Bjarney, or Disco Island, the northernmost settlement in Baffins Bay, and turning there, after a journey of a day and a night, they found a stony region, "and this they called Helluland." Another day's sail brought them to a woodland district, "and to this they gave the name of Markland." Then they sailed away to the south, and came to a keel-shaped promontory standing out between long, white shores. "King Olaf had once given to Leif Ericsson two Scotch folk, a man and woman called Hake and Hekia, who could run as swiftly as wild beasts." These were sent out as spies to explore the land, and after three days they returned with a bunch of grapes and "an ear of new sown wheat." Then they went on southward, and came to an island covered with nesting eider ducks, and they wintered there. In the spring they found a whale cast up, but it had been procured by the spells of their huntsman, "a tall, dark man like a giant," and they were all smitten with disease. When the remains of the ill gotten food were thrown away the weather cleared, and they got plenty of deer and fish, besides eggs from the island. Still they had not found Vinland, and some complained that not a drop of wine had yet crossed their lips They accordingly agreed to divide their forces and to search about in different directions. Some went north, and were driven across to Ireland. Thorfinn and the rest sailed far to the south, and came to a sandy estuary; and here at last they saw the self-sown corn and the vines along the slopes of the hills.

After a while they were visited by the savages, who came in canoes from the south, with their poles waving in the sunshine "like corn shaken by the wind." A few months afterward the black men came in crowds, so that the bay seemed to be "sprinkled with coals," so great was the multitude of their boats of hide. The Greenlanders, though successful in fight, determined to abandon the region of vines, and to go back to the estuary and the eider duck island. From this point Thorfinn made several voyages of exploration. In one of these Thorwald, son of Eric the Red, was killed by a one-legged monster. In Markland they caught some native children, who told them of a neighboring country, where men walked in white robes carrying banners and shouting aloud; and this, they thought, might be the Greater Ireland, or "Whiteman's Land."

The whole account of their way of living might have been written by anyone who had passed a summer in Greenland; and some of the incidents correspond very closely with the account of that country compiled by Ivor Bardson about the year 1349. According to the description of Thorfinn's colony, there was abundance of grass for the flocks and herds, the rivers were full of fish, and the woods well stocked with game. The settlers caught sea-fish after the Greenland fashion; they made pits and trenches in the estuary near the high-water mark, and when the tide went out they found halibuts caught in the shallows. The halibut, indeed, is a deep-sea fish; but the Greenlanders catch salmon in this way, by building stone weirs across a tidal stream, and there are places where the rocks make a natural trap of the same kind for seals. Ivor Bardson described a lake near the Church of St. Nicholas, which rises with the tide and the rain; "and when the water falls a great number of fish are left upon the sand." As to the climate in summer, he says that a fjord near the Iceblink Mountain has a number of small islands in it with nesting birds, "and on both sides extend great plains covered with green grass wherever you go." The frost in Greenland, according to his account, was not so severe as in Iceland or Norway.

"The fruits," he says, "grow there as large as apples, and are of good flavor, and there is corn of the best kind"; and it is true that there are wild service trees that bring their fruit to maturity, and pulse and oats of a sort in some specially favored localities. Modern travelers have reported of Disco Island itself, the "Bjarney" of Thorfinn's voyage, that the weather in summer is pleasant and the scenery delightful; "food is delicious and abundant, and labor an agreeable pastime."

It was thought at one time that the ecclesiastical history of the north might furnish some information as to the alleged discovery of Vinland. The Icelandic Annals have been quoted to show that one Eric of Upsi was ordained Bishop of Greenland in 1121, but soon afterward sailed "to look for Vinland," and was not heard of again. This Eric, however, seems to have been only a private missionary. Greenland became subject to the King of Norway in 1123, and Arnold, the first bishop, was appointed in the following year. The archives of the Vatican contain a few notices of the Greenland churches. There was a Papal Brief in 1275 appointing a commissioner to collect the Greenlanders' contributions toward a crusade. In 1326 an account of the duty received in Greenland, amounting, with the Peter's pence, to about a ton of walrus ivory, was forwarded from Bergen to Rome. There are very few other entries on this subject. One Alpho is mentioned as being Bishop of Gardar when the "Skraelings," or Eskimos, were first seen in the country. We are told that about 1386 the navigation ceased, but in 1408 the Archbishop of Drontheim consecrated Andrew Bishop of Greenland in case Henry, the former bishop, was dead; but it was never known whether he arrived at his diocese. It appears also from a Brief of Eugenius the Fourth that in 1433 Fra Bartolomeo de Santo Ypolito was appointed to succeed Nicholas, the bishop of Greenland, then lately deceased.

The last official recognition of the Scandinavian colony is contained in a letter written in 1448 by Pope Nicholas the Fifth to certain bishops in Iceland. The Pope speaks of Greenland as an island in the Northern Ocean, where for nearly six centuries the Church founded by St. Olaf had flourished. "But now it is thirty years since the barbarians, coming against them in a fleet from the shores of the heathen, have devastated the cathedral church and the country with fire and sword; only the parish churches were left, which they could not easily approach in the clefts of the hills." The inhabitants had been carried off into slavery; but many of them had afterward returned, and were desirous of restoring the services of religion, though they were too poor to maintain bishops and priests. The Pope ended by asking the Icelandic bishops to ordain a colleague for Greenland, and to send him out to that country if the distance were not too great.

No serious attempt was made to resume intercourse with the lost colony till the reign of Christian the Second of Denmark, when Archbishop Walkendorf endeavored to find out its situation; but he died in 1523, "and his benevolent plans were buried with him."

Martin Frobisher, in searching for the Northwest Passage in 1576, reached the coast of Greenland, which he called Meta Incognita, and an inlet known as Frobisher's Strait. He returned in the following season to look for a supposed gold mine that turned out to be only a vein of pyrites; and in 1578 he was sent to establish a colony there, though the project was soon abandoned. Crantz, the historian of Greenland, thought that the picture of Meta Incognita agreed very closely with what was afterward found in the country. But he added a remark on the wild tales told by some of Frobisher's sailors which has some bearing upon the value of the traditions about Vinland. As to the civilized natives and a king decked out with jewels, we must take it for granted, he says, "either that they consulted the prevalent taste, requiring in every new voyage gold and silver mountains, rich palaces, and a shower of impossible adventures, or else that the editors embellished the narrative out of the ballads and romances at that time in vogue."

CHAPTER XI.

> "From the north
> Of Norumbega and the Samoed shore
> Bursting their brazen dungeons, armed with ice,
> And snow and hail and stormy gust and flaw,
> Boreas and Cæcias."

ABOUT a century before Columbus crossed the Atlantic there was a great and terrible eruption of the volcano of Mount Hecla in Iceland; and about fifty years after his death distorted accounts of its fire spouts and lava floods began to be known in Italy. A great interest in the North had been revived at Rome by the labors of Archbishop Walkendorf and the zeal which he had shown in recovering the traditions of Greenland. The finding of America had given a fresh value to all the old stories of the sea. "This is an age," it was said, "most earnest in studying all kinds of new information, and especially about those countries which have been made known through the courage and energy of our ancestors."

One result of this temper of the public mind

was a fashion of dressing up the details of forgotten travels, so as to bring them into some connection with the new world, and the credit of Columbus was, of course, as much diminished as the fame of the older travelers was exalted. Lord Bacon even made the unjust accusation that Columbus had suppressed what he had learned about certain lands, which at first were taken for islands, but were afterward shown to be portions of the American continent. The admiral, it was hinted, had evidence that his plans were correct, much better than "the prophecy of Seneca," or Plato's antiquities, or "the nature of the tides and land winds"; and if he kept silence on all this it must have been because he would appear as no man's follower, but only as "the child of his own science and fortune."

The accusation was chiefly based on the statements in a book published in 1558 by Nicolo Zeno of Venice. It professed to contain the discoveries of two members of his family, who had been in the North about the year 1390, and had written letters about "Frisland" and Greenland and other far distant lands, and had indeed put together a complete book on the subject, which had, however, long since disappeared. "I am grieved," said the editor of these letters, "that this book, and many other writings on this subject, have suffered an unfortunate fate. I was but a child when they came to my hands, and I tore them up, as children will, and threw them away, not knowing what they were." He assured his readers, however, that he had put it all together again as well as he knew how. He was also in possession of a map, very imperfectly designed, which proved to be a fruitful source of mistakes to the explorers of the Northwest Passage. Of this he writes: "I have thought it well to make a copy of the sailing chart, which I have found among my family antiquities, and although it is rotten with age, I have succeeded with it tolerably well."

On examining a copy of this map it is easy to see that it contained the names of places in Shetland, which had been transferred by mistake to the coast of Iceland. This made it necessary to move the place of Iceland itself further up toward the north; and we accordingly find a volcano, a great monastery, and a town, set upon an imaginary coast line extending from the north of Greenland to the vicinity of Spitzbergen.

"Frisland," that icy region for which our sailors long sought in vain, was shown as a large island lying far out in the western ocean. The country has long ago been identified with the scattered Isles of Färöe by means of the local names, which were but thinly diguised in the Italian rendering, and especially by a very definite reference to the Monk Rock lying to the south of the group, which is still a well known resort of the North Sea fishermen. The ancient volume of letters also contained many references to a prince called "Zinco," or "Zichmni"; and he has now been clearly identified with Henry Sinclair, Earl of Orkney, who gained possession of the islands in 1390, and died about ten years afterward.

When Frobisher sailed to his Meta Incognita and the desolate coasts of Baffin's Bay, he was always looking for the kingdoms described by the Venetian merchants. In his first voyage he hoped at one time that he had come upon their track. He caught a glimpse of a country that he took for Frisland, "rising like pinnacles of steeples, and all covered with snow." It was a ragged and high land, shut in by drifts and stranded icebergs, and rendered almost inaccessible by its walls, mountains, and bulwarks of ice.

"It extends," says he, "very far to the northward, as it seemed to us, and as appears by a description set out by two brethren, who were Venetians, the first known Christians that discovered this land, about 200 years since; and they have in their sea cards set out every part thereof."

Many adventures befell the merchants in their long service with Sinclair. We must notice in particular their description of the monastery set by a burning mountain, and the visit of the fleet to a quaint kingdom near Bantry Bay; and above all, we ought carefully to examine the wonderful "Story of the Fisherman," with its pictures of life "in cold Estotiland" and among the snows of Drogio. This story contains the gist of Bacon's accusation against Columbus; and in our own time it has often been treated as a summary of what was known about Vinland by those who kept up in the North "a mercantile connection with America." It has even been praised as a very fair description of the country "as far down as Mexico," considering that it was written at the close of the fourteenth century.

Nicolo Zeno, it is said, made an expedition from Bressay in Shetland, and sailed with three ships to Greenland; "and here he found a monastery of the Order of Friars Preachers and a church dedicated to St. Thomas, very close to a hill which vomited fire like Vesuvius and Etna." There he saw a spring of hot water, used for warming the houses and gardens; and it was so boiling hot that it cooked the food, and baked the bread in stone pots "as if it had been put into an oven." The monks, said the traveler, made excellent lime out of the stones that are cast like cinders from the mouth of the burning mountain; and these same stones, when cold, are very useful for building, because they will never yield or break, unless cut with iron. "Hither in summer come vessels from the neighboring islands, and from the North Cape, and from Drontheim, bringing all sorts of goods in exchange for stockfish and hides"; and to this place, he added, the Friars resorted from Norway and Sweden, but most of all from Shetland. He describes the native boats as being made out of the skins and bones of fish in the shape of a weaver's shuttle, and as being fitted with "a kind of sleeve" for throwing out the water. The climate was bitterly cold for quite nine months at a time, and ships were continually detained by the sea being frozen round them. The Italian was not accustomed to such sharp cold, and was glad to get back to Thorshavn, where he soon afterward died. His brother Antonio, after his adventures in Ireland, went with Sinclair to the same country. They saw for themselves the mountain pouring out smoke at a considerable distance from the harbor. The soldiers sent out to explore said that they found a great fire issuing from the foot of a hill, and a spring not far off, running with a stuff like pitch, which flowed into the sea. There were multitudes of half-wild people living about the hill in caves and holes. Nothing was said on this occasion about a monastery, with its lovely garden crowded with foreign visitors, and it seems to be assumed that they had got to another volcano. This may be the reason why Olaus Magnus spoke vaguely of wild fires and flaming streams being seen in several regions of the North, and why Don Ferdinand wrote in the same unprecise way about receiving accounts of northern islands that were always on fire. But to some extent these may be reminiscences of that "Christian Odyssey" in which St. Brandan leaves the Isle of Vines and sails northward "in that clear water" until he comes to an island most dark, and full of stench and smoke, and then again blew the south wind and drove them further into the north, "where they saw a hill on fire, and the fire stood on each side like a wall."

No volcano has ever been found in Greenland. There were some warm springs at a place called Ounartok; but Ivor Bardson's survey showed that they used to belong to the bishop and to certain Benedictine nuns, and not to the Canons of St. Olaf, who owned the only establishment that could have been described as a monastery. There are many hot springs near Mount Hecla, some of which have been used for centuries for warming baths and dwelling houses, but we find no record of the Friars or of any such church of St. Thomas as is mentioned in the story. There was, however, a monastery at Archangel, which had become known to travelers about the time when the book was published; and several of the particulars in Zeno's description would suit the circumstances of the White Sea trade. It seems likely, on the whole, that this part of the story was made up out of the reports from several different places. It had reference in the main to the great eruption in Iceland; but the unlearned narrator reduced the volcanic display to effects that might have been observed in a little Italian solfatara.

The account of a visit to "Icaria" bears some signs of an authentic narrative. This country appears on Zeno's map, far off in the sea near Labrador; but it has been restored by modern research to the latitude of the "Kingdom of Kerry." Sinclair is shown arriving with his fleet at a harbor on the western side; the king is on the shore with his nobles, and a rabble of "kernes and galloglasses." The country had often been invaded before, and out of each foreign host one man had been persuaded to stay, in order to teach the natives the language and customs of his people. Now came out the long boat with no less than ten of these interpreters, but none of them could be understood except one who came from Shetland. He could, of course, talk Norse with the sailors, even if he had never heard the uncouth dialect of the Färöese. It is a pity that we are not told more of the languages of the other interpreters. They knew Irish, but not Italian, and among them they must have been ready, we suppose, with English and French and Lowland Scotch, and Erse of the Highlands, with Welsh and Manx and Cornish, and perhaps the North-Irish dialects, and Pictish of Galloway. Sinclair would have understood the talk of most of the interpreters, but only the Shetlander was taken to his ship, accompanied by the bard or "Sennachie," who could speak of the royal pedigree and receive dispatches for the king. Being asked what were the names of the place and people and by whom they were governed, he said that it was the land of Icaria, and that the king himself was called Icarus, after the first of his line, who was the son of Dædalus, one of the ancient Irish kings, and had given them a code of laws; and the sea thereabout was called the Icarian Sea, because their first king had been drowned there; which all seems like the classical jargon that an Irish bard would have brought forth. "They were all content," said the messenger, "with the state into which they had been called, and would neither alter their laws nor admit any stranger among them, and for this they were all prepared to fight to death." But they would make the usual exception, and would be glad to take one of the Italian strangers, and to make him at home, in the same way as they had done with the ten other interpreters. Sinclair, we are told, made no reply, except to ask where he could find another harbor, and so sailed off to the other side and landed a party to get wood and water. But the natives lit beacon fires to rouse the country, and came running down armed with bows and arrows, "more like beasts than men," as the Italian thought. Their rage, he says, increased more and more, "and all the way to the east cape we saw them on the hilltops and along the coast, running to keep up with us, and howling and shooting at us from afar to show their hatred."

The fleet stood out to sea and proceeded as far as Greenland. They were bound, according to Zeno, for a country in the far west which was called "Estotiland," and they had on board some of the natives of those parts to serve as guides. This, of course, is a reference to the story of the fisherman, to which the sailors, as we are told, gave full credence "from having had much experience in strange novelties," and which would transfer the fame of Columbus to the unnamed Färöese if the public were able to believe it.

The finding of the New World, said Ortelius, is not unworthily ascribed to Columbus, for by him, indeed, it was "in a manner first discovered," and was made known by him and profitably communicated to the Christian world in the year 1492. "Howbeit I find that the north part thereof, called Estotiland, which most of all extendeth toward our Europe and the islands of the same, was long ago found out by certain fishers of the Isle of Frisland, driven by tempest on the shore, and was afterward, about the year 1390, discovered anew by one Antonio Zeno, a gentleman of Venice."

Some of the local touches in Zeno's letter to his brother at home, help us to realize the story as personally related by the fisherman, and we should have known much more about it if the Italian editor had not changed the style "and some of the old-fashioned words." As it stands, it appears to contain an account of Scotland by a Färöese cast away there about the year 1370, when his native islands had no connection with the Sinclairs or anything Scottish. Four boats, it appears, had set out in winter for the deep-sea fishing, in which the Färöese used to row out forty or fifty miles from land to sink their lines for the cod and ling, or "the white fish," as they were generally called. In Sir Walter Scott's sketch of the ling fishery in Shetland he speaks of the danger and suffering which lend a dignity to the trade. The banks are distant, and the men are twenty or thirty hours away from home; "and under unfavorable circumstances of wind and tide they remain at sea for two or three days, with a very small stock of provisions, in a boat of a construction which seems extremely slender, and are sometimes heard of no more." These boats are the clinker-built "sixareens," so called from being pulled with six oars. The boats mentioned by Zeno had crews of six men apiece. They were caught by a storm on the fishing banks and driven over the sea for many days, and at last they saw lying to the westward the island of Estotiland, distant, as the fishermen thought, at least a thousand miles from their home. "One of the boats was wrecked, and the crew of six men were taken up into a fair and populous city, where there was no one who could understand their language out of all the king's interpreters, except one who spoke Latin." He had been wrecked on that coast himself, and he seems to have been able to turn the Färöese dialect into something which the courtiers could understand. But the fisherman told Zeno that he had seen Latin books in the royal library, which none of the people were able to read. They remained in that country for five years. It seemed a little smaller than Iceland, fertile in corn, and abounding in gold and other metals. In the midst of it rose a high mountain range from which four rivers came to water the country; and there were forests of immense extent. The people seemed to be very intelligent, and as well advanced in the arts as the Italians, or so the Northern fishermen believed. They were said to trade with "Greenland," by which we may understand the North of Scandinavia, and to bring back, in return for their own goods, furs and brimstone and pitch. "They also make beer," added Zeno, "which is a kind of drink that the Northern peoples take as we take wine."

They knew how to build ships, and also how to sail them, the latter being an art in which the Färöese were somewhat deficient; but we are told that they had not the loadstone, nor the needle which the Spaniards called "the messenger between the stone and the star." The compass was used but sparingly at that time, except in the Mediterranean waters, and it is somewhat difficult to believe that the Färöese were familiar with the instrument while their neighbors were ignorant of its use. The story goes, however, that the castaways were able to show the advantage of steering by the magnetic needle, and were held in high estimation accordingly.

Up to this point there has been nothing in the story that cannot be easily explained. But the account of the fisherman's later wanderings among the polar cannibals, and of temples where men were sacrificed and eaten by tribes living further to the south, appears to be compounded with fables about Scythian savages at least as old as the time of Adam of Bremen. Even in the sixteenth century we find in serious works, such as Albert Krantz's history of the North and Paolo Giovio's description of Britain, foolish stories about danger from cannibals, which can be traced through Frisian legends to early mythological Sagas, and perhaps may even be connected with the legend of Polyphemus the Giant.

Immediately to the south of "Estotiland" was a great and populous country, said to be very rich in gold, which the fisherman left otherwise undescribed. There was also a country called "Drogio," to be reached by a southward voyage; but in its main extent, if the descriptions are carefully considered, it stretched upward toward the Arctic Circle somewhere about the upper provinces of Russia. The fisherman said that he and his comrades were sent with a fleet of twelve ships to Drogio; but when they arrived they were taken up into the country, and most of them were devoured by the savages. The survivors saved their lives by showing the natives how to fish with nets. Every chieftain was anxious to learn their "wonderful art," and was ready to make war on his neighbors upon the chance of getting hold of the ingenious captives. In the course of thirteen years the fisherman was transferred in this way to at least five and twenty masters, so that he got to know the whole country, which was very large, almost like a new world. It was inhabited by naked savages, who suffered cruelly from the cold. They lived by hunting, but they had not any knowledge of metals, and used wooden lances and rude bows strung with strips of hide.

Far away from these squalid hyperboreans the wanderers found a country with a temperate climate, inhabited by nations of a more civilized kind. The further one went toward the southwest the more refinement was observed. "In those parts," said the fisherman, "they have some knowledge and usage of gold and silver; and they have cities, and temples where they offer men in sacrifice and eat them afterward."

Now after many years this man determined to make his way home, to the skerries and stacks and whirling tides of Faroe, and the fisher boys far out at sea with their songs of home,

> And we must have labor and hunger and pain,
> Ere we dance with the maids of Dunrossness again.

He pressed it upon the companions who had wandered with him for so many years, but they had given up all hopes and thoughts about home; "and so they gave him God speed! and stayed with the cannibals." But he made his escape through the forests and came upon the road to Drogio, and found a friendly chieftain who passed him on again till he came to some of his old masters, and they sent him on from one to another, and so after a long time and with great toil he got back to Drogio itself, and there abode for about three years.

One day the fisherman heard some of the natives talking about strangers having arrived, and he ran down to the port and found that there were ships from Estotiland. None of the saliors could talk the language of Drogio, so that they were glad of his services as an interpreter; and when they left he went with them, and joined their trading venture. We are told that in the end he became a rich man, and fitted out a vessel of his own, and returned home to end his days in peace. Sinclair, says Zeno, was resolved to send out a fleet to explore these golden lands; "but our great preparations for the voyage to Estotiland were begun in an unlucky hour, for exactly three days before our start the fisherman died."

The whole story has been called the puzzle of antiquarians. Some parts of it are clear enough, but others can hardly be explained without allowing that the editor wove in a few incidents from the Spanish discoveries. But it seems obvious that the original story had nothing to do with Vinland or any colony of Scandinavians surviving there into the lifetime of Columbus. The fisherman was thought to have died about fifty years before Columbus was born, and the children of the sailors from Estotiland, and of those who went out to find the New World again, or some of the very men themselves, would have met the admiral when he visited the north. This is what gives an interest to this ancient story of the sea. It seems highly probable that Columbus actually visited the Faroe Isles, and in that case we may be sure that he would touch at the port of Thorshavn. He came upon places, as he said to his son, where the tide rose "six and twenty ells," or about fifty feet according to English measurement. There is no place which seems to answer this description except that rocky group where the flood-tide is caught and entangled in deep clefts and channels and is driven to a prodigious height. There are, of course, high tides in the Severn, and on the coast of Normandy; but Columbus was referring distinctly to the North Sea, as it stretches between Norway and Iceland; and in that direction there is no place to which his words could refer except the stony and desolate rocks which were ruled by Sinclair, the "Prince of Frisland."

CHAPTER XII.

> "The slender cocoa's drooping crown of plumes.
> The lightning flash of insect and of bird,
> The luster of the long convolvuluses
> That coiled around the stately stems, and ran
> Even to the limit of the land, the glows
> And glories of the broad belt of the world,
> All these he saw."

AFTER his return from the north, Columbus appears to have lived for some time at Porto Santo. His fondness for the place is shown by certain incidents in his later career, for we know that he would go a little out of his course to spend a few hours on his favorite island. Thus, when starting on the Third Voyage, he went first to Porto Santo, "and there he heard mass, and gave orders to take in wood and water, and that very same night he sailed away to Madeira"; and on another occasion he detached one of the ships to visit the island "on a certain matter of private business."

His son Diego said that he also resided for a time at Madeira, and the same fact is mentioned by Las Casas; and an old house at Funchal was shown until lately as his home, though it is probable that he only paid visits there to one of the rich Flemish merchants. He was not concerned with the trade of the rising colony, with the fields of corn and cane, or the new vineyards which travelers described as one of the wonders of the world. He continued, no doubt, to deal in maps and charts, but his real business in Madeira was the collection of all kinds of information that bore upon his intended enterprise.

Whenever the chance occurred he would go out on a summer voyage. At one time he was the guest of his brother-in-law, Correa, who had been appointed to the captaincy of Graciosa, and sailed about the archipelago of the Azores; and on other occasions he visited the Portuguese factories in Morocco or at the mouth of Rio del Ouro. As he enlarged the circle of his observations he advanced to more distant shores, among the blacks on the River Senegal or with the pepper merchants in Malaguette or down along the Gold Coast of Benin. He is even said to have visited the islands of the torrid zone, and to have approached the equator among the hills and forests of St. Thomas. He had an early opportunity of seeing the Canary Islands, for by a treaty with Spain made about two years after his return to Porto Santo the Portuguese were allowed to trade freely with the colonists, who were already successful in sugar making, though in agriculture they had terrible difficulties in contending with the rabbits and crows. The Portuguese took in their supplies at Grand Canary, and the busy factories of Ferro and Lanzarote; and fresh venison for the sailors was occasionally procured at Gomera, where a wild population was ruled by "the huntress Bovadilla." Teneriffe and some others of the "pagan islands" were still under the rule of the Guanches.

We cannot be sure whether he visited the Cape Verde Islands at this time, though he made one or two allusions to their position in discussing the Carthaginian voyages. He described them very carefully in his journal for 1498, and it seems likely from the phrases employed that he had not been there before. His way of playing on the local names is what one would only expect from a stranger. "Cape Verde," he says, "is a fine name for a desert where nothing green could be found," as if he had forgotten that they were only named after the green cape on the African coast a hundred leagues away. When he came to Bona Vista, where lepers were sent to be cured by catching and eating turtles, "for so wretchedly," he adds, "do these sick men live, without any other employment or sustenance," he plays on the meaning of the word again. "Very far from the truth is this name, for it betokens a lovely view, whereas it is a dull and wretched place, dry and barren, with never a tree or a spring." He was evidently not familiar with Santiago, the principal settlement in the islands, for we may suppose that his description would have been more discriminating if he had been there on several occasions. The weather being bad when he arrived in 1498, he complains of "never seeing the sky or the stars," and says that "there was always a thick hot fog, so that three-fourths of the inhabitants were ill." On arriving a day or two afterward at the burning island of Fogo, he notes, as if the sight were quite strange to him, that "it looks from a distance like a great church with a steeple at the east end, and from the vast high rock there usually breaks out fire before the east winds blow, and this may be seen at Teneriffe, and at Volcano and Mount Etna." Now when he spoke to the sailors on the First Voyage about the eruption of Teneriffe, he made no mention of this burning island, though he would almost certainly have added it to his list if he had been in these parts before.

We hear much more of what he learned during his visits to the Azores. When he was at Flores the settlers told him that they had seen two drowned men in the sea with very broad faces, and "differing in aspect from Christians"; but there was nothing, of course, to show that these were not the bodies of Canarians from Ferro or Gomera. Again at Cape Verga he was told that they had seen boats drifting, as if they had been lost in a storm when crossing about between some of the distant islands; and they said that these boats were just like the African "dugout" canoes, which were called "almadias" by the Moors. All these circumstances seemed to fit in with the classical tradition, so often repeated in various forms, that certain Indians had been driven ashore in Germany, and had been sent as a gift to Metellus, the pro-consul in Gaul. The wanderings of these "Indians" had soon been found to have nothing to do with the countries beyond the Atlantic, though the story received a new importance when the English began to make plans for discovering the Northeast Passage.

Columbus seems to have approved the inferences drawn from finding the boats and corpses; but he attached more importance to the statement that large pine trees of an unknown species had been cast on shore in Correa's territory and in the neighboring island of Fayal; and his reasoning was shown to be correct when he came upon extensive pine forests on the coasts of Cuba and Hispaniola. Antonio Leme, the son of a Fleming settled in Madeira, told the admiral besides, that he had sailed out for a long way in his own ship, and had seen three unknown islands; and several captains of ships trading with the Azores confirmed the story, repeating the talk of the people at Gomera about seeing these countries every year; "and this they looked upon as most certain, and many persons of reputation swore that it was true." Columbus paid little attention to them, because he found that they had certainly not been one hundred leagues from land. They had been deceived, he thought, by meeting with isolated rocks, or masses of weed, or perhaps they had seen the burning mountains of the northern ocean, or those flitting islands in the south, which, according to the poet Juventius, "skimmed along upon the surface of the sea."

But whether their eyes had been cheated by sunset clouds, or the mirage of the Fata Morgana, or whether these were only the echoes of old traditions about the land that could never be approached, the admiral would have none of them. "If Antonio Leme saw anything, it must have been one of St. Brandan's isles, where as all the world knows many wonderful things are seen."

We find a considerable number of references to his various African voyages. There was at one time some uncertainty as to the date when his visits to the West Coast began, and Don Ferdinand himself was not quite sure whether his father went there while his wife was alive, although (to use his own phrase) "the reason of the case seems to require it." But there can in reality be little doubt about the matter. Donna Philippa did not die much before the end of 1484, nearly two years after the admiral came home from the building of Fort St. George; and it is known that he never had any opportunity of visiting the African coast again.

The admiral often referred in his letters and journals to his experiences in Senegambia and Guinea, more especially when he was describing the customs of the natives and the aspects of nature in the new countries which he had found beyond the Atlantic. In Cuba, for instance, when he gave orders to capture some of the Indians, he speaks in his journal of the detention of five young men and of the seizure of seven women and three children in a house near the shore. "I intend," he writes, "to take them with us, in the hope that my Indians will behave all the better in Spain if their countrywomen are with them; but it has very often happened that on taking men home from Guinea to teach them Portuguese, when they were brought back and one expected to get some advantage in their country in return for our favors and gifts, they ran away at once as soon as they touched land and were never seen again." Some of them, he added, did not act in this fashion, but this was because they had their wives on board; "and so these Indians, if the women are with them, will do what they are told, and the women can teach their language to our wives in Spain." In a later entry he adds: "This evening the husband of one of the women has arrived and asks leave to go with the rest. They seem to be related to each other, and now they are all consoled."

In talking of the West Indian dialects he

noticed that the people of the different islands all seemed to understand each other, which was natural enough, because they were always crossing and recrossing in their canoes. "It is not like Guinea," he says, "where there are a thousand languages, and each of them is only understood by the people of a particular neighborhood." He seems, however, to have spoken a little too generally about this uniformity of speech, even as regards the single island of Hispaniola. When the Spaniards were building their fort in a region called Maroris, Columbus sent the anchorite Romano Pane to do mission work there, and desired him to learn the language. But on going further up the country it was found that the people of Maroris had a dialect peculiar to themselves. The missionary was therefore told to reside in the territory of the chieftain Guarionex, whose language was everywhere understood. "Oh, my lord," said the anchorite, as he afterward told the story, "why will you have me go to live with Guarionex when I know no language but this of Maroris?" He begged for an interpreter who could use both tongues, and Columbus said that he might take anyone that he might choose, and he chose one

John Matthews, "the best of the Indians," who was the first native baptized in Hispaniola. Another difference of language was observed near the Gulf of Samana, where the admiral's interpreters could hardly make themselves understood in talking with the Ciguayo warriors.

In his descriptions of the physical appearance of the natives, Columbus several times referred to the black skins and woolly hair of the African negro. The West Indians in his opinion were not unlike the natives of the Canaries, being sallow or of a bright olive complexion, very tall, and with high compressed foreheads; and they had coarse black hair cut short about their ears in some places, after the fashion of the Spanish soldiers; they elsewhere wore it loose, or twisted in a network of parrots' feathers, "and their long locks were hanging down as the women wear theirs in Spain." "They are not black skinned like the men in Guinea," says Columbus, "and their hair is long; but it does not grow like that where the rays of the sun are fierce."

When he wrote to Ferdinand and Isabella about the excellence of the West Indian harbors, he declared that he had never seen anything like them for size, though he had been in all parts of

Guinea. The term, as he used it, takes in the western shores of Africa from the Senegal to Cape Coast Castle, including the Grain Coast of Malaguette, the Ivory Coast, and the Gold Coast near Ashantee, to which the name of Guinea was afterward exclusively applied.

He recognized in the New World many of the natural products which he had met with in Africa, such as palm trees of various kinds, the mangroves in the swamps, the large pearl oysters, and the oceanic birds whose habits he had observed in the tropical seas. When he saw the natives planting the yams, out of which they got meal for their chestnut-flavored cakes, the admiral said that he had seen the same roots growing in Guinea, and described the proper method of setting the tendrils; but he added that he had never seen any so large as those in the West Indies, where they sometimes grew to the size of a man's leg.

In the account of his first expedition there is an anecdote of a visit to Malaguette, where the Portuguese got the aromatic pepper called Grains of Paradise. Before the Indian pepper came into common use this spice was very highly prized, and the merchants made frequent voyages to obtain it from the desolate and dangerous coast between Mesurado and Cape Palmas, on that part of the continent where the curve of its shoulder bends eastward. Columbus considered that the cayenne pepper and red and green capsicums of Hispaniola were worth far more, either than the spice from the Indian pepper vine or the fragrant grains of Malaguette. One day he was exploring by the Rio d'Oro in the same island, where he had found gold and very lustrous ore, and when he came home he said that he had seen three mermaids, lifting themselves high out of the water; "but they were not so like fair ladies," he said, "as some people might suppose," and he told the sailors that he had seen others like them in Guinea, when he was off the coast of Malaguette. There was an officer at the Spanish court in his time who declared that he had seen a merman, with a bluish skin and bristly beard and hands like fishes' fins, and that it had been brought over from Morocco, preserved in a cask of honey; and two great scholars of the next generation, George of Trebizond and Theodore Gaza, averred that they had seen similar "tritons" in the Mediterranean. These may have been specimens of the sea wolf or monk seal, well known to the Portuguese; but the animals seen by Columbus were evidently manatees, which are fond of haunting the shores near a river's mouth; the sailors call them "sea cows" and say that when they lift their heads and breasts they have a very human appearance.

Columbus made his last voyage to Guinea soon after "John the Perfect" had come to the throne of Portugal. The factory at Saama, where the ivory and gold dust was collected, was in a very unprotected condition, and information had been received about an impending invasion. The Duke of Medina Sidonia was lord of a maritime province; and it was said that he was gathering a fleet for a raid upon Guinea. Other ships were being fitted out in England with the same object, and it was suspected that Edward the Fourth was secretly encouraging the adventure. The duke, as Columbus afterward discovered, was never of a stable mind, so that his project was soon abandoned; and it was not difficult to persuade the English king to prohibit his subjects from trading within the conquests of Portugal. King John determined to protect himself by erecting a permanent fortress. There is still a forlorn and broken castle at Elmina in the Dutch colony, a few miles from our Cape Coast settlement; and this is all that remains of the fort of St. George of the Goldmine. The king was helped in his plans by a fortunate discovery. Martin Behaim succeeded in the year 1481 in improving the astrolabe into a rude but useful sextant; and it now became easy to ascertain the latitude, and the course of a ship far from land, by taking the altitude of the sun. The Portuguese fleet started on the 11th of December in that same year. It consisted of ten caravels, and two ships of burden laden with stone, bricks, and timber work, all ready for immediate use. Columbus was in command of one of the caravels. Pedro Noronhas, his wife's uncle, was one of the king's most trusted ministers, and Columbus may have gained some advantage from the family connection. We know that he made the voyage, because the king once reminded him of his duty as a sea captain in the Portuguese service, and because Columbus himself stated more than once that he had been at Fort St. George; but he had, in fact, no opportunity of going there, except on this occasion.

The fleet was under the command of an admiral named Azumbaja. He put in first at a harbor near Cape Verde, where he had business with one of the negro kings, being commissioned to present him with certain horses and hawks, and to obtain his assent to a treaty. After leaving this country, they sailed on round the shoulder of Africa, along the Ivory Coast, and on the 19th of January, 1482, arrived at the hilly shore beyond the Cape of the Three Points, where it was intended to build the castle. In the bay they found a Portuguese merchantman, and the captain, who could speak the native language, was at once engaged as interpreter.

The presents for Caramansa, as the king of that country was called, were sent on shore at once, and an appointment was made for a state reception on the following morning. The Portuguese writers are fond of describing the scene. Azumbaja walked first in scarlet and brocade; and his captains followed in splendid cloaks and tunics, wearing their golden collars, and taking care to hide their cuirasses with abundance of silks and ribbons. Columbus, as we know, was not averse from a little display; and one may be sure that he wore his fine red coat and a necklet of amber or Indian stones. The first ceremony consisted in unfurling the banner of Portugal, which was displayed from the top of a tall tree upon the hillside. Under the tree an altar was consecrated by the priest, and a mass was celebrated for the repose of the soul of Prince Henry. Mr. Major, in his work on the Prince's life, has quoted a striking description of the subsequent meeting with Caramansa. Surrounded by his guards, armed with lances and assegais, and scantily clothed with monkey fur and strips of palm leaf, the black king sat in state; "his arms and legs were adorned with bracelets and rings of gold, and round his neck was a collar with small bells, and some sprigs of gold were twisted into his beard, so that the curls were straightened by the weight." The treaty was soon concluded, and the fortress was built within twenty days after the landing. Azumbaja remained in charge of the garrison, and the caravels were sent home with rich cargoes of gold and ivory. The merchant vessels, however, were broken up according to the king's orders, so that a report might be spread of their destruction in the whirlpools of the Ethiopian Sea. The king's plan was to make it appear that the navigation was only safe for the caravels of the royal navy. It happened one day when his courtiers were discussing the matter that a commander of great experience, who did not know of this scheme, offered to make the "Ethiopian voyage" himself, in any kind of vessel. The king broke in angrily, and said that the attempt had often been made before, and had always failed. "The man must be a rascal," he said, "and it is only worthless loons like this who boast that they can do everything, though they do little enough when the time comes." The Portuguese historians tell us another story to show how fiercely the king defended his secret. A merchant captain and two sailors, who had often been to La Mina, got across the borders of Portugal into Castile, and seemed likely to reveal to the Spaniards the information which every government in Europe was eager to acquire. King John sent certain messengers after them, to catch them and to bring them back; but the pursuers killed two of them, because it was difficult to kidnap so many at once, and brought home only one of the deserters. The king made an example of the prisoner by sawing him into four pieces; and he hoped that this would show that in no part of the world would his enemies be safe from his vengeance. When Columbus escaped into Castile he also was in some danger of being kidnapped or murdered; but when the Portuguese king wished him to return to Lisbon he was offered a safe conduct and an indemnity against a criminal prosecution. Nevertheless, again and again the dangerous secret of St. George's Fort was likely to prove his ruin, and as often as he came near the Portuguese dominions he walked in peril of his life.

CHAPTER XIII.

> " A brighter Hellas rears her mountains
>   From waves serener far,
> A new Peneus rolls his fountains
>   Against the morning star :
> Where fairer Tempes bloom, there sleep
> Young Cyclads on a sunnier deep.
> A loftier Argo cleaves the main,
>   Fraught with a later prize:
> Another Orpheus sings again,
>   And loves and weeps and dies."

SOON after his return from Guinea Columbus began to press his schemes upon the King of Portugal, who was willing at first to help him; but when his proposals were referred to the Council it was found that they involved a larger question, and the real debate seems to have turned upon the suggestion that Portugal should abandon the explorations of Africa in favor of a vague search for the lands described by Marco Polo. It was inevitable that the Council should refuse to forsake the glorious policy of Prince Henry. The king adopted their decision. He endeavored, indeed, to gain a somewhat ungenerous advantage by sending out three caravels from the Cape Verde Islands upon the route which Columbus had laid down; but the ships returned with the report that no land could be seen after a voyage of several days to the westward.

About the end of 1484 Columbus escaped into Spain. There is much obscurity about his subsequent journey. It seems probable that he made for Huelva, the home of his sister-in-law, Donna Muliar; and the better opinion seems to be that it was on this occasion that he first visited the monastery of La Rabida. We hear of a visit to Genoa; and there are traditions of his having propounded his plans to the Signoria of his native city, and afterward to the Government of Venice. It is certain that he returned to Spain before the end of 1485, since his journal for 1493 distinctly states that on the next 20th of January he would have been exactly seven years in the service of the Catholic kings.

When he first began to attend the Court at Cordova he formed an attachment for Donna Beatrix Enriquez, a lady of good family, connected with the great house of Arana. She was the mother of his son Ferdinand, who is known to have been born in 1488. But though Don

Ferdinand was scrupulously treated on the same footing as Don Diego, the elder son, it remains very doubtful whether his parents were lawfully married. It is possible that some legal impediment or flaw may have been discovered which rendered the union invalid; and in any event it is certain that Columbus was separated from Donna Beatrix after his return from the discovery of the West Indies, although up to that time she had been in charge of both his sons at Cordova.

In 1489 Columbus served in the campaign in which the city of Baza was captured from the Moors. During the next two years he lived at Seville, near the bridge upon the Guadalquivir, where he kept a small bookseller's shop, and sold charts and maps and a little treatise which he had written upon the practice of navigation.

About this time a conference of learned men was summoned to Salamanca to consider the truth of his theories and the actual value of his proposals; and in the winter of 1491 they reported against the whole scheme. This brought the matter to a point. The refusal of the Dukes of Medina Sidonia and Medina Celi to undertake so vast a task, too heavy as it seemed for the sovereigns of Arragon and Castile, fixed Columbus in his resolution to abandon Spain forever. It was natural that Queen Isabella should at that moment be regretting her decision; and a message from the Prior of La Rabida, to whom Columbus had confided his plans, determined her at all hazards to accept the offers that she had refused. Columbus rode back to the camp at Santa Fé, where a strong town had been built on land taken from the Moors in face of their beleaguered palaces. He was promised all the high offices and allowances which had seemed before too great for a subject to hold. It was arranged that he should have one-eighth of the profits in consideration of finding a like share of the expense; the town of Palos was ordered to find the ships and crews. After many delays and much resistance Columbus and his friends, two rich shipbuilders called Martin and Vincente Pinzon, procured and equipped the fleet of three ships by which the New World was found. The *Santa Maria*, a fine caravel, sailed with Columbus himself on board; the *Pinta*, the swiftest of the three, was under the elder Pinzon; and the *Nina*, a small but roomy vessel, which afterward became the admiral's own favorite, started on this occasion under Vincente Pinzon's command.

Columbus never failed to remind the Catholic kings that his whole undertaking was intended to be but an episode in a vast crusade. In Europe they had closed the war against the infidels when their banners were displayed on the Alhambra and the Moorish king had kissed hands at the gate of Granada. The time had now come to carry those banners into the East and to bring light and hope to the countless nations of Cathay. The Great Khan and his ancestors had pleaded at Rome for instruction; but the nations were sunk in idolatry and went after the "sects of perdition." "Your Highnesses," he wrote, "as enemies of the following of Mohammed have thought fit to send me to see those princes and peoples, and to judge of their present state and the proper way to convert them." He was firmly convinced that he was a divinely appointed messenger to find and reveal "new heavens and a new earth," and all the treasures of the islands that were awaiting the ships of Tarshish; and he was assured that within an appointed term he would see again the wealth of Ophir and Sheba, and bring gold by the thousands of quintals to aid in a holy war.

The journals of his first voyage are full of the indications of this belief. On the night of August 24, 1492, when sailing between the Grand Canary and Gomera, he saw the first of the signs and wonders which marked the course of his enterprise. He was passing close under Teneriffe, a volcano that had slept for centuries, when the fire suddenly "gushed out" from a ridge below the cone of the Peak, and they passed back under a flaring sky to the port where he had intended to procure a new caravel in place of the *Pinta*. But now he would have no delay; and when he learned that the ship which he meant to impress had sailed off with the Lady of Gomera he took it lightly, and "made the best of what had happened." He affirmed that since it had pleased Heaven that he should not find the caravel, it was, perhaps, because he would have lost much time about its seizure and the changing of cargoes. There must be no further hindrance; and he determined to stay where he was, and to shift with making a new rudder for the *Pinta* and cutting down the sails of the *Nina* to a proper shape. The admiral left Gomera o..

the 6th of September, and this, says Don Ferdinand, may be accounted the first setting out upon the voyage in the ocean. On the 9th they lost sight of Ferro, "the furthest Christian land," and there were many tears and groans from those who believed that they would never see home again.

For a few days they had to make head against a contrary current; but on the night of the 13th strange signs began to be seen. They had reached a "magnetic line of no deviation," a hundred leagues west of the Azores, and there was at once "a great change in the sky and the stars, the air, and the waters of the sea." The compass needle had been pointing northeast and suddenly turned a whole quarter of the card to the northwest, and remained nearly at that point through the night. The admiral was still more amazed soon afterward to see the needle pointing northeast at night and straight for the pole star at dawn. The stone was not true to the star, or the star, as the admiral said, was wheeling in a broad circle round the pole. The pilots and crews were alarmed, being in such a strange region and so far from land, and were hardly pacified by the admiral's theories on a matter beyond the scope of his science.

At this point they were within the drift of the great "Fucus bank"; it seemed as if they had returned to the weedy shores of Spain, for all the sea was covered with the orange Sargasso plant, shaped like pine branches and covered with berries like those on the mastic tree. "It was so thick," said the admiral, "that I thought it was a reef, and that the ships must run aground, whereas until I reached this line I saw not a single branch." There were also bright green leaves floating a few feet down, which looked like rock weeds from some neighboring island, but Columbus said that by his calculation the mainland must be a long way off. "I also observed," he added, "that at this point the sea was very smooth, and that though the wind was rough, the ships did not roll at all." They were borne along on an oceanic current "as calm as the river at Seville," but the sailors were alarmed at seeing nothing but the sky and the water, and looked anxiously for tokens of land. On the evening of the 15th they saw a meteor fall "like a marvelous branch of fire," and within a few hours they came into a region of balmy air and blue skies, "like Andalusia in April, if only the nightingales were singing."

"There are signs coming out of the west," Columbus writes in his journal, "where, I hope, He in whose hands is victory will bring us soon to land." A swimming crab was caught in a bunch of weed, and the crew of the *Nina* speared a spotted tunny out of a shoal playing round the ship. Some of the others caught a tern, of the kind that haunts the mouths of rivers. A white tropic bird was seen wheeling aloft, and a day or two afterward there were "boobies," looking like pelicans, flying straight out over the water, as if they were going out to fish or were making for home. When there were two or three of them together it was a sure sign that they were in their proper ground and not blown out to sea by accident; and the sailors who had been in Africa said that none of these large birds slept on the water, or were found more than one hundred miles from land. On the 20th they caught a tern, and two or three song birds came to the ship about dawn, and flew away at sunrise. It seemed as if they must have islands to the north and south of their course, but the admiral was firm in pushing on toward the Indies. "The weather is fine and, if it please God, we shall see it all on our way home."

On the 21st they sailed again into a floating weed bank. A vast sea meadow seemed to stretch away as far as the horizon. The sea was held by the yellow fondage, "as when its whole surface is caught in the ice"; and the sailors caught up the notion, and talked about the freezing seas where St. Amaro will not allow a ship to stir forward or back. Then a fine breeze sprang up and blew the weed away, the sea began to run smooth like a river, and a whale was seen spouting and this was another sign of land. Next day a flock of petrels flitted about the stern of the admiral's ship, bringing bad weather, as sailors say. The wind shifted, and blew against their course, and this, says Columbus, was "absolutely necessary for me, because the crews had been in a great excitement at the idea that there were no winds here that could take a ship back to Spain." But the sailors still grumbled at the breeze; it was only a "cat's paw," or a little flicker of wind, and if it was too weak to raise the sea it would never be strong enough to carry them home." The water was moving in a slow stream, with weed hanging round; there were little cray fishes creeping about its bunches and strings, and a booby and some white sea birds fishing, and some of the men saw a reed sparrow and a turtle dove. Suddenly the sea rose, though there was no longer a breath of wind, and rolled so high that they were all amazed. "This great sea," the admiral repeated, "was quite necessary for me; but such a thing has never happened before, except when Pharaoh went forth after Moses, who delivered the Hebrews from bondage."

Next day, said the journal, they spied another booby flying out, and several small birds coming from the west, and tunny fishes, "whereof the men of the *Pinta* and *Nina* stuck some with harping irons, because they would not bite at the hook." Columbus now signaled to Pinzon to bring the *Pinta* alongside, and to give back the copy of Toscanelli's map, which he had borrowed three days before. Pinzon came up accordingly, and said that the map showed islands thereabouts. The admiral replied that he thought the map was right, but that the current had been thrusting them away from the islands, and they had possibly not gone so far as the pilots made out; and when Pinzon had put the map into a case and heaved it to the admiral on a line, Columbus and the pilot Juan de la Cosa, and some of the sailors near them, began to stoop over the map and point their fingers to the islands. Pinzon was watching the sunset from the poop of his caravel, when all in a moment he leaped in the air and shouted, "Good news, good cheer, Lord Admiral! Land ho! and good luck to the news!" His hand pointed to a dark smear on the sky line which loomed like distant land. Columbus fell on his knees in prayer. Pinzon led off a *Gloria in Excelsis* which was taken up by both the crews, and they could see the men of the *Nina* climbing her masts and crowding out in the rigging. But by noon next day they knew that they had been deceived by a sunset cloud.

Now came tokens of a new kind. On the 27th several doradoes were harpooned. Two days after that they saw a frigate bird chasing some boobies, and the sight reminded them of the world behind, for some of them remembered the same thing in the Cape Verde Islands. The tropic birds and boobies were gathered in little flocks and companies. A shoal of "emperor fish" passed by, very brilliantly colored, "but with a hard skin, and not fit to eat." But however much the admiral attended to these signs he still more carefully watched the deviation of the needle and the movements of the stars round the pole, and he was confirmed in his belief that the load star moved in a wide circle, but the compass was always true. .

There was heavy rain on the 1st of October, and Juan de la Cosa came up and announced in a dolorous voice that they were now five hundred and seventy-eight leagues from Ferro. The admiral had learnt by watching the water and the sand glass that their run was about five hundred miles further than the pilot supposed; but he winked, we are told, at this mistake, "that the men might not feel quite dejected at being so far from home." The sailors were now almost ripe for a mutiny. They muttered at their leader's foolish fancies; he wanted to be a lord at their expense, while he was but a foreigner, hated at court and despised by all the wise and learned. Some said that the best plan would be to throw him overboard, and to say that he lost his footing when he was taking an altitude. "It pleased Heaven," says the biographer, "to send fresh signs." Birds and fishes came round the ships, and the sea went in a smooth stream again, for which Columbus rendered "infinite praise." There was a great quantity of weed, some of it with green leaves and berries and some all withered and going to powder. No less than forty petrels were playing about the admiral's ship; "but, thanks be to God," he writes, "the sea is still running like a river," and he compares it more than once to the calm waters of the Guadalquivir below the bridge at Seville. The flying fish were now beginning to be seen. A modern traveler says in describing them that "the first little fish may be mistaken for a dragon fly, and the next for a plover," "and their flight is almost exactly like that of a quail or partridge." Columbus called them "water swallows," and said that they were about a span long, with little wings like a bat; "they fly about the height of a pike and for a musket-shot in length, more or less, and sometimes they drop into the ship."

On the night of the 6th of October Pinzon brought the *Pinta* alongside, and proposed to turn toward the southwest. He may have thought that they were near the rich island of Cipango. Columbus still thought it best to make straight for the mainland of Cathay; but he consented to change their course on seeing a large flock of birds flying to the southwest, and either making for their home or beginning a winter migration. The air now became as balmy as the gardens round Seville in springtime. Twelve birds with bright plumage were singing and fluttering about the mast; there were daws and ducks flying to the south, and all night long they heard the flocks of birds whistling and crying overhead. The men were so sick of delay that none of these things would comfort them. Day and night they complained, and the admiral argued and threatened. "Be it right or wrong," he said, "and tokens or no tokens, they had to go on with the Indian voyage by order of the Catholic kings."

Then they suddenly changed their minds. There were green rushes floating, and the men on the *Nina* saw a dog-rose briar covered with bloom, and a little stick with curious carving. Now they were all racing to earn the reward for the man who should first see land. On the evening of the 11th of October, after the *Salve Regina* had been sung, Columbus said that he would add a velvet coat as a special prize of his own. Looking out from the poop cabin about ten o'clock, he thought that he saw a light moving up and down and vanishing sometimes, as if a torch were being carried about in a village. He called others to look at it, but they could not be quite sure about the matter. About two o'clock in the morning the *Pinta* fired a gun. The coast had been seen about two leagues off by a sailor called Roderigo de Triana. "Being now arrived the ships all lay by, and it seemed a long time before the morning came." The New World was found, and the reward was afterward adjudged to Columbus, "because he had been the first to see light in the midst of the darkness."

CHAPTER XIV.

> " A fleet of glass,
> That seemed a fleet of jewels under me,
> Sailing along before a gloomy cloud
> That not one moment ceased to thunder, passed
> In sunshine ; right across its track there lay
> Down in the water a long reef of gold,
> Or what seemed gold."

WHEN the dawn broke they saw that they were fronting "a little island of the Lucayos," flat and tufted with high towering trees. They had reached the archipelago of the Bahamas, and they hoped and believed that they were in Indian waters and already among the Golden Cyclades. About two leagues off lay a rich-looking coast, with a white sandy line of beach, and here they determined to land and enter into possession. When the boats were hauled ashore the admiral knelt and kissed the sand, and gave thanks with tears. The royal standard was unfurled, the cross was set up and the banners raised; the name of San Salvador was given to the island, and Columbus formally assumed the offices of viceroy and governor. When they looked round they must have felt bewildered, like men in a dream. The forest stood like a wall round the blue curve of the bay, with its masses of metallic green or the soft and liquid color of the acanthus, silvery or golden or gleaming with blue and topaz, "ever changing," to use Kingsley's words, "and iridescent like a peacock's neck." There were strange naked people groveling and crawling, or pointing to the armed and bearded Spaniards and their three ships, and then to the sky and the sun. After a time a crowd of them came round and tried to talk with the interpreters. They were the warriors of the Isle of Guanahani, having only one woman with them. Some had their faces smeared with a blood-red stain, others were striped and checkered or plastered with a chalky white; one had his nose painted, another had bright rings round his eyes, and they all looked like "madmen or clowns." Their skins, where the natural color could be seen, were neither white nor black, but somewhat of an olive color, like the complexions of the natives in Gomera or the faces of sunburned laborers in Spain. They were tall and well-shaped, and with good features, except that their foreheads had been squeezed too high, "which made them look rather wild." Most of them had gray eyes, with specks of blue or brown about the iris. Their hands were small, with polished nails, and when they began to laugh and talk their teeth were as white as ivory. Their thick black hair was cropped and worn in a straight fringe above the eyebrows; "some few let it grow down about their shoulders, and held it back with a string, as women tie back their tresses." They carried bundles of darts made out of the stems of reeds or canes, and tipped with spikes of hard wood or sharks' teeth and thornbacks' spines. Before the Spaniards returned to their boats the admiral distributed a few red caps and strings of beads among them. A crowd now followed them to the water's edge and swam out to the ships, carrying all their treasures to exchange for memorials of the white men who had sailed from a land beyond the sun. They had parrots and reed darts and large balls of cotton; and they possessed a greater treasure than all the rest in the dried tobacco leaves, which the Spaniards did not know how to use. "The Indians," they said, "value these dry leaves as being sweet-scented and wholesome, and use them as a sort of incense for perfuming themselves." Next day the bargaining went on again, the Indians clustering round the ships in their dugout canoes, which turned out after all to be very like the African "almadias." They seemed very poor, Columbus said, but they had plenty of spun cotton, and would give it by hundredweights for scraps of broken pottery or a Portuguese half-farthing. One or two, however, had little plates of gold hanging to their nose rings, and being asked where they got them they showed by signs that it was "toward the south," and told of a king there who had great pieces and platters of gold. On the 14th the admiral completed the circuit of the island. Like most of the Bahamas, it was girt in on almost all sides by coral rocks; but the reef in one part opened into a harbor "which would have held all the navies of Christendom." On going in with the longboat he found several houses, and captured some of the natives to act as interpreters. There were lovelier gardens than he had ever seen before, with water rippling in a green shade and trees with fresher foliage than the cork woods of Castile in May.

On setting sail again they saw a multitude of other islands, and the Indian guides were able to repeat the names of more than a hundred of those in sight, all flat and fertile, as they reported, and all of them thickly inhabited. The Indians said that in the nearest, which seemed much closer than it was in that clear atmosphere, the chiefs wore bangles and bracelets of gold. When the Spaniards arrived there about sunset they found nothing but naked Indians again, but Columbus landed and took possession, and gave it the name of Santa Maria de la Concepcion.

A larger island stood a few leagues off toward the western horizon, and it was here, as the guides explained, that the people wore bracelets and bangles, and golden necklaces and earrings. Columbus named this country Fernandina, and determined to explore it thoroughly in hopes of finding a gold mine, but he was once more disappointed, and was told that he would find it in "Saometo," which he afterward called "Isabella" in honor of the queen. In Fernandina the people were somewhat more civilized, and they seemed to be sharper than the other Indians at a bargain. The women wore cotton mantillas and aprons. There were villages with ten or twelve houses together, tent-shaped, with air shafts standing out from the roofs. Inside were slung hammocks covered with cotton rugs. There were dogs kept for food and for hunting the rabbit-like agoutis; but the Spaniards saw nothing alive in the maize fields, except parrots and lizards and a snake found by one of the ship boys. Columbus took many notes about the fauna and flora, as the place seemed suitable for a colony. What struck him most was the marvelous entanglement of the bush and the abundance of creepers and parasitic plants. Out of the trunk of one forest tree grew branches of other kinds, orchids and creepers, a pine growing on the bough like a mistletoe, "one branch like a reed and the next like a mastic bush," and yet there was no sign of grafting; and indeed the natives had no feelings about these astonishing sights, and apparently no reverence for anything; and this might make it easier to convert them, since they showed no lack of intelligence.

The admiral describes one of his walks in the forest. The verdure of the foliage reminded him of the gardens round Granada, but the trees themselves, the fruit, the grass, the very stones, were as different from anything in Europe as the day from the night. It is true that there were mastic trees and others that reminded him of the woods in Castile, but one could always see the difference. The sea round Fernandina was full of life. There were whales spouting in the bay. The natives caught all sorts of sea birds, and land crabs, and fishes of many strange kinds. These fish were of the strangest shapes and painted in most fantastic colors—pink and silver, or scarlet, or striped like a zebra. There were "yellow fins" and "hog fish," and the parrot fish, and "sea cocks" of a silvery red, "shaped just like Chanticleer" and with all his brilliant coloring. "There is no one, I am sure," said the admiral, "who would not be amazed and delighted at seeing them."

After a while the flotilla made for Saometo. This was the finest place which they had yet seen, with a bold cape and swelling hills covered with groups of enormous trees. "It is all so fine," wrote the admiral, "that I do not know where to begin. My eyes are never tired of looking at the green foliage, so different in its colors from ours at home. I expect that trees and plants grow here which are of a high price in Spain for dyes, and medicine, and spice; but I do not know them, and this gives me great concern. When I arrived at this beautiful cape the flowers and trees on shore sent out to us such a sweet and soft perfume that it was the most agreeable of all offerings to our senses. To-morrow, before leaving these parts, I shall go ashore to see what there is on the cape. The village is further off in the interior. It is there, according to my Indians, that the king lives who carries so much gold about him. I must go early enough to find his palace to-morrow; and I shall speak to this king, who, according to the guides, holds all these islands under his sway, and wears rich robes, and covers himself over with gold." He adds that he does not much believe in the story. The cape seemed to form an islet by itself, and there might be still another to be passed before they could approach the royal domain. "When I have found the spots where the gold and spices abound, I shall stay there until I have collected the greatest possible store, and that is why I am going round only to look for these productions."

On October 21 he walked about the island with his two captains. "How beautiful it is!" he cried, "and how full of great green forests, and lakes set round with groves! The grass at this moment is like the herbage of Andalusia in the springtime." There was a concert of singing birds, "so sweet that he could hardly depart." Great flocks of parrots darkened the sun, and the air was full of the odors of fruit and flowers. "I was in despair," he says, "at not knowing the different kinds, because I am quite sure that they are all very valuable, and I am bringing home specimens of every kind, and even of the grasses." As he walked by the lake side he saw an iguana run down into the water, and they killed the great lizard, or "serpent" as they called it, and brought back the skin to Spain. It was just there that he thought he recognized the lign aloes or "eagle wood," which was used in making frankincense. It was probably one of the euphorbias, which always burn with a pleasant smell. "They tell me it is very precious," he writes, "and I shall take down ten quintals of it to my ship to-morrow." Then they found a village with empty houses, and thought that the people must have carried off their clothes and property into the hills. One or two Indians came round, and brought a little water in their poor calabashes. "I wish," said Columbus, "I could see this king, and try to get the gold that he wears, and then start off to the other great island, which must be Cipango, if the guides are right." They called it Cuba, and talked of its broad havens and the multitude of its sailors. There was another great country near it called Bohio, which turned out afterward to be Hispaniola. The admiral determined to visit all the islands, and to act according to the quantity of wealth which they might find. "At present," he said, "I am resolved to go to the Terra Firma and the City of Quinsay, to remit your Highness's letters to the Grand Khan, to ask for an answer, and to return home as soon as I become its bearer."

All night and all the next day he was waiting, wondering why the king or some noble person did not arrive with gold and treasures. In the morning came the waking from his dream. All round came groveling and staring the naked men with blood-red faces, or spotted with black and yellow, or plastered with chalky white, holding out their reed darts and balls of cotton in exchange for potsherds and bits of glass. Some had morsels of gold on their noses, which they gave away for almost nothing; and the pieces, indeed, were so small that they were in fact worth nothing at all. The same things began to happen over again. The Indians talked about the ships sailing down from Heaven. Martin Pinzon killed another serpent five palms long in the same lake, and the sailors continued to cut down all the lign aloes that could be found.

"I see," said Columbus, "that there are no gold mines here, and I shall not stay to go round the island, or to find the village where I had intended to see this king or chieftain." "I must go on to some country," he added, "where I can manage some great commercial operation; this island seems to be fertile in spices, but I do not know them. I am truly grieved at this, for I see a thousand kinds of trees with different fruits, and as green as our woods in June; and it is just the same with the herbs and flowers, and yet we have recognized nothing except the lign aloes, of which I have ordered a great quantity to be loaded to-day."

Next day he was more cheerful. They were sailing for Cuba with a fine breeze, and there he said that, according to the Indian guides, the natives had a very extensive trade, and gold and spice, and great ships and crowds of merchants. "I think it must be Cipango, which lies somewhere about here, according to my maps and globes." There were pearls too in great plenty, said the Indians, and this made Columbus sure that he was right. When they came near Cuba the pink cliffs and blue mountains in the distance reminded him of Sicily. The foliage and the face of the earth still seemed like the gardens of Granada. This island, he says, is the fairest ever seen by the eyes of man. They were anchored at the mouth of a broad river. "I never saw anything so magnificent," he repeats. There were palms unlike any that he had seen in Spain or Africa, and giant trees covered with strange fruits and flowers, and there were chirping sparrows and birds singing so sweetly that he often longed to hear them again. The Indians said that they were near the gold mines and pearl beds, and Columbus thought that he saw a place suited to the growth of pearls and several of the right kind of shells upon the shore. They all agreed that this must be the place where the Great Khan's navy came, and, if that were so, they would be at a distance of about ten days' sail from the Continent.

Passing by one broad river, they reached another, still finer than the first, and they named it the Rio de Mares. There were large tent-shaped houses, thatched with palm-leaves, set here and there about the banks. The inhabitants all fled away on seeing the strangers. On landing, the Spaniards found that the houses were very neat and clean, and there were masks of faces and carved figures of women set up inside. There were dogs that could not bark, and tame parrots; they saw nets of a marvelously fine texture, and hooks and other implements of fishery. "These must be the fishermen," they said, "who carry up the fish into the rich interior of this lovely land." The admiral thought that there were flocks and herds, for he saw bones in one of the houses that seemed to be those of a cow, though, in fact, they must have belonged to a sea cow, or manatee. All night long they heard the song birds, the sparrows, and the grasshoppers, and everyone rejoiced. The sea, Columbus declared, was always calm, "as smooth as the Guadalquivir," and such waters must be of a nature to favor the growth of pearls. He looked about, and found twisted conch shells on the sands of a kind that was new to him, and they tried the meat, but found that it had little flavor; and when they left the flat coast they passed some very high rocks, of which one was like a fine Moorish mosque and another like the Lover's Leap.

After passing a cape covered with a thick palm grove, they arrived at a bay with a poor anchorage, and they determined, as the weather was threatening, to return to Rio de Mares in order to careen the ships; and while they were engaged on this work they noticed that all the wood used for the fire was of the lentisk kind, and was full of the precious gum mastic. The admiral knew that one of his sailors had carried letters to a native king in Guinea, and this made him think of sending an embassy to find the ruler of this new country, and to give him greeting from their Catholic Majesties. The painted savages were beginning to come round again. Columbus was still in hopes that he was within a hundred leagues of Quinsay, and he now thought it possible that all these naked Indians were at war with the Grand Khan. Some of the natives came out to his ship with cotton and hammock nets for barter. The admiral had sent off two of his men to find out what the people of the interior were like. One was Rodrigo de Jerez from Ayamonte; the other was a converted Jew named Luis de Torres, who knew the Hebrew and Chaldean tongues, and could speak a little Arabic. They were well supplied with guides and provisions and samples of spice for comparison, with a string of beads to exchange for food if they ran short; and they carried with them a letter of recommendation from Ferdinand and Isabella, and a present for the native king. While they were away the admiral made notes on the productions of the country, which seemed very pleasant and fertile. There were fields full of the yuccas and manioc plants, from which they got the meal for making cassava cakes; and in others there were crops of maize and yams or "sweet potatoes." They did not cultivate the cotton plant, but got their supplies from the great ceiba trees that stood like sentinels at the mouths of the deep ravines. Columbus himself saw some of these trees with ripe pods and flowers upon them at the same time, as if they bore cotton all the year round. Martin Pinzon came in with a story of having seen an Indian carrying clusters of red nuts and three bundles of sugar cane, and he produced two pieces of the cane, added that he had talked to an old man, who said that the gold and pearls were at a place called Bohio, where the natives were covered with jewels. He understood them to say that there was much shipping and merchandise there, and they had spoken about one-eyed monsters, and men with dogs' faces, who were cannibals.

These rumors determined Columbus to sail to the new country if the embassy should not come back with good news; and he went on meanwhile with the collection of eagle wood and mastic. On the 6th of November the messengers returned without much information of importance. They had come upon a village with fifty large houses, or wigwams, and about a thousand inhabitants. These houses were of the usual conical shape, and were made of boards thatched with palmetto. The Indians had lodged their visitors in one of the largest of these lodges, and had made them sit on chairs carved like animals, with the tail set up for a back and the head projecting in front with eyes and ears of gold. There was no sign of sugar cane or pepper, but there were immense quantities of cotton, which the natives used for aprons and hammocks. Besides the crops which the admiral had already seen, they had a grain called maize, with grains like millet and as large as hazelnuts, which tasted very well when ground and baked. All the men and women carried about fire and smoked tobacco, wrapping the leaves together into little rolls "like the toys which the children play with at Easter." They lit one end and sucked the smoke in by the other, "making themselves drunk through their nostrils," and they said that it took away all sense of fatigue. Being asked whether they had any gold or pearls or spice, they made signs that there was great plenty toward the east in a country which they called "Bohio." "They seem very simple people," said the admiral, "and not too black, not quite so black, in fact, as the people in the Canaries"; and he noted for the queen's behoof how docile her new Indians were, and clever at remembering with exactness, so that there was every hope that in a little while the whole race would be converted to the faith. "As for me," he writes, "I am getting ready to start on Thursday for the southeast to search in God's name for the gold and the spices and the undiscovered lands."

"Bohio" and "Babeque" were the birthplaces of the gold, and according to the Indians' pantomime one might see a crowd there going by torchlight to pick up nuggets on the shore, or standing at great fires to hammer out the yellow lumps and beat them up into bars and ingots.

Some days were spent in exploring Our Lady's Sea and the multitude of islets called the King's Garden. They lay hardly a musket shot apart, with deep channels between, and towered aloft in airy pinnacles out of the tangled forests of palm. These, he said, must be the Eastern Islands of the maps, that lie by thousands in the Indian Sea, and he considered that they held great wealth in spices and precious stones. There seemed to be an abundance of lentisks and lign aloes, and there was even gum mastic in the roots, out of which the Indians made their bread. The sailors were set to look for pearl shells, and found plenty of them; but there were no pearls, because the season for their production was past. In one of the islands the men killed an animal like a badger with their swords; they saw guinea pigs, and found signs of some beast like a musk deer; and they caught a coffer fish in their net, which exactly resembled a swine, and was covered all over with a hard mail, except at the eyes and tail. On November the 19th Columbus made a strong attempt to get across to Bohio, or Hispaniola, as he afterward named it, and he saw

"Babeque," or Jamaica, in the distance, but was driven back once more into Our Lady's Sea. Not far from the haven was a promontory, where the admiral landed and saw a stream of clear water falling down a mountain side with a mighty noise, and running up he saw in its bed a number of stones with stains of a color like gold, and at the moment of his picking up the ore, as he believed it to be, the sailors shouted out that they saw a forest of pine trees. The pines were tall enough to make masts for the largest ships, and there were oaks growing near, and other timber trees like those of Castile, and a river for turning the saw mills, if it should be necessary to build a navy there. "The infinite number of green trees," said the admiral, "the birds, and the verdure of the plains, tempted me to stay there forever." He declares that he felt as if he were moving in a dream or a whirl of enchantment, and as though a thousand pens or tongues would not avail to depict the wonders around him.

In a few days he was steering for Bohio, with the *Nina* as his only companion. Martin Pinzon had carried off the *Pinta* without leave, and was exploring on his own account. In the clear air of a tropical region they saw the blue mountain ranges sixty miles away, higher as they thought than anything that the Old World could show, visible to all the islanders around, gigantic sea marks,

> Known to every skiff,
> As that sky-scraping Pike of Teneriffe.

"They are all most beautiful," says Columbus, "and of a thousand different shapes, and they are covered with trees of a multitude of kinds, and of such great height that they seem to reach the sky."

He arrived on December the 6th at a large, deep haven, which he named in honor of St. Nicholas. The country seemed to be rocky, and the hillside was covered with oaks and myrtles like those of Castile. In a bay further to the north a gray mullet leaped into the admiral's ship, and when they cast a net they took soles and fish like salmon and dories, and they saw a shoal of sardines, and they were all just like the fish of those kinds at home. A bird like the nightingale was singing, and many song birds of other kinds, with notes that recalled the April evenings in Spain. The fields reminded them at once of the fertile Vale of Cordova, and for all these reasons they were moved to give to the strange island the homelike name of Hispaniola.

The Indians seemed to be of a higher type than the natives of the other islands. Their habits and customs were much the same, but they were better made, and of a fairer complexion. Two of the girls, it was noticed, were as white as any ladies in Spain. "They were all tractable and courteous; and they said that the country where the gold was found lay further to the eastward." They brought in parrots and cassava bread for presents, but they seemed to have nothing of any value, except small grains of gold hanging at their ears and nostrils." Columbus gave them the highest of characters in his journal. "So loving, tractable, and free from covetousness they are, that I swear to your Highnesses there are no better people, nor any better country in the world. They love their neighbors as themselves, and their conversation is the sweetest in the universe, being pleasant and always smiling. True it is they go unclothed; but your Highnesses may believe me that they have many commendable customs; and the king is served with great state, and he is so staid that it is a great satisfaction to see him, as it is to think what good memories these people have, and how desirous they are to know everything."

In describing the visit of the Cacique Guanacagiri, the admiral enlarges on this theme. "There is no doubt but your Highnesses would have been very much pleased to have seen his gravity and the respect that his people paid him. They were all wonderfully grave, and spoke but few words, and those that they uttered, by what I could gather, were very deliberate and staid."

On the night of the 24th the admiral's ship was wrecked on a flat, "in a dead calm," as he says, "and with the sea as still as the water in a dish." The Cacique, with tears in his eyes, expressed his grief at the loss, and sent out all the people in the place to help with their large canoes. "From time to time," says the admiral, "he sent some of his kindred weeping, to beg of me not to be cast down, for he would give me all he had. I do assure your Highnesses that better order could not have been taken in any part of Castile to secure our things, for we lost not the value of a pin."

The Indians now began to bring in small supplies of golden plates and ornaments, and assured the Spaniards that they would procure as much more as was required, "and the Cacique, perceiving that this was pleasing to the admiral, said that he would cause a great quantity of gold to be brought from Cibao, a place where much of it was found." He offered to cover Columbus with gold, if he would wait, "and gave him some masks, with eyes, noses, and ears of gold, and some of the ornaments which they hang round their necks." Some said that the king had ordered a life size statue of the admiral to be made of the solid metal. All the information about Cibao seemed to be genuine, and Columbus felt sure that he had gained his quest, and had at last discovered the wealth of Cipango. Finding such signs of gold, he almost forgot his grief at the loss of the ship, and he determined to return at once in the *Nina*, without trying for further discoveries, "lest some other misfortune might befall him which might hinder their Catholic Majesties from coming to the knowledge of these newly acquired kingdoms."

A few days were enough for building the fort of La Navidad, where a garrison of forty-two men, well equipped with arms and stores of all kinds, was left to maintain possession and to find out the position of the gold mines. There was talk of a supposed discovery of the rhubarb plant, and of other spices which might be found in the mountains. But Columbus was in a hurry to be gone. He writes that he hoped to find a barrel of gold when he returned, and so much spice, that before three years had passed they might be preparing for the new crusade; "and to this effect it was that I showed your Highnesses my desire of seeing the profits of my adventure employed on the conquest of Jerusalem, and your Highnesses smiled, and said it would please you well, and even without those profits you would have a good heart for the enterprise."

On the 4th of January, 1493, Columbus took leave of the little garrison, and started on his voyage home. The next day they were coasting by the fertile slopes of Monte Christi that rose in the shape of a huge pavilion from the plain. There was a fine line of mountains inland, looking like the range that hangs over the Vale of Cordova; the air was bright, and the sea like sapphire. "The whole place is so smiling," they said, "that no words of praise could be in the least degree exaggerated." Yet Columbus felt presentiments that the omens were threatening, as if the powers of evil were baffling him in the moment of victory. Pinzon came in at last with a poor set of excuses, and the admiral was sorely tempted to embark on a dangerous quarrel. The men of the *Pinta* had found gold, and had heard of rich ground in Jamaica, where there were nuggets as large as beans, instead of mere specks and grains. But, after all, it appeared that the best place was the country round La Navidad, where Columbus himself had seen so much free gold in the river sand that he did not trouble to take home specimens from the rich bed of the Rio del Oro. He was bent on sailing home without the least delay, and he wanted to get out of bad company as soon as possible; "but there must be no more quarrels with Pinzon till the news of the voyage reached home." It was difficult to avoid anger. The *Pinta* wanted a mast, which could easily have been cut out of a great pine tree if her captain had not deserted his duty in Cuba. By the 10th of January they had reached a river which still bears Pinzon's name, and the water was full of boring worms; the *Pinta* had come back riddled with them, and quite unsafe for sea. It was easy to see where Pinzon had stayed when he was gathering gold. The unruly captain tried to kidnap some Indians at the last moment. Columbus rebuked him fiercely, and showed how worse than foolish were acts of violence upon the borders of the Land of Promise, and so close to their new-built town.

On Sunday the 13th, being near the Lovers' Cape, the admiral sent a boat ashore, where the men found some Indians of a fierce countenance, armed with great bows and arrows, like the English bowmen whom he had seen in the army at Dartmouth; they seemed to be ready to engage, and yet were in some consternation. Their faces were all daubed over with charcoal, and their speech was as fierce as their looks. There was a skirmish in which the Indians were easily repelled, and the admiral was not at all displeased, thinking that these were "the bold and resolute Caribs." They seem, however, to have belonged to the Ciguayo tribes, with whom the Spaniards were destined to have much trouble in days to come.

One of these Indians pointed out the way to the Carib Islands and the country of the Amazons, and said that there were masses of a golden alloy there as large as the stem of the caravel. Columbus noticed that there was a great deal of gulf weed drifting about the shore, and it occurred to his mind that this might be a sign of land to the eastward, and if this were so, he might find that some parts of the archipelago were not very distant from the Canaries, and creeping from island to island, they might in this way diminish their dangers, and find at last a gap of perhaps four hundred leagues for their battered ships to traverse.

On the 16th he actually started from the "Bay of Arrows," as he had named the Gulf of Samana, and made for the Cannibals' Land. But he was uneasy in his mind, believing that an approaching conjunction of planets betokened great changes in the weather, and they had gone but a short distance when a fresh breeze sprang up and blew right for Spain. So sad were all the faces round him, and so terrible was the condition of the ships, that he dared not reject the sign; and so they put about and changed the course, and sailed nearly fifty miles toward home before the sun went down.

Cape St. Elmo was the last land seen. "Twenty leagues further there appeared abundance of weeds, and twenty leagues further still they found all the sea covered with small tunny-fish, whereof they saw great numbers the two, following days, and after them an abundance of sea fowl, and all the way the weeds ran with the current in long ropes lying east and west, for they had already found out that the current takes these weeds a long way from land." The signs were still favorable. Although the skies were lowering, "the sea ran soft and smooth like a river," for which the admiral offered thanks to Heaven. On the 25th food was beginning to run short. There was nothing left but bread and wine and some of the Indian cakes, but the sailors harpooned a tunny fish and caught an enormous white shark. "Holding on their course with a fair wind, they made so much way that in the opinion of the pilots on the 9th of February they were south of the Azores; but the admiral said that they were a hundred and fifty leagues short, and this was the truth, for they still found abundance of weeds, which as they went to the Indies they did not see till they were two hundred and sixty-three leagues west of Ferro. As they sailed on thus with fair weather, the wind began to rise more and more every day, and the sea to run so high that they could scarce live upon it," and on Thursday, the 14th, they were driving which way soever the wind would carry them. The *Pinta* had disappeared, and all was despair among the admiral's crew. They cast lots which of them should carry a candle in pilgrimage to Our Lady of Guadaloupe, and the lot fell on Columbus, and henceforth he was a pilgrim, as he said, and bound to perform his vow. A second time they cast lots which of them should go or send a pilgrim to Our Lady of Loretto, and the lot fell on one Pedro de Villa, who came from the port of Santa Maria. And again a third time they cast lots which of them should go on a pilgrimage to Santa Clara of Moguer to watch by night and procure a mass, and again the lot fell upon Columbus. Then they all vowed together that they would go in their shirts upon the first land that they might see to one of Our Lady's churches; and everyone was making vows for himself, because they thought that they were all lost in that terrible sea. The *Nina* could hardly keep upright for want of ballast, because all the provision casks were empty. The admiral had intended to take in ballast when he reached the Amazons' Island; and when the course was changed it was too late to do anything but hope for the best. He hit upon a plan, however, for staving off the danger, by filling all his empty casks with sea water so as to steady the ship.

Of this violent storm the admiral wrote these words: "I had been less concerned for the tempest had I been alone in danger, for I know that I owe my life to the Creator, and have been at other times so near death that the merest trifle was wanting to complete it. But what infinitely grieved and troubled me, was the consideration that, as it had pleased the Lord to give me faith and assurance to go upon this undertaking wherein I had now been successful, so now that my opponents were about to be convinced and your Highnesses served by me with honor and increase of your mighty state, He should be pleased to prevent all this by my death. Even death would have been more tolerable were it not attended with the loss of all those men whom I had carried with me upon promise of a happy success; and they, seeing themselves in that affliction, cursed their going out upon the voyage and cursed the fear and awe which my persuasions had cast upon them, dissuading them from going back when outward bound, as they had often resolved to do. But above all my sorrows were multiplied when I thought of my two sons at school in Cordova left destitute of friends in a strange land, before I had performed, or was known to have performed, such service that your Highnesses might be inclined to relieve them." It seemed as if all the good work had been lost when it was almost brought to perfection, and all the honor snatched away at the very moment of enjoyment. "Being in this inward confusion," he wrote, "I thought about your Highnesses' good fortune; though I were dead and the ship lost, yet your fortune might find for you some way of saving a conquest so nearly achieved, and bring the success of my voyage by some means or other to your knowledge. For this reason, as briefly as the time would permit, I wrote on a parchment that I had discovered those countries as I had promised, and in what way I had done it and in how many days, and about the goodness of those lands and the nature of the inhabitants, and how your Highnesses' subjects were left in possession of all that I had discovered. I folded and sealed the writing and addressed it to your Highnesses, with a written promise upon it of a thousand ducats to anyone that should deliver it sealed to you."

Having made a copy of the memorandum, one

of the documents was packed with great care in oilcloth and wax and sent adrift in a cask; the other was packed in the same way, and set upon the top of the poop, so that when the ship sank the cask might have a chance of floating. "Sailing on in such mighty danger and through so great a storm, on Friday the 15th at break of day, one Ruy Garcia saw land from the round top." The admiral concluded that it was one of the Azores. On the same day they saw another island; "and they ran struggling against wind and weather, with continual labor and no respite, but were not able to get to land." Next evening they succeeded in beating up against the wind, and lay at anchor off the island of Santa Maria.

The town lay at some distance off, and they saw a little hermitage upon the shore, but no other building. The boatmen who came out with provisions said that this hermitage was dedicated to the Virgin, and Columbus at once determined that the crew should go barefooted in their shirts to hear a mass according to their vow. Half the ship's crew being landed for this purpose, as soon as they were engaged in prayer, the governor broke out upon them with horse and foot, and took them prisoners; and he afterward said that he was acting under strict orders received from the Court of Portugal. In parleying with the admiral alongside the caravel, the governor laughed at the commission and letters patent from Spain. He said that he knew nothing about Castile, or the king or queen, but he would very soon let Columbus know what it was to deal with Portugal. The admiral at first negotiated and then threatened in his turn, and declared that he would never leave his caravel till he had depopulated the island and carried off a hundred of its chief inhabitants as hostages. On the 20th he went across to St. Michael's to find shelter from a sudden tempest, and on his return to Santa Maria he was able to recover his men.

In describing the violent storms which seemed to haunt the neighborhood of the Azores and Canaries, Columbus says that he never could understand why they should occur in those latitudes, when all the way to the Indies, after passing a certain line, the air and sea were always serene and calm. It must be, he thought, that the theologians and philosophers were right who placed the Earthly Paradise in the ends of the East, because the climate was so fair; and he concluded that the lands which he had found were not far from Paradise, and quite close to that extremity of the world.

When they sailed from Santa Maria the sea became smooth again, for which the admiral again offered thanks and praise. But another storm was brewing, as if the powers of evil must prevail in the end, and on March the 3d the tempest was so great that all their sails were split and carried away. Again they cast lots which of them should send a pilgrim, in his shirt and barefoot, to Our Lady of La Cinta in the town of Huelva, and the lot fell on Columbus again. "They were running on without a rag of cloth; it was a mighty sea, with high winds and frightful thunder." The rain fell in torrents, said Columbus, and the clouds were ablaze with lightning. "It was a ghastly and terrible sight; but it pleased Heaven at that moment to render aid and to grant me the sight of land." Then they made shift to set the mainsail and to bear up against the storm until daybreak; and after "a night of anguish" they found themselves off Cintra at the mouth of the Tagus, and were forced by a surprising chance to run into the port of Lisbon; "and this to my mind," says the admiral, "is the greatest marvel in the world."

CHAPTER XV.

> "It was roses, roses, all the way,
>   And myrtle mixed in my path like mad;
> The house-roofs seemed to heave and sway,
>   The church-spires flamed, such flags they had,
> A year ago on this very day."

KING JOHN was at Torres Vedras when he heard the news, and received a letter from Columbus asking leave to move up to Lisbon for fear of an attack by pirates. Assurances were given that the ship had not been anywhere near Guinea, but had found the Indies, and returned by a route hitherto unknown. The king was ill at ease in body and mind. He had but just recovered from a disease attributed to poison, and was moving restlessly about to escape the threatened approach of the plague. A rival's success was a bitter disappointment, and revenge seemed hopeless when he heard of the excited crowds going out to stare at the Indians and talk about the gold, some shouting for joy at the good news, and others storming in the streets because Portugal had lost the prize. The royal officers were as eager as the rest, and the captain of the port had visited the caravel in a state procession "with trumpets, fifes, and drums." The king saw that Columbus had escaped the toils. If the ship had been detained at the Azores no man on board would ever have seen Europe again; but as things had turned out it seemed advisable to put a good face on the matter, and to join in the popular welcome.

Columbus himself was gratified at the manner of his reception. The nobility were sent out to meet him, and on coming into the presence the king treated him with all respect. He bid the admiral sit by him with hat on head, as befitted a grandee of Spain. The king, we are told, heard the story of the voyage with a cheerful countenance. Late into the night the admiral told his tale, much in the same words, we suppose, as those on the parchment cast into the sea, and in the letter written to the Chancellor of Arragon in the terrible storm off the Azores. Thirty-three days out from the last Christian land he had reached the Indies with a fleet from Spain, and had found a multitude of countries of which he had taken possession in the name of the Catholic Kings. Besides the great islands of

Cuba and Hispaniola, there were four others to be specially mentioned as forming the first fruits of the enterprise. They were coral islands studded about the great Bahama Bank, thickly peopled with strange Indian tribes, and bright even in winter with palm woods and orchids and flowering trees, but they were bare of gold, and not worth much to Spain. To everyone he had given a significant name. Guanahani had become San Salvador, "in remembrance of those things so marvelously brought to pass." Opposite lay Guanima and her islets, now dedicated to Santa Maria de Concepcion. For ten leagues they had sailed along the southern shore, and had crossed to Fernandina, where he found two main islands of wonderful beauty, with a chain of coral rocks behind. The fourth he had called Isabella; it was the Indian "Saometo," a long island on the rim of the bank, by the channel that leads to Cuba. To the Portuguese king there would be little interest in hearing of the Indians and rocks and trees. To ourselves the subject comes nearer home when we speculate, amid the conflict of theories, which of our outlying settlements was the island where the light was seen, and where was the exact point where Columbus landed.

Guanahani has now been clearly identified with Watling's Island. Almost all the names were at one time transposed. The natives were massacred or taken to work in the mines and fisheries abroad; the islands were lost again in their forests till they became the lurking-places of the pirates; and when the pirates were expelled and negro slavery was introduced, the details of the ancient story were all confused. The journals of Columbus show that the larger island "opposite to Guanahani" was probably the island now called "Rum Cay"; that he crossed over to Great Exuma with its chain of detached rocks, which he called "Fernandina"; and that our settlement of Long Island is the country of "Saometo," where he saw the groves of "lign aloes" surrounding a shining lake.

The story of Columbus was concerned with still greater things. To Cuba, "the fifth island," he gave the name of Juana, in remembrance of the Prince in Spain. "When I reached Juana I followed the coast westward, and found it so large that I felt sure it was the mainland of Cathay." After going many leagues, and finding nothing but deserted hamlets, he had returned to a certain harbor, where two men were sent away to explore. "Meantime I had learned from the Indians that this part of the country was surrounded by the sea, and I followed the coast for a hundred and seven leagues eastward till it came to an end, and there I saw a great island, which I called Hispaniola." "The land runs high, and there are sierras and peaks to which Teneriffe itself is not to be compared, all most beautiful, of a thousand different shapes, and all accessible to man and covered with trees of a myriad kinds." The land contains many gold mines and the inhabitants cannot be numbered. "Hispaniola is a marvel; in plain and mountain, in meadow and field, the lands are so fine and rich for crops and cattle and the building of towns." This, he said, is something worth coveting, and worth taking pains to keep when found. "All these islands," he added, "I have taken for their Highnesses' absolute use. And there was one large town of which I especially took possession, being well situated for the gold mining and for commerce with Europe or with the countries near the Great Khan's land, with which there will be abundance of business and gain."

According to the Portuguese historians, the courtiers found Columbus so prolix and so full of the praises of his golden land that he seemed to be triumphing over the king and casting up again the rejection of his former offer; and the king, they say, was so stung by this thought, and by a feeling that his laws had been broken, that he listened with a darkening brow and returned but cool replies. But Columbus noticed nothing amiss, and reported that King John had offered him any help that might be required on behalf of their Catholic Majesties. The king began to talk about Prince Henry's time, and the Pope's Bulls that gave to Portugal all the lands from Cape Nun to India; there was a solemn treaty besides, which would bar the Spaniards from invading his rights. Columbus himself, after all, was a captain in his navy, and he supposed that all these new conquests belonged to the Portuguese. The admiral said that he knew nothing about such things; he had most strictly obeyed his orders, as given to him in Spain and published in every port of Andalusia, and those orders had been, not to go near Fort St. George, or any other part of the king's dominions in Africa. "It is very well," the king replied, and added that he had no doubt but justice would be done in the end.

"Having spent a long time in this sort of discourse, he commanded the Prior of Crato, as the greatest man then about the court, to entertain the admiral, and to show him all civility and respect; and having stayed there all Sunday, and Monday till after mass, the admiral took leave of the king, who expressed great kindness and made him great proffers, ordering Don Martin de Noronhas to go along with him; and many other gentlemen went for company, and to hear an account of his voyage." On his way back he passed the monastery of San Antonio near Villafranca, where the queen was lodging, and received a message begging that he would visit her; "and she was much pleased to see him, and did him all the favor and honor that was due to the greatest lord."

As soon as his visitor was gone, the king summoned a council, at which it was openly debated whether Columbus should be killed in order to check the Spaniards. Some offered boldly to see to the work themselves. Some urged the proposal as a matter of public policy. If the prime engineer were removed, the only man in fact who knew the work, who would ever persuade Ferdinand again to start such a dangerous undertaking? "When the good of the state is concerned, everyone knows that morality must give place to wisdom." Many were shocked at this outrageous doctrine, but held that Columbus had forfeited his life by breaking the sea laws and by deceiving both nations about the matter. But King John was reminded that it would be a shocking thing to receive a guest one day with favor, and to kill him next day without any new offense. "Would it not be safer and wiser to send out a fleet at once to take possession by force of arms of all that properly belonged to Portugal?" The wiser counsel prevailed, and orders were given to get the ships ready at once. But a long negotiation began as soon as the news reached Spain; the astute Ferdinand persuaded the Pope to fix the boundary line a hundred leagues west of the Azores, and though this limit was afterward extended in favor of Portugal, the lands found by Columbus were justly secured for Spain.

For an account of the homeward voyage we return to the journal again. At the very moment that he was leaving Llandra to go on board his ship, an equerry rode up with a message from the king. If Columbus would go by land to Castile, the officer would go with him all the way, and would provide for lodgings and changing horses and everything that might be required. Again, when the offer had been declined, the officer came back with presents from the king, a mule for the admiral, and another for his pilot, Juan de la Cosa. Columbus adds that the equerry, as he heard afterward, had brought the pilot a splendid fee of twenty "spadines" in gold, and he notes the remark of some of the bystanders that these favors must have been given in hopes of impressing the king and queen at home. On Wednesday, the 13th of March, he started in the morning "on a mighty tide," and set sail with a favorable wind for Seville. The next morning he found himself off Cape St. Vincent, and turned east with a view of putting in at the port of Palos. At sunrise on the Friday he was opposite to the Bar of Saltes, waiting for the tide, and about noon he passed the bar, and arrived safe at the haven which he had left some months before. Here his journal ends. He speaks of making a voyage to Barcelona, where Ferdinand and Isabella were making a royal progress, wishing to tell them with his own lips the whole story of the voyage, and of the signal miracles which had been wrought in favor of one who had been so long derided and treated as a dreamer of dreams.

As the *Nina* was casting anchor in the port, the *Pinta*, by a strange chance, was seen creeping past the bar. Nothing had been heard of her since the storm off the Azores, and it was feared that Pinzon and all his crew were drowned. Pinzon himself could not face the admiral. His tragic story is known to all. He thought that Columbus would never reach land, and was prepared for a glorious reception; he seems always in his own mind to have claimed the chief merit of the enterprise. He designed, says Don Ferdinand, to go by himself to Barcelona, to carry the news to their Catholic Majesties; but they sent him orders not to go there without the admiral under whom he had been sent to serve, "at which he was so concerned and offended that he returned indisposed to his native place, where within a few days he died of grief." Before Pinzon reached Palos, Columbus had started upon his triumphal progress through Spain.

The first thing of all was to fulfill the vows made in the storm. Their pilgrimage to the hermit's chapel had been rudely interrupted by the Portuguese; but it was now carried out in every detail at the church of Santa Maria in the convent of La Rabida. Now followed a journey to Santa Maria de Guadalupe, and another pilgrimage to Santa Clara's convent at Moguer, close by the port, and whatever else was due to carry out their promises; and when all these duties were accomplised the admiral set out on his journey. He was forced to stay a little by the way, "for so great was the admiration of the people through Andalusia and all the way to Catalonia that they ran out from all the towns and villages to see the procession go by; and, thus holding on his way, he got to Barcelona about the middle of April, having sent their Highnesses an account of the happy success of his voyage, which was extraordinary pleasing to them, and they ordered a most solemn reception, as for one who had rendered them a singular service." Through the streets, waving and flaming with banners, the crowds poured out to meet Columbus. First marched Juan the Pilot beneath the standard of Castile, and next to him the painted Indians decked out with feather cloaks and plumes; the sailors carried palms and fruits, and birds of gay plumage, strange fishes, conchs, and turtle shells, and hideous lizards on poles; and there were others with fruits and spices, and huge fagots of the "lign aloes," and gold dust in calabashes, and coronets and masks of gold, and whatever else would show the wealth of the world beyond the sea. The admiral rode last:

> The air broke into a mist with bells,
> The old walls rocked with the crowds and cries.

Ferdinand and the queen were on their thrones under a canopy of cloth of gold, "and when he went to kiss their hands, they stood up as to some great lord, and made a difficulty to give him their hands," and bade him be seated at their side; "and he was so highly honored and favored," says his son, "that when the king rode about Barcelona, the admiral was on one side and the Infante Fortuna on the other; but before that time, none had ever ridden beside his Majesty, except the Infante, and he was the king's near kinsman."

CHAPTER XVI.

> " O hundred shores of happy climes,
>   How swiftly streamed ye by the bark !
> At times the whole sea burned, at times
>   With wakes of fire we tore the dark ;
> At times a carven craft would shoot
>   From havens hid in fairy bowers,
> With naked limbs, and flowers and fruit,
>   But we nor paused for fruit nor flowers ;
> For one fair vision ever fled
>   Down the waste waters day and night,
> And still we followed where she led
>   In hope to gain upon her flight."

AFTER the feasting at Barcelona was over, the business of founding a colony began. The Portuguese had been forestalled, and Hispaniola, with its clusters of Indian isles, was to be annexed to the crown of Castile. A short way had been found to the mountains of Ophir, where Solomon's navies had gathered wealth in a three years' voyage, and the gold and silver were waiting to be hurried across another ocean by a new fleet from Tarshish.

Seventeen ships were equipped at Cadiz with all the stores required for building a city at La

Navidad, where it was hoped that the garrison left by Columbus had already laid up an abundance of food and treasure. A sufficient number of artisans and husbandmen had been engaged under contracts with the government, and live stock, seeds, and plants of many useful kinds were collected for the use of the settlement. There was also, unfortunately, a wild rush of adventurers excited with "the fame of the gold." The ships were crowded with more than five hundred unauthorized passengers, besides the thousand to whom license had been given; and it was certain that great troubles would arise as soon as the provisions began to fail.

"Furnished in this way," says Don Ferdinand, "the admiral weighed anchor in Cadiz Roads on the 25th of September, 1493, about an hour before sunrise, my brother and I being there, and stood southwest for the Canaries." The fleet took in provisions and another supply of live stock for breeding purposes at Gomera, and then sailed out with a fair breeze toward the islands where rumor said that they would find the Amazons and the cannibals. When they were quite a month out from Spain, Columbus observed with astonishment that they had met with none of the floating weed and had seen no signs of land. About that time the sailors saw a swallow flitting up and down among the ships. Within a few hours a violent storm broke on them, but the men were cheered at seeing the electric flames, which they called the "corposant," or body of St. Elmo. "Seven lights were seen on the roundtop, and there followed mighty rains and frightful thunder. The ancient Romans used to say that these flickering meteors would settle on the yards, and whistle and leap like birds on a bough. If one came alone, they feared the "disastrous Helena"; with two or more they sailed secure, protected by the sea-gods and Helena's brothers,

Et fratres Helenæ, lucida sidera.

A few days afterward several frigate birds were seen wheeling aloft about sunset, as if designing to make a flight for some neighboring shore; and Columbus, taking into account the movements of the needle, the continuous rain, and all the other signs, concluded that they were close to land. Within a few hours, on Sunday, the 3d of November, they saw at daybreak the mountain mass of Dominica, and its cliffs green with foliage to the water's edge; and in the distance rose other peaks and volcanic cones along the great curve of the Windward Isles. Columbus was tempted to explore the rocky stronghold of the Caribs, but there was no convenient harbor; and he moved the fleet a little northward to an uninhabited island, which he called "Marie Galante," after the name of his ship.

The country seemed to be covered with a tangled forest into which the sailors could hardly cut their way. There were huge trees wrapped in creepers and covered with flowers and fruit; there were shrubs that smelt like the finest cloves, and some of the men were so rash as to taste the green apples of the manchineel, which drove them nearly mad with pain. The next morning they passed on to Guadalupe, making straight for the high crater, with its waterfalls "dropping from the sky." Here the fleet stayed for several days, delayed by the necessity of waiting for an exploring party who had lost their way in the bush. They said, when they returned half dead with fatigue, that the woods were so thick and close that they could never see the sky. Some of the men had climbed the trees to get a glimpse of the stars, but it had been of no use, and if they had not come accidentally upon the coast they would never have reached the ships. A search party, following their traces, brought back reports of the riches of the island. They had seen silk-cotton trees, and cinnamons of an inferior variety; there were yellow mirobolans on the ground, and roots which looked like ginger, aloes, and mastic in abundance, and lign aloes fit for making the brown kind of frankincense. The villages near the coast were deserted, but the Spaniards succeeded after a time in capturing a few of the Caribs and in saving a number of their miserable prisoners; and they were able to form a clear notion of the modes of life in the savage community. The Caribs were in appearance not very unlike the Indians seen on the former voyage. The men and women alike were bulky and muscular, and they seemed to be as fierce as wild beasts. The warriors had black patterns tattooed on their faces, and they stained their bodies red with anatto, and drew circles of black and white round their eyes. Their heads were pressed into a high square shape and shaved up to the crown, with the hair hanging loose behind. They were all expert archers, using stiff bows and poisoned arrows with barbed tips of bone. They had very little knowledge of metals, except copper and a base alloy of gold used for ornaments; their hatchets and cutting tools were made of polished stone, and with these, it was said, they could cut down great ceiba trees for making canoes, which six men together could scarcely grasp. They lived in small wigwams, but there was a great hall in every village with walls of plaited cane and well trimmed beams; here they took their meals in public, and here they fixed the great looms for weaving the coverings of their tents, like those used at Genoa for tapestry, and others for making fine cloth from the silk cotton and stuff for their hammocks. Columbus noticed that they seemed to be more intelligent than the natives of Hispaniola. "In other parts the people only reckon the day by the sun and the night by the moon, but the women here know the other stars, and say that it will be time to do such a thing when the Bear rises, or when such a star has moved into the north." As to their food, they were undoubtedly cannibals when they had the opportunity. They had strange superstitions about abstaining from the flesh of the manatee and the turtle. Some of their little foxlike dogs were kept for hunting, but more were fattened for food. For domestic pets they kept macaws of gorgeous plumage, as large as barn-door fowls. They seem to have been clever at gardening and agriculture. They had fine crops of maize, and yams, and the farinaceous yucca roots, and "manioc" for their cassava cakes; and they grew large crops of pineapples. "These look like our green pine cones," the sailors said, "and they are as full of meat as a melon, but much sweeter in taste and smell, and they grow about in the fields on long stalks like aloes or lilies."

On the 10th of November the fleet made a fresh start. Columbus was anxious to reach Hispaniola, and he now determined to run up the long line of islands without any further delay. Every few hours new lands appeared, all very high and full of woods, rising in pyramidal masses out of the smooth blue sea. To each, as he passed, the admiral gave some appropriate name. Montserrat reminded him of the jagged sierra near Barcelona; a steep dome of rock took the name of Santa Maria de Redonda. The cone of Nevis may have received its title either from its snow-white shore or from a floating cloud of steam. The "fertile country," as the Caribs called it, a few leagues to the north, was called St. Christopher from the shape of Mount Misery, which resembled a giant stooping under a burden. On their right hand they could just see the barren land to which they gave the title of Santa Maria la Antigua.

They rested for one night at St. Martin's, and as they started again found pieces of coral entangled in the anchor flukes; but, though the discovery seemed to be valuable, they had no time to search for treasures on the way. At Santa Cruz there was another garrison of the Caribs. They rescued some of the wretched prisoners, and experienced in the skirmish that ensued the untamable ferocity of the painted warriors and the amazonian archers. The ships were now getting near the rainless zone, and as they were passing the desolate Virgin Isles the admiral named them in a group after St. Ursula and her maidens. But now, turning to the west, they came into a pleasanter region, and found a harbor on the farther side of St. John's, or "Porto Rico," as it was afterward called, and here for two days the weary crews had rest. The island seemed more beautiful than any which they had seen before. The shore was full of creeping vines, the trees were covered with fruit. Some sat among the flowers, and watched the large falcons hovering; others went fishing, and caught skate, and bream, and scads as large as mackerel, and other fishes like those in Spain, but finer and more delicate in flavor; some tried in vain to get speech with the Indians, who were too much afraid of the Caribs to stay within sight of a stranger. From the prisoners whom they rescued the sailors heard that the natives were learning to defend themselves and to imitate the Caribs' archery; and it was said that they were even beginning, by way of revenge, to adopt the vile practices of the cannibals. Some of the Spaniards found an empty village containing large wooden halls, with a square in front, and a broad road down to the sea; "and there were towers plaited with cane on two sides and interwoven with foliage atop, like the arbors in the gardens at Valencia; and on the sides looking toward the sea were raised balconies for ten or twenty people, very lofty and well built."

"It was at dawn," one of the officers wrote, "that we left the island, and before nightfall we caught sight of land, which we knew to be Hispaniola from what we were told by the Indian women." The coast near Mona Island, which was passed in their course, is very low and flat, and this caused some doubt in the admiral's mind; but the mountains rose into sight, and he soon reached the Gulf of Arrows, where they had fought their first battle with the Indians, and the haven near the promontory of Monte Christi, where he had thought of founding a settlement.

At Monte Christi they stayed for several days, looking about for a convenient site; but though the river was all that could be wanted, the ground in the neighborhood was swampy and unwholesome. On one of the little islands the sailors hunted an alligator without success; they said that it was "as big round as a calf, with a tail as long as a lance." Some of the others made a dreadful discovery. They saw two bodies in the river tied with ropes of fiber; one had the rope round his neck, and his arms were stretched on a kind of cross; and next day two more corpses were seen in the water, and one seemed to be that of a man with a beard. They could not be quite sure if these were the bodies of Spaniards or of Indians; but there was evidently great cause for alarm. It seemed incredible that any harm could have come to a strong garrison from the fawning, childish natives. The affectionate young Cacique who had helped them after the wreck, and the peaceful Guarionex, on whose land they were standing, would never have joined in any such bloodthirsty treachery. The admiral had himself seen a thousand Indians run away from one or two sailors, and he had said that one might as soon expect an attack from them as from so many sheep or rabbits. But when they arrived at the sandy bay and the site of the town of La Navidad, the worst of their fears was justified. They could not see the walls of the little fortress. The place was silent and deserted. No sound came in reply to the roar of the guns from the fleet; and when the admiral landed, he found that the fort and the Indian houses near had all been burned, "and nothing left that had belonged to the Christians, but only rags and cloths and such like things, as is usual in a place taken by storm." Some of the Indians made timid approaches, and showed where many of the Spaniards' bodies were laid, and, from the look of the vegetation about them, they seemed to have been dead for more than a month. The Cacique's brother next arrived, and showed how the friendly Indians had suffered in defending the Spaniards. The Cacique himself was wounded, and his house destroyed. As for the Spaniards, they had certainly been unfortunate. They had quarreled among themselves about their gold and Indian wives, and had broken up the garrison to go in quest of treasure. Some of the men from Biscay had gone up to the mountains of Cibao to visit the mines, but they had been killed by Caonabo, the King of the Golden Mountains; and Caonabo had come down with his Caribs, and had burned some of the Christians in their huts, and the rest he had driven into the sea. The armies of "Marien," which the Cacique's brother ruled, had found that they could do little against the archers of Cibao; but Columbus, if he pleased, might visit the wounded Cacique, and see the gashes which his men had received from the spikes in the Caribs' clubs and their barbed arrows and poisoned darts.

Columbus visited the wounded king, and became convinced of his innocence. He knew at the same time that no words were enough to describe the ill-conduct of his lost garrison or the exquisite pain of his disappointment. Making the best of what had happened, he determined to leave the Cacique's dominions, and go back to the neighborhood of Monte Christi, within the territories of Guarionex. It may be mentioned for the sake of clearness in the story that the whole island was divided into five kingdoms. The northwest end belonged to Guacanagiri, the friendly Cacique, who died in misery, loathed by his countrymen for having cleaved to their oppressors to the end. Next to him, and all along the eastern coast, were the domains of Guarionex, a peaceful and easy-going man, who was afterward seduced into a guerrilla war, and who perished in the great storm which destroyed the fleet returning to Spain; and Caonabo the Carib held the inland range of Cibao and all the lands down to the southern coast. The region looking eastward to the cannibals' islands was called Higuey; and here also the king took part in the civil war, and died in one of the greater massacres. The western part of the island was called Xaragua, where there were shadowy woods and a lonely lake with which many ghostly legends were connected. This country had no such rich savannas as the plain of the Vega in the north, or as the famous pastures of Higuey; but it was celebrated for its flowers and sweet "mamee fruits," on which the dead were supposed to feed, for the size of its trees, and for the abundance of game in the forest. This was the birthplace of the famous Anacoana, the wife of the Carib Caonabo, who went back after her savage husband's death and became the Queen of Xaragua; and she, too, died a horrible death by public execution, after her chieftains had all been destroyed in a massacre that followed one of her famous banquets.

We must now go back to the time when the Spaniards and Indians were still friends, before the gold was found, or the war broke out, or the natives were reduced to slavery.

Now, at last, in the neighborhood of Monte Christi, as had been before proposed, a site was found for the new city of Isabella, intended to be the seat of government and the capital of the island. There was a fine haven, we are told, "and a most delicate river not a bowshot away"; it was not far from the wonderful pastures of the Vega, fringed with forests of mahogany and basil wood; and when once the plain was reached, one had only to climb the mountains on the other side to be among the mines of Cibao. The Spaniards had been cooped up for nearly three months on shipboard, and required rest in a healthy air, with plenty of nourishing food. But they found, upon landing, that their hardships were actually increased. Their provisions were already running short, and they were called upon to toil at grinding meal and drawing water, or at carpenters' and masons' work. All this hard living, and the heat of the steaming swamp, soon caused an outbreak of disease. The situation of the city was ill chosen, as they might have known by looking at the seaside villages, where the filthy huts were sodden with damp, and overgrown with a rank vegetation. The admiral was ill on board his ship, too weak even to write his journals, and barely able to keep up authority over his disappointed and mutinous followers. The best chance of restoring order was to send an expedition to search for treasure in the mountains, where Caonabo was said to be enthroned in a golden palace with his fair queen clad in garlands of flowers, whom the Indians called Anacoana, or "the Bloom of the Gold." Ojeda and Gorbolan, two gallant young officers, were sent out to explore the mines in the region of Niti and the auriferous streams of Cibao. Ojeda was completely successful. Every brook that came from the stony range was found to contain gold-dust or grains of ore in its channel. Ojeda himself picked up a nugget of nine ounces' weight; "but the finest thing of all," it was said, "was when one of the rocks was struck with an Indian's club, and the gold flew out on all sides in a sparkling shower." Gorbolan's party was almost as fortunate. They had some difficulty in fording a great river, "broader than the Tagus, and swifter than Ebro"; but they succeeded after some days in reaching a hilly region where the natives talked a great deal about their mines. One day a chieftain took Gorbolan into a workshop where a smith was making ornaments out of a plate of gold which one man could hardly carry, and this man readily took them to a place not far from his cabin, where four streams ran near together, all very rich in nuggets and glittering ore. This news, says the biographer, much rejoiced the admiral, who was then recovered from his illness. "Accordingly on the 12th of March, 1494, he set out from Isabella for Cibao to see the mines, with all the people that were in health, on foot and on horseback, leaving a good guard in the two ships and three caravels that remained of the fleet, and causing all the ammunition and tackle belonging to the other ships to be put aboard his own, that none might rebel with them, as they had attempted to do while he was sick." Leaving, therefore, his brother Diego in charge of the fleet, he started toward Cibao, carrying along with him all the tools and materials for building a fort, to keep the province under and secure the Christians left there to gather gold against any attempt of the Indians; "and to appear the more formidable he made his men march under arms in rank and file, with trumpets sounding and colors flying, as is usual in time of war." On Sunday, the 16th of March, they entered Caonabo's country, "and found it rough and stony, full of gravel, with plenty of grass, and watered by several gold-bearing streams; and there were very few trees, and those mostly pines and palms growing near the rivers." The admiral, now considering that they were eighteen leagues from Isabella, with a craggy country between, thought it well to build a fort there, to be called the Castle of St. Thomas, to command the country round the mines. He waited to see the foundations laid, and the walls of clay and timber begun, and returned to Isabella by easy stages; and they were glad to find on their arrival that all the green crops and the vines and canes were doing well. The admiral, we are told, was well enough pleased with the air, the soil, and the people. He had found several indications of mineral wealth besides the great treasure of the gold: a little amber near the coast, a vein of lapis lazuli, and signs of copper in the mountains; he had found ebony, cedar, and mulberry trees in the forest, and a kind of fig tree that was said to produce scammony, besides the frankincense and spices. We are not surprised, therefore, to find him writing, even before his successful expedition, that the beauty of the country was such, in mountains and rivers and well watered plains, that "there is no land on which the sun shines that can make so fair a show."

A few days after his return the admiral received a sudden request for more soldiers at Fort St. Thomas. The savage Caonabo had come home, and was gathering his armies to sweep the invaders away. Columbus, it is said, paid very little attention to these threats, knowing how inconsiderable the Indians were, "and especially confiding in the horses, by which they feared to be devoured." He did, however, send up seventy men with ammunition and stores, because he was about to start with the three caravels to seek for the neighboring continent, and thought it well to leave all things in security behind him. While the ships were being fitted out, he superintended the building of the city, "dividing it into streets, with a convenient market place," and endeavored to bring the river to it by a new channel, making a dam to serve the mills, because the people were "weak and indisposed," and could not carry water so far.

The government of the colony was placed in the hands of a council, of which Don Diego was the president, and the admiral set out upon his journey to explore the coast of Cuba, "not knowing, indeed, whether it was an island or a continent." He left the port on the 24th of April, and touched again at Monte Christi and the site of La Navidad, and afterward at the neighboring Isle of Tortuga. On the 29th he crossed over to Cuba, and found a harbor with a narrow entrance, spreading out between the mountains into a grassy lake. A trivial story is told of their finding a quantity of broiled fish and oysters, with iguanas and agoutis hanging up to the trees on the shore, and of the shy Indians stealing back to say that the fish had been cooked in preparation for the banquet of some neighboring chieftain. This bears out what has been said of Hispaniola, that fish could not be kept there uncooked from one day to another, because of the alternations of heat and damp. The physician who discussed the matter was no admirer of the Indian ways; he liked the maize cakes and fish with capsicum sauce, and had heard people praise the meat of the agouti; but as to the rest, he says, "They eat all the snakes and lizards and land crabs, so that to my mind they are more brutal than any of the beasts." The Spaniards seem to have first tasted the iguana at a banquet given by Anacoana to Don Bartholomew in 1496, after which they were always talking about "the sweetness of those serpents."

Before going far along the coast, Columbus determined to pay a short visit to Jamaica, remembering what he had heard on his former voyage about a country called "Babeque," where much gold had been found. Approaching the island on its northern side, he thought that it was the most beautiful place in the Indies. A foreground of rolling hills was covered with groves of pimento. Every valley, as a modern historian has said, has its rivulet, and every hill a cascade, and the rocks overhanging the sea are veiled with transparent waterfalls; behind the low hills appears a vast amphitheater of forest, the outline melting into the distant Blue Mountains, with their summits lost in the clouds. Columbus was astonished at the multitude of Indians, the crowd of archers, and the huge canoes of cedar and mahogany. The natives at first showed fight, but after one sharp skirmish they were peaceable and inclined to trade. But it soon appeared that the story of the gold was a delusion, and Columbus started off again to look for the cities of Asia. As he passed along the coast of Cuba he met with violent storms, which broke out night by night, as soon as the moon arose. "But the worst of it was," says his son, "that all over that sea, the further they went, the more low little islands they met with; and though there were trees in some of them, yet others were sandy, and scarce appeared over the surface of the water." The nearer they sailed to Cuba, the pleasanter the islets appeared, and the admiral gave them all one name together, and called them the "Queen's Garden." They saw many strange and interesting sights. In one of the deep channels there were Indians fishing for turtle with a remora, or sucking fish, after a fashion well known in Africa. On some of the sand banks stood regiments of scarlet flamingoes, on others there were gray cranes like those in Spain, and sea crows, and an infinite number of little singing birds, "and all the air as sweet as if they were in a garden of roses."

Columbus had expected by this time to have found the Golden Chersonese, or some civilized country near the Ganges; and he had dreamed, with a bold flight of fancy, that he might bring his little fleet to the Red Sea, or sail home round the cape which the Portuguese had discovered in Africa. But after wandering about the flats and shoals for weeks in great perplexity, he found his food running short. He never knew that he was at that moment quite close to the open sea beyond Cuba. He thought it was now well proved that this land which they had followed for hundreds of miles was part of the Asian Continent. His captains and crews were ready to swear to the fact, and they all undertook to suffer the severest penalties if they should ever say anything to the contrary. While he turned the matter over in his mind, the men began to find prodigies and omens in the natural phenomena of the tropics. On one day there was a migration of turtles "of a vast bigness and in such numbers that they covered the sea"; the next morning a cloud of sea crows darkened the sun; and for the whole of the day after that the air was black with swarms of butterflies. Within a few hours afterward they began to retrace their course. On June the 13th they anchored at the Isle of Pines, and sailing to the south again went up into a clear, blue channel, which turned out to be an inland lagoon. They found it shut up, as if it had been suddenly closed in despite of their efforts; and the terrified crews thought that the forces of nature were hemming them in on all sides. But the admiral kept a cheerful countenance, and thanked Heaven that he was forced back the way he came, "for if they had continued on that course they might have run themselves into some place where they could hardly get out, when perhaps they might have neither provisions nor ships for returning, which now they might easily do." Back again they sailed to the high cliffs of the Isle of Pines, and then passed with amazement into strange seas, patched all over with green and white, or thick like milk and dazzling to the eye, and then through waters as black as ink, until at last they came again to the eastern end of Cuba. The men by this time were much spent for want of provisions; "they had nothing for food but a pound of rotten biscuit in the day, with a half pint of wine, unless they happened to catch some fish," as the admiral wrote in his journal, "and I myself," he added, "am on the same allowance. God grant it may be to His honor and for your Highnesses' services, for I shall never again for my own benefit expose myself to such sufferings and dangers, since never a day passes but I see that we are all on the brink of death."

About the middle of July they met some friendly Indians, who relieved them with supplies of yams and cassava bread, and soon afterward they pushed across to the southern coast of Jamaica. "The country all along was most delightful and fruitful, and all the coast full of towns, the people following the ships in their canoes, and bringing such provisions as they eat, which was much better liked by the Spaniards than what they had found elsewhere." Columbus noticed the magnificent scenery on this coast, the gigantic cliffs, and the Blue Mountains rising "in stupendous and soaring ridges." The land, he noted, was as high as any that he had ever seen, and he believed that it reached far above the region that breeds the storms. On the 20th of August they reached Cape Tiburon, the nearest point of Hispaniola, and coasted afterward as far as the island of Alto Velo, where the ships parted company for a time. They proceeded shortly afterward to a "delightful country" near the Bay of Ocoa, and here they heard that some Spaniards had arrived, and nine men were landed to carry news of the admiral across the country to Isabella, while the fleet proceeded to Higuey. The weather seemed inclined to break, and one day a monstrous fish was seen, which seemed to be the harbinger of a storm. The description is confused and evidently exaggerated, but it may well have been one of the great horned rays which are sometimes found in those seas. "It was as big as a whale," the men said, "and had a great shell like a turtle; there were two fins like wings, and a tail like a tunny, and the head, thrust out of the water, seemed to be as large as a wine cask." The admiral sought at once for a harbor, and was so fortunate as to find the channel behind the island of Saona, where he saw an eclipse of the moon, by which he endeavored to calculate his distance from Spain. When the ships got together again they made for the Mona Passage, the admiral having formed a rash plan of visiting the Carib Isles, and of killing some of the cannibals and breaking up their war canoes. But at this point he was overtaken by illness. His journals came to an end. He could only say afterward that in going from Mona to Porto Rico his fatigue, and weakness, and want of proper food "cast him into a dangerous disease between a pestilential fever and lethargy, which deprived him of his sense and memory." His men took him back to the colony, where his health at last came back, after a sickness of five months, attributed to his great sufferings and extraordinary weakness; "for sometimes he had not slept three hours in eight days, which seems almost impossible, were not he himself and his men witnesses of its truth."

CHAPTER XVII.

"Chains for the Admiral of the Ocean! chains
For him who gave a new heaven, a new earth,
As holy John had prophesied of me;
Gave glory and more empire to the Kings
Of Spain than all their battles! chains for him
Who pushed his prows into the setting sun,
And made West East, and sail'd the Dragon's Mouth,
And came upon the Mountain of the World,
And saw the rivers roll from Paradise."

FIVE days and nights Columbus lay crippled and blinded, and when he woke he saw the faces of both his brothers at the bedside. The admiral was rejoiced to see Bartholomew's tall shape and sturdy countenance. Diego's gentle spirit had been too weak to deal with a turbulent soldiery; but the powers of the president had been re-enforced by his brother's timely arrival. When Columbus had first started from Palos Bartholomew had been working for his cause in London, and it was only when bringing back the English king's acceptance that he heard how the task was already done. Too late to join the second expedition, he was sent out a few months afterward in charge of a squadron. He found the colony in a sad state. The admiral was away, and Diego could hardly control his colleagues. The forces placed under Margarite were mutinous, and their commander soon afterward went home, and left the soldiers to rob and kill as they pleased. The natives were not slow to retaliate. Straggling pillagers were cut off in the woods; a vassal of Gaurionex killed ten in this way, and burned a hospital with forty patients. The same chief was blockading the fort in the Vega. The bold Ojeda still held his own at St. Thomas, but was hard pressed by the armies of Caonabo.

Columbus soon received a visit from the Cacique who had befriended him before. He spoke of his own grievances against the Caribs, and revealed a general plot for taking the city and driving the white men into the sea. Columbus at once rose to the occasion. By a bold exercise of power he appointed his brother to the new office of Adelantado, or Lord Deputy of the Indies. The fort in the Vega was relieved, and Ojeda, in a dare-devil adventure, brought in Caonabo in the shackles which he had mistaken for ornaments. The Carib's brother raised an army for his rescue, but was beaten and captured in the opening skirmish. Notwithstanding these defeats, a huge Indian force assembled in the woodlands of the Vega; and on the 24th of March, 1495, Columbus and the Adelantado marched out with two hundred men-at-arms and twenty horsemen, besides friendly natives, and they took with them a score of Majorcan hounds, as terrible to a naked foe as the firearms or the steel-clad cavalry. The Spaniards divided their force so as to attack on two sides at once, but the Indian lines broke at the first volley, and the "faint-hearted creatures" fled. It was like the ancient comedy of the Greeks fighting against the Sparrow-folk armed only with fish bones. To Columbus it seemed like a miraculous victory. The country was thenceforth regarded as a fair prize of war, and a tribute of gold or cotton was imposed, according to the nature of the district. The Indians were forced to labor, and were fast sinking into slavery. As a last resource they tried to starve their masters, ravaging the fields and taking refuge in the clefts of the mountains; but they were hunted like wild beasts, with only the choice of death by famine or by the edge of the sword, and the feeble remnant came in at last and yielded a sullen obedience.

The king and queen had written to the admiral in gracious terms; but his enemies filled the air with complaints of the harshness of his government, and they railed at the scarcity of the gold, picked out in grains from the stream, or welded into small plates, perhaps after ages of labor. The movement had a double result. Licenses for discovery were offered to private adventurers, and it was determined to send out a commissioner to inquire into the alleged abuses. Juan Aguado was chosen for the post. He was believed to be the admiral's friend, and his instructions were drawn so as to give the least possible offense. But he took up such an arrogant attitude on arriving at the colony, as if it were his chief business to collect accusations against Columbus, that all the Spaniards were convinced of the admiral's approaching downfall.

Columbus felt that it was time to meet his enemies face to face. He announced that he would return with Aguado, and began to get together a collection of rarities and valuable produce. The queen had told him of her delight in studying these samples of another world, and he was anxious besides to prove the value of his latest discoveries. There were amber and coral and shells, and flamingoes and macaws, with a great store of cassia, and precious gums and spices. He had specimens of ebony and mahogany, and "brasil wood" for dyeing; there were specimens of copper and lapis lazuli, and golden coronets and masks, with gold ore in pieces like pigeons' eggs, and Caonabo's heavy chain and necklace, in which the prisoner was to be paraded before the court in Castile.

When the ships were just ready for sea, the port was swept bare by a hurricane, and Aguado was compelled to wait while a new caravel was constructed from the wreckage. During this interval the good news arrived of a discovery of a gold mine at La Hayna, in the south of the island. A Spaniard, convicted of stabbing in a duel, had fled beyond the mountains of Cibao, and had married the queen of a rich country through which the Ozama flowed. The Lady Catalina, to use her adopted name, showed a gold-field to her new friends where the ore was abundant and fine in quality; and Columbus felt sure that he had found the storehouse of Solomon and the sources of wealth that had adorned the Temple.

The two vessels sailed on the 10th of March, 1496, carrying a number of invalids and disappointed adventurers. Caonabo, who died on the voyage, and about thirty other Indians, were on board the admiral's ship. It was long before they could clear the eastern cape, and for many days afterward they beat up against the trade wind, and were forced at last to make for Marie Galante and Guadaloupe. On the 20th of April they set out again, "with the wind very scant." A month of misery had passed, with food very short, and the pilots "going like blind men," when Columbus made out by the variation of the compass that they had reached the "hundred league line." Then came a few days of great distress, and the crew were for killing the Indians, "but the admiral used all his authority against it, saying that they were human creatures, and ought not to be used worse than the rest"; and that night, while the pilots were disputing, he told them to take in sail, because they were near Cape St. Vincent, and in the morning they saw the sands of Odemira and the cape itself in the distance.

The king and queen received him at Burgos with undiminished favor. He was allowed to exhibit his samples of produce, and to give his own account of his troubles and victories. The queen was especially interested in the Indians, and their customs and beliefs. She learned that "they were not the worst kind of pagans," since they had some notion of a Deity and a future state. Their creed was embodied in barbarian songs, which they sang in their moonlight dances. The chiefs had amulets and wooden figures by which they claimed to control the forces of nature. They had childish legends about the origin of mankind, and the transformation of ancestral beings into birds or frogs or trees. They were chiefly guided by oracles taken by their sorcerers, or "medicine men," who made themselves mad for the time by inhaling the powder from a species of acacia.

When Columbus landed he found a squadron setting out for the colony under Pedro Nino, whom he had known at Huelva, and he dispatched a letter to Don Bartholomew asking for more gold, and suggesting that all natives concerned in the murder of Spaniards should be shipped as slaves. The ships came back with nothing but prisoners of this kind, though Nino foolishly boasted that he had "a cargo of gold in bars." The disappointment caused a grievous delay. The admiral was eager to explore the continent, and hoped by taking a southerly course to avoid the network of the islands. But the whole scheme had become hateful to the public mind. The king was deeply engaged in an expedition to Naples and the projected marriages of his son and daughter, on which the greatness of Spain appeared to depend. It was difficult to get crews together for a fresh voyage, and the admiral had to be content in the end with a fleet of six vessels manned almost entirely by convicts.

He sailed from San Lucar on the 30th of May, 1498, taking a circuitous course to avoid the French cruisers off Cape St. Vincent. After spending a few hours at Porto Santo, he went to Madeira and thence to Ferro, where he sent some of his caravels across by the ordinary route. He himself proceeded with half the fleet to the Cape Verde Islands, intending to strike the equator and to find his way through the torrid zone. The cross currents and the hot mists compelled a change of course, and they sailed into a region southwest of Fogo beyond the range of the trade wind. For eight days there was a calm, with violent heat; the casks burst and the provisions were spoiled, "and had it not rained sometimes they thought that they would have been burned alive." When the wind revived they made toward the Carib Islands and saw land one day about noon, and then three peaks together, and Columbus named the new country after the Trinity.

Trinidad lies near the mouths of the Orinoco, and is divided from the continent by two narrow straits. The sea inclosed between the promontories is known as the Gulf of Paria. To Columbus it was the "Golfo Triste," or the "Golfo de Balena," a place where he was in peril of the leviathan; while the names of the Serpent's Mouth and Dragon's Mouth recalled the memory of his escape from "the heads of the dragons in the waters." As they passed along the south of the island the country looked green and fresh, with palms by the water's edge. "It was like the gardens of Valencia in March"; and soon afterward they found themselves under an April sky. They anchored by a smooth strand "and took water from a delicate brook"; and they noticed that the sea ran like a turbid river, as happens at San Lucar when the Guadalquivir is in flood, "which never ceases flowing toward the bay, however the tide may rise." Anchoring next day at the sandy cape, just within the narrows of the Serpent's Mouth, they were nearly overwhelmed by a sudden flood advancing against the current. "In the dead of the night," writes the admiral, "I heard an awful roaring, and saw the sea rolling mast-high, with a great wave and a noise of breakers." The anchors gave away, and the mountain of water passed under the ships without much harm being done; but it was necessary to leave that dangerous roadstead without delay, and so with much labor they struggled through reefs and shoals into the landlocked gulf. Going northward for a few leagues they reached two headlands, with green islands between them, and here they felt the current plunging into the Dragon's Mouth, and heard the uproar of the fresh waters struggling against the tide. This was, in fact, the only way by which they could reach the open sea, but to evade the danger they crossed the entrance of the channel, and coasted down the opposite shore, hoping that Paria might prove to be an island, and that they might escape on its further side. The coast at first was wild and broken, but after a time they passed a sharp promontory, called "the Needle's Point," and came into a region of tropical verdure, which seemed to be "the loveliest country in the world."

The natives of Trinidad and Paria were fairer in complexion than any of the people seen on the previous voyages. Columbus had expected to find them as black as negroes in a country so near the equator, and he had feared, indeed, that the whole region would have been parched up like the African deserts. He met some of the islanders on his passage into the Serpent's Mouth. A chief came out with a score or more of warriors in one of the long cottonwood canoes. The Indians negotiated, and hung off and on, but seemed willing to take the toys held out to them over the side of the ship. The admiral, to draw them nearer, set a musician on the poop with tabor and pipe, and told some of the young men to dance. The natives, taking it as a challenge, seized bows and bucklers, and let fly a few arrows at the dancers. The sailors ran for their crossbows, and began to give the Indians a lesson; but the canoe moved off to another vessel, "clapping close to her side without the least apprehension," and the warriors were soon enriched with tin bowls and bits of looking-glass, while their chief was exchanging his gold coronet for the pilot's red cap. They wore their hair rather long, and cut in the Spanish fashion, and they had bright scarfs about their heads and bodies, which looked like the silk handkerchiefs that form part of the Moorish costume. When the ships reached Paria the natives came out "in countless numbers." Most of them wore ornaments of gold or colored stones on their breasts, and some had strings of pearls on their arms. The Spaniards thought that the pearls were bred in the oysters which they saw hanging to the roots of the mangroves, but the Indians said that they came from a sea beyond them in the north. Two boats' crews were sent ashore to procure fine specimens for the queen. The sailors were very hospitably received; they said that there were two large houses in the village with balconies and rows of seats, and that they had been regaled with white maize beer and a darker drink tasting like cider, made from the honeyed sap of an aloe.

The little vessel called the *Postman* was sent on to look for a channel into the ocean, but the captain soon came back and reported that no outlet could be found. He had reached another fresh-water sea of a circular shape, to which Columbus gave the name of the Gulf of Pearls, and there were four bays set at equal distances, with rivers opening into them, so that Paria was clearly part of the continent. There was no exit except through the Dragon's Mouth, so the ships were turned toward the headlands again, and were borne swiftly along the current, and thrust out by the help of a strong breeze through the rolling masses of water. After a journey of some days along the Pearl Coast they crossed over to Margarita, "the jewel of the islands," and the sandy wastes of Cubagua, where the pearl fishery was afterward established. They bought a large quantity of pearls from the fishermen, and made arrangements for a future trade. There is a mention of two groups of rocks, called the Guards and the Witnesses, and of the coast stretching on toward Venezuela; "but the admiral said that he could not give such an account of it as he desired, because through too much watching his eyes were inflamed, and he was forced to take most of his observations from the sailors and pilots."

He seems to have connected his misfortune with a vision of triumph, as if it was through these pains that he had visited the outgoings of Paradise. In the travels of his favorite, "Mandeville," he found the picture of what he witnessed in the Gulf of Paria. The Fathers had agreed that Eden was in the ends of the East; so held St. Ambrose, and Isidore, and the Venerable Bede. The most learned scholars were of opinion that it was the highest point in the world; thus said Scotus, and Strabus, and the writer of the "Historia Scholastica," and Mandeville even thought that it reached near the Circle of the Moon. By its rivers, he said, no man might go, their shock is so rude and sharp; the water came down "outrageously in great waves," so that no ship could move against it; and he described the "awful roaring," and said that "many had become blind, and many deaf, for the noise of the water." Columbus was convinced that he had seen these gigantic cataracts. "There are great signs," he said, "that this is the place of Paradise; I have never read or heard of fresh water so abundant and so mixed with the sea." He thought that his new "heaven and earth" were different from the old world in their nature. At the line of a hundred leagues from the Azores there had been strange frondage in the sea, new motions of magnetic force, and a change in the courses of the stars. When he reached the islands he found a rich verdure and "a most pellucid air"; and as he went deeper into the tropics the people were lighter in color, and the climate grew daily more genial. He imagined that this part of the earth was the highest and closest to the firmament. He supposed that there was a gradual rise for some thousands of miles over a circle comprised in the new hemisphere. Its outer line was reached at the point where the face of nature changed, not far from the Azores, and its center might be found on the equator, below Paria and the fresh-water sea. "I have no doubt," he adds, "that if I could pass beyond the equator, after reaching the highest point I should find a mild climate again and fresh changes in the sea and the stars." If the great stream that he had seen was not one of the rivers of Eden, it must come from "a vast land in the south," of which nothing was known; "but the more I reason on it," he concluded, "the more I hold it true that the Earthly Paradise is there."

He reached the colony by the end of August,

and moved forward to the Ozama River, where Don Bartholomew was building the new city of San Domingo, so named in memory of old Domenico Colombo. Here the admiral heard the story of all the quarrels that had followed his return to Spain. Guarionex had attacked the fortress in the Vega, because some of his subjects had been burned for blasphemy. There was a plot to massacre all the Christians at the full moon, which came to nothing from the Indians' ignorance of such calculations. Roldan, to whom the admiral had intrusted the "rod of justice," had set himself up as a protector of the disaffected. His crew of desperadoes had twice threatened the fort, and had plundered the stores at Isabella. They were now idling in Xaragua, the land of fruit and flowers, and had been joined by many of the sailors of the ships last sent from Spain. The admiral's own relations, Arana and Giovanni Colombo, were in command of two of these ships, and they were now awaiting orders in the port.

Columbus found it almost impossible to pacify the rebellious alcalde, but after months of parleys and bargaining a peace was arranged on very disastrous terms. The mutineers were allowed to send home their prisoners, including even the daughters of several chieftains, shamefully torn from their homes to be sold for slaves at Seville; and one of the main causes of the admiral's disgrace was the queen's wrath at this outrage on her "Indian vassals." Roldan himself, as if in burlesque, was appointed chief justice of the colony, and a catastrophe was certain to occur when he began to wield his powers against his wild companions. In September, 1499, the bold adventurer, Ojeda, arrived with four ships laden with slaves from the Carib Islands. This was the famous voyage in which Juan de la Cosa served as pilot and Amerigo Vespucci as general adviser. They had followed the admiral's track by the Pearl Coast, and far to the west had found a warlike people who fought them on equal terms, and they had nothing to show for spoils but a few hides and jaguar skins. They had now come across to Hispaniola to lay in cassava bread and to load a cargo of logwood. Ojeda gave out that Columbus was in disgrace at home and that the queen, his only friend, was already at the point of death. "This Ojeda troubled me much," the admiral said, "for he announced that he was sent with promises of gifts and liberties, and collected a large band around him." Roldan was charged to watch his proceedings and keep him in play, and he succeeded at last in persuading the visitors to continue their voyage.

Columbus was now nearly worn out with his troubles. The Spaniards, he complained, made war on him as if he were one of the Moors. "On Christmas Day, being forsaken by all the world, the Indians and rebel Christians fell upon me, and I was reduced to such distress that to avoid death, leaving all behind, I put to sea in a little caravel." He fell into a trance, and heard mystical words of comfort; all his enemies were to be scattered, and all his hopes fulfilled; and on that very day he heard of a broad tract of land "with gold mines at every step." This field was in fact so rich that it employed nearly the whole population. One man collected as much as forty ounces in a day. A huge mass of gold was found lying in the bed of a brook when Bobadilla had assumed the government. It was lost in the storm of 1502, when Bobadilla was drowned with Roldan and the unfortunate Guarionex:

> The hurricane of the latitude on him fell,
> The seas of our discovering over-roll
> Him and his gold.

About this time a more serious rebellion broke

out. Hernando de Guevara, a young nobleman in disgrace, had retired with hawk and hound to a hunting lodge belonging to his cousin, Adrian de Moxica. Their sport led them to the forests near the salt lake in the territories of Anacoana. Guevara had visited her court and had betrothed himself to her child, almost as celebrated for beauty as her mother, "the Bloom of the Gold." The young man was under Roldan's supervision. There were elements of danger in the proposed alliance, and the consent of the government was refused. Guevara sent for a priest to baptize the princess, with a view to immediate marriage; but Roldan arrested him in her very presence, and sent him as a prisoner to San Domingo. Adrian de Moxica made off at once to his old haunts and collected a large force, intending to rescue his relation and to put Roldan and the admiral to death. They were foiled by Roldan's activity, and were captured at a midnight council; and Columbus, to whom the matter was referred, reluctantly sanctioned their execution. "I could not have acted otherwise," he afterward said; "even toward my own brother, if he had sought to slay me and rob me of the lordship which the king and queen had placed in my charge,"

There was a painful scene when Moxica was led out to be hanged. He struggled and delayed to make confession, and Roldan at last lost all patience, and ordered him to be thrown from the battlements. Guevara and several of Moxica's other companions were also convicted, and were left for execution in the fortress.

Columbus was now quite ready to leave the island, and "to give up the government of this dissolute people." But Bobadilla was already on his way as a high commissioner with plenary powers; and on the 2d of August, 1500, his two ships sailed into the harbor of San Domingo. As he passed between the banks of the Ozama he saw on either side a gibbet with a dead Spaniard, and the first thing he heard on landing was that several more were lying under sentence of death. The air was full of complaints against Columbus and his brothers, and a mob of witnesses came forward to charge them with horrible cruelties. Bobadilla seems to have completely lost his head. Assuming the whole power of the government, as he had a right to do in case of need, he seized the fortress, and placed Don Diego under arrest. The admiral was in the Vega when he first heard the news of Bobadilla's strange conduct, and he had moved to the neighborhood of La Hayna when he received a peremptory summons to attend at San Domingo for trial; and the messengers showed him a letter from the king and queen requiring implicit obedience. Don Bartholomew was away in Xaragua, chasing the last remnant of the rebels, when he received a note from Columbus advising him to yield without resistance. As each arrived they were thrown into irons amid jeers and shouts and blowing of horns, and after the pretense of a trial they were all convicted and sent home in chains by separate ships.

The insults offered to the great admiral, the finder of a world for Spain, were received at home with an outburst of anger and indignation. His own wrath was expressed in a letter sent to a lady at the court, in which he showed the meanness and vulgarity of the measures adopted against him. If he were to be arraigned he had hoped to be treated in a manner becoming his great office, as when a proconsul of old was impeached for exactions in his province, or some valiant captain for what he had done in a conquered territory. The king and queen accepted all his explanations, acquitted him of all charges, and among other marks of their favor invited him to visit them at Granada. The admiral appeared, erect in his fine dress, and attended by his squires and pages. He seemed fierce and angry as he faced the king, but when he met the queen's looks, as he knelt before her, they both burst into tears.

CHAPTER XVIII.

> "In the end
> I learned that one poor moment can suffice
> To equalize the lofty and the low.
> We sail the sea of life: a calm one finds,
> And one a tempest; and, the voyage o'er,
> Death is the quiet haven of us all."

SEVERAL months were spent at Seville in preparing the mystical "Book of Prophecies" showing that Columbus was destined to recover the Holy Places as well as to carry light into the dark regions of the world. The admiral had renounced his visions of wealth and honor, but after a time he began to feel the need of another voyage, in order to find the strait leading past the Southern Continent into the expanse of the Indian Sea. He thought that the stream which hurried past Margarita must have an outlet not far from the equator. He intended to make the attempt from Jamaica, being still prohibited from visiting Hispaniola; and indeed Ovando, the new governor, had orders not to allow a landing unless the admiral was actually returning to

Spain. From Jamaica he meant to sail on a direct line to the neck of water drawn on his map and placed near the point where he was afterward barred by the Isthmus.

In the spring of 1502 he went out with four ships. One of these was under Don Bartholomew's command, and he took with him on his own vessel his son Ferdinand, then barely fourteen years old. The boy's notes of the voyage are to be found in the close of the biography; and a singular charm is added to the story by his fresh descriptions of strange lands, and fishing adventures, and hand-to-hand fighting with rebels and savages.

From the Canaries they ran with a fair wind to "the Woman's Island," as the natives called Martinique, and took in wood and water, and "made the men wash their linen," as Ferdinand notes. They lay for a few hours in a quiet roadstead off Dominica, and then moved upward along the chain of islands till they reached the Carib settlements in Santa Cruz. In the last week of June they were coasting by Porto Rico, "the island of St. John," and rested in the sunny bay which had so delighted the sailors in a former voyage. Here Columbus determined at all hazards to pass over to Hispaniola. One of his ships was almost useless, even under the skillful guidance of Don Bartholomew. "She could carry no sail, and her side would lie almost under water"; and it seemed almost impossible that she could keep up with the others in the passage to Paria. Columbus arrived at the port of San Domingo on the 29th, and sent in a request to exchange the ship for a small caravel at his own cost. He saw that a fleet of eighteen sail was just ready to start for Spain, carrying his enemies, Bobadilla and Roldan, as it turned out, with a treasure of £80,000 sterling, besides his own humble fortune. He felt sure from signs in the sea and air that a great storm was coming, and begged that the fleet might be detained and his own vessels allowed to run in for shelter. His requests and warnings were treated with contempt, and almost the whole of the king's fleet was destroyed by the predicted hurricane. Columbus found a safe anchorage, but his three consorts were carried far out to sea. "They all suffered very much, except the admiral;" and they agreed afterward, on comparing their adventures, that "Bartholomew had acted like a good sailor in going out to weather the gale, but the admiral had hugged the shore like a wise astronomer, because he knew which way the blast would come."

After the storm, says Ferdinand, they had a little breathing time, and the men were allowed to go fishing; they harpooned a sunfish asleep, that looked like a church bell half out of the water, and they caught a young manatee, which some took for a real "calf of the sea," because it was grazing on the herbage by the shore. Another gale seemed to be approaching, and they moved on to the "port of brasil wood," where Ojeda's freebooters had cut their cargo of logwood, and on starting again they were so becalmed that they could not make the coast of Jamaica, but drifted to certain sandy banks which Columbus called the Wells, because the men got water by digging pits on the beach. The weather became very bad, but they struggled on till they reached Jamaica. "There the sea became calm," writes the admiral, "but there was a strong current that carried me as far as the Queen's Garden without seeing land."

He succeeded in reaching the island of Guanaga in Honduras Bay, sailing in darkness under torrents of rain, or driving before the thunder storms. Here they found a people looking like Caribs, but with foreheads less compressed. There was a forest of pines as tall as those of Cuba, and in walking through it the sailors found a heap of calamine, or zinc ore, used for making brass, which some of them mistook for gold. One morning a large trading canoe came alongside, making up the gulf with goods from Yucatan. "It was as large as a galley, eight feet in breadth, and all made out of one tree; in the middle was an awning of palmetto leaves, looking not unlike those of the Venetian gondolas, which kept all under it so close that neither rain nor sea-water could do any harm. Under the awning were the women and children and all the goods." There was a crew of twenty-five men, says the young Ferdinand, but they had not the courage to defend themselves against our boats; and the admiral blessed the Providence that gave him samples of all these commodities without exposing his men to danger; and he ordered such things to be taken as appeared most sightly and valuable. There were bright-colored quilted stuffs, and painted jerkins, and cotton wrappers like those of the Moorish women at Granada. There were bundles of swords of a peculiar kind, intended apparently for the Mexican market. They were very long, and made of a hard palm wood, with channels where the edge should be, in which were sharp blades of obsidian fixed with fiber and elastic gum, "as good to cut naked men as if they were made of steel." Besides these weapons the Indians had hatchets for sale, shaped like the common stone axes, but made of brass or hardened copper, with plates and bells of the same mixed metal, and molds for castings. The provisions for the crew included maize and yams and other Indian roots. They had a store of cocoa nibs, which the Spaniards now saw for the first time, and on these the Indians seemed to put a high value for making chocolate, and also as a kind of money, or medium of exchange; and it was noticed that they all stooped at once to pick up any of the berries that fell down upon the deck; and they had maize beer for drink, which looked like bright English ale. The men were asked about the strait between the two oceans, and seemed to know it well. They said that it was close to Veragua, not far to the eastward; but it became obvious afterward that they had been speaking of an isthmus, and not of a channel from sea to sea. By a curious freak of imagination, Columbus thought that he had found the Massagetæ described by Herodotus, whose savage queen had once defeated the Persian armies and given Cyrus his "fill of blood." They made much use of gold and brass, according to the Father of History; "their spears, arrowheads, and battle-axes are made of brass; their helmets, belts, and breastplates are adorned with gold; they tie plates of brass on their horses' fronts, and use gilded reins and harness." The same description recurs in the works of Strabo and Mela, and was repeated in the "Cosmography" of Pius the Second, to which Columbus gives a reference. "The nation of which Pope Pius writes has now been found, to judge by the situation and other signs, except indeed the horses with poitrels and bridles of gold; but this is not surprising, because the lands on the coast are only inhabited by fishermen, and I did not stay there very long, being in haste to proceed."

After leaving Honduras they came to a forest land, where the Indians were almost as black as negroes, with tattooed skins and ears distended so as to hold stones as large as a hen's egg. The guide from Honduras called them cannibals, and

Columbus was ready to believe it of people so repulsive in their looks. But when Bartholomew landed with the other captains to hear mass, and again when they were taking possession of the country for Spain, the natives came down loaded with fat geese, and fowls with woolly crests like the hens of Mandeville's Indian travels, with roasted fish, and beans, and large, yellow plums, and a fruit with a prickly husk like a chestnut. The forest seemed to be full of life. The Spaniards heard of pumas and jaguars, and saw deer of different kinds. The coast swarmed with fish of every sort, as it seemed to the travelers, that could be found either in Spain or the Indies. The natives, for the most part, went naked, but a few chiefs wore tunics or short frocks without sleeves, and red and white cloths twisted about their heads. They all had tattooed skins, "looking very odd," as Ferdinand said, "with jaguars or deer, or houses and towers painted all over the body;" "but when they want to be fine against a festival day, their faces are colored black or red: some have streaks of several colors, some paint their noses and others blacken their eyes, and so they adorn themselves to look beautiful, when in truth they look like so many devils."

For sixty days they tried to make head against the Gulf Stream in weather so fierce that it seemed "like the end of the world." Columbus has recorded that his very soul was grieved at the distress of his little son, "though he worked as if he had been eighty years at sea." "I myself," he added, "had fallen ill, and was many times at the point of death, but I directed the course from a cabin that I ordered them to set up on the deck." In all this time they only made seventy leagues, but afterward they reached a point where the land trended southward and the east wind was no longer such a hindrance, "and they all gave thanks to God together, for which reason the admiral gave to the cape the name of Gracias a Dios."

The travelers were now in the land of Cariari, a region of enchantments, as the Spaniards supposed, and inhabited by sorcerers of terrible power, whose spells they could hardly cast off. The Indians came down in great numbers, and seemed ready to defend their country. Some of them were armed with clubs, or bows and arrows, and others carried palm-wood spears "as black as coal and hard as horn" and tipped with the poisonous spines of the sting ray. The men, as Ferdinand noted, had their hair braided and twisted round their heads; "the women wore it short like ours." As the Spaniards seemed to be peaceful, the natives proposed to trade, and brought out weapons, and cotton jackets and wrappers, and pieces of the baser kind of gold, which they hung upon their necks, as the Spaniards wore their medals and relics. Columbus was unwilling to take anything from their hands, and the Indians, in the same spirit, returned all the trinkets that were given to them. Two young girls who were brought on board were found to have "magic powder" concealed in their dress; and at a conference on shore the witch doctors threw some of the powder at the Spaniards, and blew the smoke of a burning resin against them. "They would have given the world," said Columbus, "to prevent my remaining there an hour." On October the 2d he directed his brother to visit the Indian town, and to find out the secrets of the land; but the explorers found little that was remarkable, except a public hall with walls of plaited canes, and tombs with embalmed bodies in them, and gilt headboards, painted with the likeness of the persons buried there, or carved into the shapes of animals. An incident which happened as they were leaving the coast is interesting as a point of natural history, though Columbus seems to have regarded it more seriously as a warning of strange events. One of the archers had shot an "arguato," or "howling monkey," in the woods, and the creature was at that time strange to the Spaniards, though they soon afterward saw them in greater numbers, leaping and swinging among the trees. These creatures, according to Humboldt's description, resemble young bears: "the fur is tufty, and reddish brown, and the face a blackish blue." The Indians brought two peccaries, or wild wood swine as a present; and they were so savage that the admiral's Irish hound would not face them; but the "arguato," though dreadfully maimed, caught the nearest peccary's snout with its prehensile tail, and held it like a vise till the boar was completely beaten. The young Ferdinand took the monkey for a kind of catamount; "it frightened a good dog that we had, but frighted one of our wild boars a great deal more"; and he notes that it showed "how these cats go hunting, like the wolves and dogs in Spain."

Columbus took two of the men of Cariari on

board to serve as guides, but the sailors said that the ships had no more luck after feeling the presence of these accursed necromancers. The Indians took them to the Land of Carambaru, and the ships sailed between the islands as through narrow streets, with the boughs of the trees striking the shrouds. The people here all went naked, and had golden mirrors and ornaments shaped like eagles round their necks. They offered next to show the Spaniards the way to the wonderful country of Ciguare, about which they told the most fantastic tales. Not only were the people rich in gold, but they wore coral necklaces and coronets, and also inlaid their chairs and tables with the same material. They had fairs and markets, where they traded in pepper from India; they had ships with cannon, and the men had rich clothes, and wore swords and cuirasses, and rode fine chargers into battle. The country was surrounded by the sea, and the River Ganges was at a distance of ten days' journey. "These lands," says Columbus, "seem to have the same bearings compared with Veragua, as Pisa has to Venice, or Tortosa to Fontarabia." All down the "trade coast" for fifty leagues he was shown where the gold mines lay, and the towns where the metal was smelted, of which Veragua was the chief. The natives seemed to be hostile for the most part, "brandishing their spears and blowing conchs and beating drums," and using strange incantations; but once or twice the Spaniards went ashore and traded. When they landed at Catiba they found a multitude of Indians with their king, "who differed in nothing from the rest except that he was covered with a large leaf because it was raining hard"; and here, in exchange for a few toys, they procured nineteen plates of solid gold. The admiral, without making any stay, went on to the Isthmus of Panama, where he put into a haven which he called Porto Bello, "because it is beautiful and well peopled, and encompassed by a well tilled country." The place was full of houses a stone's throw or a bowshot apart, and it looked, said Ferdinand, like the finest landscape that a man could imagine. On the 9th of November they sailed out of Porto Bello eight leagues to the east; but were soon forced back among the islands, near the place where Nombre de Dios was afterward built. Here a boat's crew chased a canoe, from which the Indians leaped out and could not be overtaken; "or, if one were overtaken, he would dive like a duck and come up again a bowshot or two away; and this chase was very pleasant, seeing the boat labor in vain and come back empty at last."

The weather had broken by this time, and the ships took shelter in the little creek of Retreta, about ten leagues east of Porto Bello, "with risk and regret"; and on leaving it the storm began again, "and wearied me," says Columbus, "so that I knew not what to do." "An old wound opened, and for nine days I had no hope of life; no eyes ever saw a sea so high and fierce with foam." It seemed, he wrote, as if it were a sea of blood, seething like a caldron on a mighty fire. The sky burned like a furnace, and flamed with lightning for a day and a night. When the storm abated the ships were followed by a multitude of sharks; and some thought that they boded mischief, because they can smell out death like ravens; but they turned out to be very good food for the men, who had nothing but biscuit, "so full of weevils," said the boy, "that, as God shall help me, I saw many that stayed till night to eat their sop for fear of seeing them."

They could hardly keep count of the storms that thwarted them on this "Coast of Contradictions." If they trimmed their sails for Veragua the west wind rushed out against them "like a man waiting for his enemy." If they made for port again, the east wind rose and thrust them from shore. At one time the crews were resting at the end of a large bay when they made a strange discovery. "We went ashore," says Ferdinand, "and saw the people living like birds on the tops of the trees, laying sticks across from bough to bough and building their huts upon them; and, though we knew not the reason of the custom, we guessed that it was done for fear of their enemies, or of the griffins that are in this land." The last words seem to contain a reference to the admiral's new theory that they had found a Scythian people belonging to the northern parts of Asia.

When the new year began, all hopes of finding the strait were abandoned. Columbus now became anxious to see the mines of which he had heard so much when he was skirting the shores of Costa Rica. Arriving at a river near Veragua, he named it Bethlehem, because they landed there on the Feast of the Epiphany, and prepared to establish a small settlement there, leaving Don Bartholomew in command while he returned home for supplies. An exploring party went up to Veragua and found a large, open town, like the straggling villages in Biscay. They were hospitably received by Quibio, or "the Quibian," as they called the lord of the district, and were taken up to a mountain, where the gold lay on the surface or entangled among the roots of the trees. This "Quibian" was showing the riches of a country belonging to his enemies; but it turned out that there were mines in his own district where a man might collect in a few days "as much ore as a child could carry." The admiral remembered the saying of Josephus that the treasure of the Temple had been brought from a golden peninsula a few days' journey from India, and he felt sure that he had found this rich region at Veragua, where he saw more signs of gold in two days than in all the years in which they had known Hispaniola. "I think more," he wrote, "of this opening for trade, and the lordship over these great mines, than of anything else in the Indies; and this, indeed, is such a son as must not be left to the care of a stepmother."

The natives seemed to lead an easy life. The chiefs strutted in fine robes and feather crowns braided with gold. They did little but chew cocoa paste, "mixing a powder with the leaf in a singular fashion," and their followers chewed another leaf which made their teeth very black. They had little game or venison, but plenty of grain, roots, and fruit of many kinds, and a great variety of liquors. They made one kind of wine from the pineapple and another from the peach-like "mamee," and had drink brewed from palm nuts, besides the sharp and brisk maize beer and the cider-like "pulque" from the aloe. Their chief business was to lay in stores of baked fish, which they prepared with wonderful patience, wrapping it up in dry leaves "as apothecaries do with their drugs." For the large fish they made hook and bait in one out of turtle shell, which they cut by sawing it up and down with a fiber; and they had seines for the shoals in the bays and contrivances of mat work and netting for the swarms of fry. The flying fish were mostly taken at the mouths of rivers with canoes fitted up with palmetto screens, against which the fish leaped when the water was beaten with paddles.

A few houses were built for those who were to stay behind, and a scanty store of provisions was placed out of reach of danger. Columbus himself was getting ready for sea, though his three available ships were leaky and worm-eaten, and as full of holes as a honeycomb. It was suddenly discovered that the Indian chief was preparing to massacre the settlers as soon as the fleet had sailed, and the admiral determined as a counterstroke to carry him off with all his wives to Spain. Don Bartholomew captured "the Quibian" with his own hands after a desperate struggle, and he was carried down to the boat with his wives and children and principal followers. Their captivity was of short duration. The indomitable Indian, though shackled hand and foot, plunged overboard and dived to the shore; some of the other prisoners burst open the ship's hatches and swam to land through the surf, and the rest hanged themselves in the hold, though the beams were so low that their feet and knees were dragging on the floor.

The settlement at Bethlehem was at once attacked. Accounts of the fighting have come down to us from Don Ferdinand, and from the brave Diego Mendez, who afterward carried a message from Jamaica to Hispaniola in a frail native canoe. Their stories are full of a frolic humor and a gay courage in face of death and disaster. The first that they knew about the assault was a sudden shout at their doors, and the javelins coming through the thatch. Don Bartholomew, they said, ran out at once with his spear and laid about him, and the Indians danced to and fro with their darts, like the picadors at a bullfight; they ran forward to cast, and then rushed back, as the young men do at home when they tilt with the bulrush spears. But they soon made for the woods when they felt the edge of the Spanish swords and the teeth of the Irish wolf dog. One comical fellow, says Ferdinand, ran straight back into the house. "This way, this way, Sebastian!" cried Mendez. "Where are you off now, in such a hurry?" "Let me be," said the sailor in his Italian: "*Lasciarmi andar, Diavolo!* I am going to put myself away." They laughed again at the pedantry of Diego Tristan, who was on the river close by with two boats' crews, and who would not join in the fight for fear of losing part of his force. The battle ended with an advance of the picked warriors armed with heavy palm-wood clubs; "but none of them got home," says Mendez, "for with our swords we cut off their arms and legs." Next day the austere Diego Tristan went up the river to get water for the fleet, and came to a terrible end. His boats were in a bend of the stream between woods too thick for a landing, when they were surrounded by a fleet of canoes with four or five Indians in each, and every man of the crews was killed, except one who dived to the shore and made his way home through the forest. "The Indians took the boats and broke them to pieces," says Mendez, "and this caused us much vexation, for the admiral was at sea without boats, and we were on shore deprived of the means of going to him." "We were all in the same trouble and confusion," as Don Ferdinand wrote from the ship, "as those who were left on land." The admiral, he adds, was lying in an open roadstead, with very few men; and those on shore, "seeing the bodies drift down, covered with wounds, and followed by swooping and screaming crows," took it as a bad omen, and feared the same end for themselves. They accordingly abandoned the village and encamped upon the open beach, making a shift to defend themselves behind casks and boxes. The Indians were gathering in great strength, and the woods were full of the noise of their conchs and drums; "but we had two good brass falconets with plenty of powder and ball, with which we frightened them off." The admiral, as it turned out, had one boat left, and after some days he succeeded in sending a message ashore by one Peter Ledesma, a man of gigantic strength, who was rowed within a short distance from land, and then plunged and swam through the surf. The party on shore were taken off on a raft, their ship being useless, and the little fleet set out once more toward Porto Bello, where Columbus was forced to abandon one of the three remaining vessels, "being all worm-eaten through and through."

In the Jamaica letter, Columbus records the agony of mind in which he abandoned his golden dreams. He was almost alone, outside the Bethlehem River, consumed by a raging fever, and worn out by fatigue. "All hope of escape was gone. I toiled up to the highest part of the ship, and with quavering voice called on your Highnesses' war captains to come from the four quarters of the heavens to succor me, but there was no reply, and I fell asleep lamenting, and heard the voice of compassion"; and these were the concluding words which he heard or seemed to hear: "Fear not, but trust; all these tribulations are graven in the rock, and not without cause." On this the weather had cleared, and he was able to rescue his men. He would have remained to defend the fort, but he doubted whether any ships would ever again come that way, and his action was decided by the thought that he might help himself, instead of waiting for help from others. On May 10, 1504, they arrived at the Queen's Garden, about ten leagues from Cuba, or as Columbus thought, "at the province of Mango, next to Cathay"; they were battered by storms, and lost almost all their tackle, and the crews were almost dead with fear. The two ships collided and all but sank, the water rising nearly to the decks, though all hands were at the pumps and baling with pans and kettles. "My vessel," says the admiral, "was on the very point of sinking, when the Lord miraculously brought us to land. Who will believe what I write? I say that in this letter I have not told the hundredth part of the wonders that happened on the voyage."

They saved themselves by putting into a harbor on the coast of Jamaica, "but though good enough as a shelter in a storm," the port had no fresh water in its neighborhood, and they could not see any Indian village. "We made the best shift that we could," says Ferdinand, "and moved eastward to another harbor, called Santa Gloria, which was inclosed by rocks on three sides; and having now got in, and being no longer able to keep the ships above water, we ran them ashore as far as we could, stranding them close together, board to board, and shoring them up so that they could not budge; and in this posture the water came up almost to the decks, upon which, and upon the poops and forecastles, sheds were made for the men to lie in, to secure themselves against the Indians." They had come to their last ration of biscuit and wine, but the natives were peaceable, and brought in plenty of food. "The Indians sold us two little creatures like rabbits for a piece of tin, and cakes of bread for a few glass beads, and when they brought a good store they had a hawk's bell, and sometimes we gave a great man a little looking-glass, or a red cap or pair of scissors, to please them." There was a danger, however, that this peaceful state of things might come to an end, and Columbus was anxious to let his position be known in Hispaniola. We have a record of his conversation with Diego Mendez, who was now his chief secretary. The admiral, says Mendez, called me aside, and spoke of his peril, addressing me as follows: "Diego Mendez, my son, not one of those who are here has any idea of our great danger, except myself and you, for we are but few in number, and these wild Indians are numerous, and very fickle and capricious; and whenever they may take it into their heads to come and burn us in these two ships, which we have turned into straw-thatched cottages, they may easily do so by setting fire to them on the land side, and will so destroy us all." He then proposed that Mendez should make his way to Hispaniola in a canoe, and should buy a ship and stores at the admiral's cost. The secretary doubted if success were possible, but finally agreed to make the attempt. The admiral, he said, rose and embraced him, kissing him on the cheek, and saying, "Well did I know that there was no one here but yourself who would dare to undertake the enterprise." After one failure, in which he nearly lost his life, Mendez succeeded in reaching the colony, where he found Ovando engaged in the campaign against Xaragua. "He kept me with him," said Mendez, "until he had burned or hanged eighty-four Caciques, and with them Anacoana, the principal lady of the island; and when that expedition was over I went on foot to San Domingo, and waited there till the storeships should come from Spain." In the course of the spring, three vessels sailed in together; and Mendez bought one of them on the admiral's account, and sent her off to Jamaica, well supplied with meat and biscuit.

During the year which Columbus spent at Santa Gloria he was confronted by troubles of all kinds. The Indians became tired of supplying food, "being a people," said Don Ferdinand, "that takes little pains in sowing, and we eating more in one day than they did in twenty"; but their childish minds seem to have been subdued by the admiral's prediction of an eclipse "with an angriness and color of blood in the moon," since they believed that such eclipses had always brought disaster upon them. Only one short message had been received from Hispaniola in answer to his demand for assistance. A small caravel put into the port one evening with a dispatch from Mendez and a curt message from the governor of the colony, who regretted that he had no ships ready for the relief of the shipwrecked crews. The captain handed down a cask of wine and two sides of bacon as a compliment, and, having received a letter for Ovando, went back that same night. His sailors had been forbidden to speak to anyone on shore, and there was an air of mystery about the whole transaction. Columbus endeavored to make the best of the case, declaring that ships would be sent to carry them all away, but many of his followers persuaded themselves that he had practiced an illusion, and that "this was no true caravel, but a phantom of that black art in which the admiral was well skilled." They had long been convinced of his supernatural powers, thinking that his "rough magic" had raised the great storm in which his enemies had perished at Hispaniola, as though he were the master of such powers as he who cried:

> I have bedimmed
> The noontide sun, called forth the mutinous winds,
> And 'twixt the green sea and the azured vault
> Set roaring war.

This idea seems to have influenced the proceedings of the mutineers, who did not dare to attack the admiral themselves, though they continually incited the Indians to kill him. At the beginning of the year 1504, Francisco de Porras, one of the ship's captains, had broken into open rebellion. He took command of a band of fifty mutineers, and insisted that Columbus should take them home. "What is the meaning, my lord, that you will not go to Spain, but keep us all perishing here?" He demanded that they should all be embarked at once, crying out, "I am going to Spain with all who will follow me," and his men began to shout, "We will all go with you!" or "Death! death!" and "Spain! Spain!" They possessed themselves, says Ferdinand, of the forecastle, poop, and roundtops, all in confusion. The admiral was in bed, so ill of the gout that he could not stand. "Yet he could not forbear rising and stumbling out at this noise; but two or three of his servants laid hold of him, and with much trouble put him on his bed that the rebels might not murder him. They then ran to his brother, who had courageously come out with a half-pike in his hand, and thrust him in to the admiral, desiring Porras to go about his business, and not do a mischief that they might suffer for. The desperadoes went off with the canoes which Columbus had been collecting, and lived upon what they could take from the Indians, "waiting for fair weather and destroying the country." After several vain attempts to pass over to Hispaniola, they came back to the neighborhood of Santa Gloria, where Don Bartholomew went out with about an equal force to meet them. The rebels, thinking themselves to be the stronger party, charged in a body, with shouts of "Slay! slay!" Six of their best men, including the gigantic Ledesma, and Sanchez, who had been the first to draw his sword on the admiral's deck, were banded together under an oath to kill Don Bartholomew. "If he were killed," they said, "they would make no account of the rest." But Bartholomew fell on them so fiercely that most of their picked men were killed in the first charge. Porras himself was taken prisoner; Sanchez was among the killed, and Ledesma was found at the foot of a rock from which he had fallen, with a crowd of Indians round him, amazed at his desperate wounds. The other rebels soon afterward came in, and bound themselves with many vows to do their duty in the future.

The admiral's ship, with a caravel lent by Ovando, arrived a few days afterward, "and on the 28th of June, 1504," says Ferdinand, "we proceeded with much difficulty, the winds and currents being very contrary, and arrived at San

Domingo on the 13th of August in great need of rest."

The letter which Columbus wrote from Jamaica in the previous year expresses the sense of disappointment and defeat that darkened the close of his life. "The honesty of my service and these unmerited affronts would not let my soul be silent, if I wished it. I pray your Highnesses' pardon. I am lost, as I have already said. For others I have wept before; but now let Heaven have mercy upon me, and let the whole earth weep!"

His son describes the final troubles of the voyage. Of their two ships, one had soon to put back, but the other pressed forward through a terrible storm. On the 19th of October, the weather being fair, the mainmast split into four pieces; but they managed to rig up a jury-mast, though the admiral could not rise from his bed to direct them. The foremast went soon afterward, but crippled as they were, they managed to sail for seven hundred leagues, and arrived on the 7th of November at the harbor of San Lucar.

While Columbus was at his old home in Seville, he heard of the good queen's death. He writes sadly to his son Diego, grieving at the loss of his protector and best friend: "We trust that she rests in glory, far from all care for this rough and weary world." Columbus made repeated applications for the arrears due to his men, and the restitution of his dignities. He could get no answer of any kind. King Ferdinand had assumed the regency, but he had no real power to control the revenues of Castile, and his mind was engrossed in the attempt to postpone his daughter's accession. In the spring of 1505 Columbus had an audience at Segovia, and followed the court from that time, pleading for his rights, and offering to serve the State again, "though the gout was working him without mercy." He was always received with the same cold politeness. The restitution of his dignities was delayed, and all questions of revenue were referred to a tedious arbitration, though Columbus was fast sinking into poverty. He was pressed to exchange his claims for an estate and a pension in Castile, "the Indies showing daily more and more what they were like to be, and how great would be the admiral's share." Columbus wrote that, if the king would not keep his word, it was useless to contend with him. "I have done all that I could, and I leave the rest to God." There was one last gleam of hope when he heard that Philip and Juana had landed. Don Bartholomew carried a letter to Corunna, tending the admiral's homage, and offering to do such service as the world had never seen. A few days afterward all hope was gone. The disease that had so long oppressed Columbus took a sudden turn for the worse, and he died in the inn at Valladolid upon Ascension Day, the 21st of May, 1506. He was buried in that city in the Church of Santa Maria la Antigua; but his body was removed six years afterward to Seville, and King Ferdinand built him a tomb, in which his remains rested for a time before their removal to the Indies. "An epitaph," writes his son, "was cut upon the tomb in Spanish, and the words were these: '*A Castilia y a Leon, Nuevo mundo dió Colon*': words well worth observing, because the like cannot be found either among the ancients or the moderns."

INDEX.

A

Acacia, 318
Acunha, Trisdan d', 78
Adam of Bremen, 131, 161, 201
Adelantado, Office of, 313
Æthicus, Cosmography of, 42, 94, 172
Agouti, 245, 304
Aguado, Juan, 315–16
Ailly, Pierre d', 133
Albania, 163, 173
Albisola, Orbisola, 7, 17
Alciati, 36
Alexander the Great, 162, 173–4, 176
Alexander the Merchant, 129
Alfragan, 130
Almadia, 210, 243
Aloes, 20, 58, 290, 292, 350
Alto Velo, 310
Amaricus, 131
Amazons, Isle of, 161, 265, 268, 287
Amber, 59, 127, 220, 303, 316
Amico, Antonio de, 26
Anacoana, 300, 305, 330, 358
Andalusia, 231, 279, 284
Angelfish, 152

Antilla, 107, 115, 136, 157
Antigua, 293
Antipodes, 32, 124
Antwerp, Trade of, 59
Arabia, 155
Arana, Family of, 225, 327
Archangel, 194
Archers, English, 202, 265, 342
—— Indian, 294, 297, 306, 242
Archil, Orchilla, 100, 101
Arctic Circle, 121, 131, 133, 140, 151, 155, 165
Arguato, 344
Arguin Island, 112
Aristotle, 43, 45, 108, 116, 118, 125
Arngrim, The Learned, 167–8 169
Assegai, 221
Astrachans, 58
Astrolabe, 219
Atalanta, 117
Atlantis, 109, 117
Attila Lay, 177
Azores, 105–8, 118, 158–9, 207–11, 230, 267, 271–2, 275, 281, 283, 326
Azumbaja, 219

INDEX.

B

Babeque (*see* Jamaica),256, 258, 305
Bacon, Francis, 188, 191
Bacon, Roger, 95, 133
Bahama Bank, 276
Baltic, 50, 155, 161
Baldo, 31, 36
Bambothus River, 113
Bantry Bay, 191
Barbadoes, 115
Barbary, trade of, 60
Barcelona, 282-6, 292
Bardson, Ivor, 182
Battles—
  Bethlehem River, 351
  Brest, 50
  Cape St. Vincent (1470), 57, 71-74
  Cape St. Vincent (1485), 12, 57, 72-3
  Cyprus, 57
  Genoa, 46
  Guinegette, 50
  Navidad, 296-7
  Ravenna, 78
  Rif, 149-50
  Samana, 265, 295
  Santa Cruz, 293
  Santa Gloria, 361
  Santa Maria, 271
  Stamford, 67
  Tunis, 55-6
  Vega, 314-15
  Viverro, 50, 52-5
Bavarello, Giacomo, 22, 30
Beccaria, Antonio de, 116
Bede, The Venerable, 325
Beer, 200, 323, 339, 350
Behaim, Martin, 219
Behemoth, 43, 113
Bellini, Gentile, 77
Benin, 207
Bergen, 146, 149, 153, 184
Bernadigio, Antonio di, 44
Bernardo of Sestri, 18
Béthancourt, 96
Bethlehem, River, 348-54
Bissagos, Islands, 113
Bjarney, or Disco Island, 179, 183
Bjorn of Scardsa, 178-9
Bjorn Thorleifsson, 149, 165-6
Bjorn Heriulf's Son, 169
Blue Mountains, 306, 309-10
Bogliasco, 7
Bohio, Hispaniola (*see* Hispaniola), 249, 254, 256-9
Bojador, Cape, 97-8, 112
Bona Vista, 209
Booby, Gannet, 102-3, 233
Bobadilla, 329, 331, 336
Book of Prophecies, 324
Bovadilla, The Huntress, 208
Boverio Family, 26
Bracciforti, 87
Brasil wood, 299, 316, 337
Bressay, 191
Bristol, 138, 141, 149-51
Bruges, Trade of, 59
Bryniulf of Skalholt, 165
Burgos, 318

C

Cadamosto, 100
Cadiz, 57, 109, 117, 119, 123, 154, 286-7

INDEX. 367

Calais, 20, 149'
Calamine, 328
Camara dos Lobos, 93, 96
Canary Isles, 96, 101-4, 114, 127, 207, 215, 229, 256, 266, 272, 287
Candia, 19, 101
Cannibals, 161, 201-3, 255, 266, 287, 291, 294, 298, 311, 340-41
Canoes, West Indian, 210, 261, 306, 309-11, 322, 328, 346-7, 350, 353, 357, 360
Canynge, William, 149
Caonabo, 297-300, 302-3, 313, 317
Cape Coast Castle, 216, 219
Cape Verde Islands, 114, 129, 208-10, 225, 235
Capiscum, 217, 305
Caramansa, 220-1
Carambaru, 346
Cariari, 342-5
Caribs, 205, 289-90, 297, 313, 320, 328, 335, 338
Carthage, 39, 97, 107-9, 114, 208
Casenove, Coulon (*see* Columbus)
Caspian Sea, 163, 173, 176
Cassava, 257, 260, 292, 328
Cassia, 316
Catalina, the Indian, 316
Cathay, 3, 107, 135-6, 156, 228, 237, 277, 359
Catiba, 346
Cattigara, 83, 129
Cazel, Robert de, 49

Ceiba-tree, 254, 291
Chariot of the Gods, 113
Charles the Bold, 50, 54, 65-7
Charles the Eighth of France, 72
Cibao, 262, 297-302, 316
Ciguare, 345
Ciguayo Indians, 215, 265
Cinnamon, 20, 40, 58, 122, 290
Cipango (Japan), 99, 107, 134, 136, 157, 237, 249, 262
Clear, Cape, 158
Cloves, 122, 289
Coca, 350
Cocoa, 329, 350
Cod-fishery, 140-1, 152, 198
Coffer-fish, 257
Colombi, of Cogoletto, 7, 9, 10, 16
—— of Corsica, 9, 17-18
—— of Cuccaro, 10
—— of Montferrat and Piacenza, 10-11
Colombo, Giovanni, 327
—— of Oneglia, 13, 17-18
Colombo of Terra-Rossa, 15, 24
—— de Terra-rubea, 24
—— Antonio, 24
—— Bortolomeo (*see* Columbus)
—— Battestina, 25
—— Biancinetta, 18, 22, 30
—— Cristoforo (*see* Columbus)
—— Domenico, 10, 24-9, 327
—— Giacomo (*see* Columbus)
—— Giovanni, 24-5
—— Giovanni-Pelegrino, 18, 28
—— Susanna (*see* Fontanarossa)

Columbus, Bartholomew—
—— —— born at Quinto, 18
—— —— journey to England, 312
—— —— appointed Adelantado, 313
—— —— in Hispaniola, 305, 313, 327-8
—— —— arrest of, 332-3
—— —— voyage to Honduras, 335-6, 340
—— —— at Veragua, 349-50
—— —— in Jamaica, 361-2
—— —— at Corunna, 364
Columbus, Christopher—
    his family, 3-17, 24-30, 87, 327
    his father and mother, 10, 15-18, 24-30, 327
    at Genoa, 21, 46
    at Pavia, 31-9, 43-5
    at Savona, 17, 26-7, 48
    at Porto Santo, 106, 206
    serves with privateers, 48, 52, 56-8, 70-4
    Mediterranean voyages, 5, 17, 47-8, 106
—— to the Azores, 106, 207, 210-11
    Canaries, 207
    Cape Verde Islands, 208-9
    English Channel, 67-8
    North Sea, 71, 106, 150-5, 205
    Arctic Circle, 5, 138-40, 150-2
    Senegambia and Guinea, 207, 212-20

Columbus, Christopher—*cont'd.*
    at Lisbon, 47, 73-4, 81-2, 85-90, 134, 273
    marries Philippa Moniz, 87-90
    his portraits, 76-81
    settles in Spain, 225-7
    Beatrix Enriquez, 225
    First Voyage to West Indies, 103, 215-16, 227-66
    return by the Azores, 267-73
    Second voyage, 39, 71, 102, 120, 286
    Third voyage to Paria, 320-5
    his arrest and return, 331-2
    Fourth voyage, 335-62
    at Honduras, 337-41
    in Veragua, 346-54
    flight to Jamaica, 356-62
    final return, 362
    last illness and death, 363-4
Columbus, Diego—
    Christopher's eldest son, 91, 226, 362
    at Porto Santo and Madeira, 106, 206
    at Cordova, 270
    makes payments at Savona and Lisbon, 28-85
    sees beginning of second voyage, 287
    his last will, 90
Columbus, Ferdinand—
    son of Beatrix Enriquez, 225

INDEX. 369

Columbus, Ferdinand—*cont'd.*
  at Cordova, 270
  Conversations with the Admiral, 4–5, 33, 73, 128–41
  writes on pedigree of Columbi, 6, 7, 9–10, 12–14
  Essay on the Zones, 139
  on battles at Cape St. Vincent, 12, 72–4
  on his father's marriage, 90
  on Carthaginian voyages, 117–19
  on early life of Columbus, 103–4, 134–5, 159, 193
  on the first expedition, 229, 285
  sees second fleet start, 286
  his adventures on the fourth voyage, 325–61

Columbus, Giacomo (Don Diego)—
  born at Genoa, 18
  voyage to Hispaniola, 28
  in command of fleet, 302
  President of Council, 304, 312
  sent back to Spain, 331

Columbus, French Vice-Admiral—Coulon de Casenove, 13, 14, 48–55, 62, 70
  his family, 49, 51
  services under Louis the Eleventh, 49–50

Columbus, (Coulon de Casenove) *cont'd.*
  his action at Viverro, 50, 52–5
  imprisoned, 62

Columbus the Younger—
  Nicolo Griego, or Colombo, 12, 13, 48–9, 51, 55–7, 64–5, 68–73
  known as Pirate Colombo, 13
  in English Channel, 65, 67–70
  at Cape St. Vincent (1470), 71–74
  off Cape St. Vincent (1477), 71, 154
  takes Flanders galleys (1485), 12, 57, 72
  his action off Cyprus, 57

Como, 7, 77
Concepcion Island, 244, 276–7 (*see* Guanima)
Copenhagen, 149, 165
Copper, 291, 303, 316, 339
Coral, 243, 276, 293, 345
Cordova, 226, 259, 270
Correa, Pedro, 90, 92, 104, 207, 211
Corsica, 9, 17
Corunna, 364
Cosa, Juan de la, 234–6, 282, 284, 328
Cosmas, 43
Costa Rica, 348
Cotton, 242–4, 249, 253–5, 315, 343
Crab, various species of, 103, 232, 246, 305
Crane, 307
Crato, Prior of, 280

INDEX.

Crayfish, 253
Crispi, Alberto di, 45
Cristofano dell' Altissimo, 79
Cuba, 211-13, 250-8, 264, 276-8, 355 (*see* Juana)
Cubagua, 324
Cuccaro, 10, 11
Cuneo, Corrado di, 28
Cyprus, 19, 57

D

Dædalus, 196
Dartmouth, 69-70, 265
Decio, Filippo, 37
Degree, measure of, 130-1, 139-40
Denmark, 140, 149, 168, 185
Desertas, 99
Dicuil, 131
Diodorus Siculus, 39, 44, 108, 110, 120, 174
Diogenes, voyage of, 128
Disco Island, 179, 183
Dittmar Blefken, 168
Dog-faced Tribes, 161, 255
Dogs, Indian, 245, 252, 291
—— Irish, 344, 352
—— Majorcan, 314
Dominica, 288, 335
Dorado, 235
Dragon's Blood, 93
Dragon's Mouth, 320-1, 324
Dragon-tree, 92-4
Drift-ice, 132, 142-3, 152, 190
Drogio, 191, 201-3

E

Eaglewood, 248, 255

Ebony, 303, 316
Edward the Fourth of England, 65-6, 70, 218
Elmina, 218-19, 222-3 (*see* St. George's Fort)
Emperor-fish, 235
England—
  negotiations with Columbus, 2, 24, 312
  trade with Genoa, 19, 59
  —— —— Iceland, 139, 140, 150-51, 165-6
  —— —— Norway, 153-5
  —— —— Venice, 56-61, 63-6
  Wars of the Roses, 66-70
  Wool Trade of, 20, 59-60, 149
English Fleet at Calais, 67
—— —— at Havre, 69
—— —— at Dartmouth, 70-1
Enriquez, Beatrix, 225
Eric the Red, 163-72, 174-9, 181
Esdras, Book of, 41, 43
Eskimo, 173, 175, 184
Estotiland, 191, 199-204
Etna, Mount, 209
Eudoxus, voyage of, 97
Eugenius the Fourth, 135, 184
Euphorbia, 248
Exuma 244-6, 277 (*see* Fernandina)

F

Färöe Isles, 132, 140, 164, 190, 198-205
Fata Morgana, 212
Faventia, Stefano di, 44

INDEX. 371

Fayal, 157, 211
Ferdinand of Arragon, 47, 71-2, 76, 281, 318-19, 363-4
Ferdinand and Isabella, 2-3, 34, 226-8, 238, 282
   at Barcelona, 282-4
   letters from, 254, 315, 332
   letters to, 215-16, 228-9, 260-2, 269-70, 309, 304-5, 362
Ferdinand of Sicily, 52-5
Ferdinandina, La, 55-6
Fernandina Exuma, 244-6
Ferrariis, Theophilus de, 116
Ferreri, Giovanni, 24
Ferro, 208, 210, 230, 236, 267, 319
Fisheries—
   Icelandic, 140, 147-9
   Lofoden, 151-2
   Färöese, 198
   Scotch herring, 140
   West Indian, 246-7, 350
Fisherman, Story of the, 197-205
Flaccus, Septimius, 128
Flamingo, 307, 316
Flanders Galleys, 19, 57-61, 63-6, 70-4, 154
Flatey Book, 164-8, 179
Flitting Islands, 211-12
Flores, 157-8
Flying fish, 237-8, 350
Fogo, 209, 320
Fontana-Rossa, 15
   —— family of, 15-16, 26
   —— Susanna, mother of Columbus, 15-17, 28-9

Fortuna, the Infante, 285
Fortunate Isles, 114, 120, 174
Fox grape, 163
Frankincense, 127, 248, 303
Freydisa, 177-9
Frigate bird, 235, 288
Frisland, 139, 188-90, 198
Fritalo, Giovanni di, 25
Frobisher, Martin, 185, 190
Frozen Sea, 233
Funchal, 94, 206
Furtada, Beatrix, 90
—— Caterina, 90
—— Iseult, Hizeu, 90, 104

G

Gallo, Antonio, 82
Garcia, Ruy, 271
Gaza, Theodore, 217
Genoa, home of Columbus, 2, 7-11, 17, 25-6, 46-7, 225
—— description, 20-24
—— Black Sea trade, 47
—— Olive Gate, at, 21
—— St. Andrew's Gate, 8, 18, 21, 26, 30
—— spice trade, 16, 20, 47
—— trade with Lisbon, 82, 86
—— weaving trade, 21, 23, 291
—— early voyages from, 96
George of Trebizond, 217
Ginestreto, 22, 24
Giovio, Paolo, 38, 77-82, 201
Girardi, 134
Giulio Romano, 78
Giustiniani, 6, 82

Gold, discovery of, 217, 254, 297, 300-3, 305-6, 315-16, 329-30, 338, 343
Gold mines, 257, 262, 278, 345-9
Gold ornaments, 221, 243-4, 247, 249-50, 260-61, 316, 323, 340, 345, 349
Gold Coast, 207, 216, 219
Golden Chersonese, 43, 129, 307
Gomera, 208, 210-11, 229, 241, 287
Gorbolan, 300-1
Gorgon Islands, 115
Gorillas, 113
Gracias a Dios, Cape, 342
Graciosa, 207
Grain Coast, 216-17
Granada, 2, 228, 333, 338
Greenland—
—— Bishops of, 183-5, 193
—— invasion by Eskimos, 184-5
—— Norwegian settlements in, 144-6, 161-2, 181-3, 204-5
—— the voyages to Vinland, 162-5, 169-81
—— voyage of the Zeni, 188-93, 194, 197-200, 204
Griego, family, 51 (*see* Columbus)
Griffins, 163, 348
Guacanagiri, 261, 298
Guadaloupe, 289-91, 317
Guanaga Island, 337

Guanahani, 240-1, 276-7 (*see* Watlings Island)
Gaunches, 208
Guanima Islands, 244, 276-7, (*see* Concepcion and Rum Cay)
Guardafui, Cape, 128
Guards, Islands, 324
Guarionex, 215, 296-8, 313, 329
Guevara, Hernando de, 330-1
Guinea Coast 5, 212-34, 253, 274
Gulf Stream, 105-6, 342
Gulf weed, 103-5, 231-4, 236-7, 265-6, 288

H
Hair, mode of dressing, 215, 242, 290, 323, 343
Hake and Hekia, 180
Halibut, 152, 182-3
Hammocks, 245, 253-5, 291
Hanno, 112, 120
Hanse League, 141, 153
Hayna, La, 316, 332
Hawk's Book, 178-9
Hecla, Mount, 187, 194
Heimskringla, 167
Helena, meteor of, 289
Helluland, 170, 180
Heriulf's Ness, 169-70
Henry the Seventh, 72, 155, 312
Henry the Navigator, 97, 113, 157, 221, 224, 279
Herodotus, 43, 340
Hesperides, 107, 114-15
Hesperus, 113-14, 115

Higuey, 210, 298
Hispaniola—
    building of La Navidad, 262–4
    —— of Isabella, 299–300
    —— of San Domingo, 327, 331
    civil wars in, 327–31
    conquest of, 312–15
    dialects in, 214–15
    discovery of, 116–17, 259–60, 276–7
    foundation of colony, 286–7, 299
    hurricanes at, 316, 329, 336–8
    last visit of Columbus, 359
    mastic-trees in, 47
    Mendez, visit of, 351, 356–8
    pine forests, 211
    return of Columbus to, 310–11
    shape of, 123
    skirmish at Samana, 265–6
    spices found in, 216–17, 316
    (*see* Bohio)
Himilco, 108
Historia Scholastica, 325
Hogfish, 246
Honduras Bay, 327–8, 340–1
Honeydew, 174, 176
Hot springs, 192–4
Houses, West Indian, 248, 252, 255, 291, 294, 323, 343, 346–8
Huelva, 90, 225, 273, 318
Hull, 149
Hundred-league line, 230, 281, 317, 326
Hyrcania, 163, 172–4, 176

I

Iambulus, 120
Icaria, 195–7 (*see* Kerry)
Iceblink, Mountain, 182
Iceland, taken for Thule, 131–3, 138–40, 154
—— confused with Shetland, 189
—— English trade with, 138–51, 165–6
—— calendar used in, 143–4, 151
—— literature of, 165–9, 177–9
Ireland, 124, 158–9, 181, 193, 195
—— Greater, 173, 181
Isabella, Queen, 215, 227, 244, 256, 315–18, 323, 328, 332–3, 362–3 (*see* Ferdinand and Isabella)
—— City of, 299–304, 310, 327
—— Island, 243, 246–50, 277 (*see* Long Island, Saometo)
Isidore, 325
Ivory Coast, 216–18

J

Jamaica, 256–8, 264, 309, 324, 337, 351–8, 362 (*see* Babeque)
Jerez, Rodrigo de, 253
John the Second, 155, 218–23, 274–6, 279–82
Josephus, 43, 349
Juana, Island of, 277 (*see* Cuba)
Juana, Queen, 364

Juba, King, 94
Juventius, 211

K

Kerry, 195-7 (*see* Icaria)
Khan, Great, 228, 249, 251-3, 278
King's Garden, 257

L

Labrador, 158, 175, 195
Lanzarote, 208
Lapis-lazuli, 303, 316
Ledesma, Pedro, 354, 361
Leif Ericsson, 163-5, 169-70, 177, 180
Leme, Antonio, 211-12
Leviathan, 43, 320
Lign-aloes, 250, 257, 277, 285, 290
Lisbon, 47, 73-5, 81-2, 85-6, 102, 104, 134, 154, 223, 273-4
Lizards, 92, 245, 250, 284, 305
Llandra, 281
Lofoden Islands, 151-2
Logwood, 328, 337
London, 59, 147, 149-50
Long Island, 244, 246-50, 276 (*see* Isabella Island, Saometo)
Louis the Eleventh, 13, 49-50, 63-4, 68-70
Lover's Cape, 265
Lucian, 109, 119, 120
Luigi, Scotto, 86

M

Macaw, 292, 316
Machico, 93, 97
Machin, Robert, 98
Madeira, 93-103, 114, 206-7, 211, 319
Magnus, Olaus, 95, 141, 152, 155, 173, 193
Magnussen, Professor, 142-4
Mahogany, 299, 306, 316
Maino, Giasone, 37-8
Maize, 162-3, 254-5, 292, 305, 329
Maize beer, 323, 329, 350
Malaguette, 207, 216-17
Mamee fruit, 298-9, 350
Manatee, 218, 252, 291, 337
Manchineel, 289
Mandeville, 43, 95, 173, 325, 341
Mangrove, 216, 323
Manioc, 254, 292
Mantegna, Andrea, 77-8
Marco Polo, 133, 224
Mares, River, 252-3
Margarita, 324, 334
Margarite, 313
Marie Galante, 289, 327
Marien, 297
Marinus, 83-4, 127-31, 133
Markland, 170, 181
Maroris, 214-15
Martinez, Fernando, 134-5
Martinique, 335
Martyr, Peter, 44
Masks, Indian, 252, 262, 285, 316
Massagetæ, 340
Mastic, 47, 231, 245, 253, 255, 257

INDEX.   375

Maternus, 128
Mazer wood, 177
Mecca, 155
Medina Celi, Duke of, 226
Medina Sidonia, Duke of, 218, 226
Mendez, Diego, 352-3, 356-7
Mesurado, 217
Meta Incognita, 185, 190
Metellus, 210
Middleburg, 59
Mirobolans, 58, 290
Misery, Mount, 293
Mona, 294-5, 311
Moniz, Brigulaga, 90
—— Gil, Family of, 91-2
—— Isabel, 90-93, 97-8, 100-3, 106
—— Donna Muliar, 90, 225
—— Philippa, 87, 93, 102, 104, 212
Monk Rock, 140, 190
Monkfish, 152
Monk seal, 95, 218
Monelone, Nicola di, 27
Monte Christi, 263, 295, 298-9, 304
Montserrat, 292
Moon, eclipse of, 83, 311, 358
Moors, 2, 112, 207, 226
Moxica, Adrian de, 330-1

N

Navidad, La, 262-4, 286-7, 296, 304
Nearchus, voyage of, 129
Negro, Paolo de, 86
Nervi, 7, 22

Nevis Island, 292
Nina, The, 227-9, 232, 234-5, 238, 258, 262, 268, 283
Nino, Pedro, 318
Nombre de Dios, 346
Noronhas, Archbishop of Lisbon, 88
—— Martin de, 280
—— Pedro de, 219
North Sea, 142, 150, 163, 184, 190, 205
Northeast Passage, 155, 210
Northwest Passage, 189
Norway, 141, 146, 161-4, 168-9, 183-4, 192

O

Obsidian, 329
Ocoa Bay, 310
Odemira, 71, 327
Ojeda, 300-1, 328, 337
Olof, Lady, 149, 166
Orkneys, 126, 164
Oro, Rio d', 217, 258, 264
Orinoco, 320, 326
Ounartok, 194
Ouro, Rio del, 112, 207
Ovando, 324, 357-9, 361
Oysters, 304, 323
Ozama River, 316, 327, 331

P

Palm, 216, 252-3, 257, 276, 284, 302, 329
Palmas, 217
Palos, 3, 90, 157, 227, 282-3, 312
Pamir, 128

Panama, 346
Paradise, site of, 3, 4, 95, 272 325
Paria, 320-5, 336
Parrot, 73, 242, 245, 248, 252, 260
Parrot fish, 246
Pavia, 31-8, 44-5
Pearls, 216, 251, 254, 257, 324
Pearl Coast, 324, 328
Pearls, Gulf of, 324
Peccary, 344
Pelegro, Antonio, 22
Pellacano, Francesco, 44
Pepper, 207, 216-17, 345
Perestrello, Bartholomew, 87-8, 92, 97, 100, 104-5
———, Bartholomew the younger, 90, 104-5
Petrel, 233, 237
Pewter trade, English, 59
Phœnician voyages, 97, 110-11
Piacenza, 7, 10-11, 87
Pimento, 305
Pine woods, 211, 258, 264
Pines, Isle of, 208
Pineapple, 292, 356
Pinning's Judgment, 155
Pinta, La, 227, 234-5, 237, 258, 264, 268, 283
Pinzon, Martin, 227, 234-8, 250, 254, 264-5
Pinzon, Vincente, 227
Pirates, Easterling, 65
——— English, 60, 65, 277
——— French, 71-2

Pirates, *cont'd*.
——— Mediterranean, 12, 13, 19, 51, 57, 62-5, 67-8, 70, 72, 73-4
——— Norwegian, 156
Pitto family, 26
Pius the Second, 340
Pliny, 109, 114-15, 130, 143, 161
Porras, Francesco di, 359-60
Porto Bello, 346, 354
Porto Rico, 293, 312, 335
Porto Santo, 87-90, 92-101 104-6, 206, 319
Portuguese, Atlantic expeditions of, 87, 100-1, 156-9, 224-5
  colonies of Porto Santo and Madeira, 87-90, 92-104
  West African settlements, 97-100, 106
  trade with Malaguette, 216
  settlement on Gold Coast, 72, 218-22
  voyages to India and China, 87
  ——— to the North Sea, 155
  treaties with Spain, 207-8, 279, 281
  opposition to Columbus, 222, 271-2, 279-81
Posidonius, 124
Postman, the ship, 223-4
Poti, 20, 47
Ptolemy's Geography, 33, 43-5, 83, 114, 122-3, 130-1, 138
Puerto, Geronimo del, 85-6

INDEX. 377

Pulque, 350
Pytheas, 132

Q
Quarto, 22, 25
Queen's Garden, 306, 337, 355
Quezzi, 16, 22
Quibian, Quibio, 349-51
Quinto, 8, 15-17, 22-5, 28
Quinsay, 136, 249, 253

R
Rabbits, 92, 208
Rabida, La, 91, 157, 225-7, 284
Rainless zone, 293
Ravenna, geographer, 43-4
Rays and skates, 152-3, 294, 310, 342
Redonda Island, 292
Reed sparrow, 234
Remora, 307
Réné of Provence, 46, 55-6, 68-9
Retreta, 347
Rhipæan Hills, 161-3
Rhubarb, 20, 263
Rincon, Antonio del, 76
Roldan, 327-31, 336
Romano Pane, 214-15
Rorqual, 151, 175
Rosato, Ambrosio, 40
Rum Cay, 277 (see Guanima)

S
Saama, Factory of, 218
Sabæans, 39-40
Saffron, 58
Salamanca, 226
Salineri, 24
Salmon, 170, 182, 259
Saltes, 90, 282
Samana, 215, 266, 295
San Antonio, monastery, 280
San Domingo, town, 91, 327, 330-2, 336, 358, 361-2
San Lucar, 319, 321, 362
San Pietro, island, 56
San Remo, 17
San Salvador, 103, 240-1, 276-7 (see Guanahani, Watling's Island)
San Stefano, abbey, 18-21
Sanchez, 361
Santa Clara de Moguer, 268, 284
Santa Cruz, 293, 335
Santa Fé, 227
Santa Gloria, bay, 356, 358-61
Santa Maria, island, 271-3
—— —— port, 268
Santa Maria, ship, 227
Santa Maria la Antigua, church, 293, 364
—— —— of Guadaloupe, church, 268, 284
—— —— of Loretto, church, 268
—— —— of La Rabida, 284
—— —— of Redonda, 292
Santiago, 209
Saometo, 244, 246-50, 277 (see Isabella Island, Long Island)
Sargasso Sea, 108, 231

Sagres, Cape, 113
Savona, 6, 7, 17, 26-9, 47-8, 52
Scammony, 58, 303
Scandinavian Voyages to Greenland, 182, 183, 205
—— —— to Vinland, 162-6, 169-81
—— intercourse with America, 191
Scillacio, 39-41, 101, 120
Scio, 47, 58
Scotland, 122, 140, 198-200
Scotus, 325
Sea cock, fish, 246
Seals, 95, 182, 218
Segovia, 363
Seneca, 125, 188
Senegambia, 97-9, 113, 207, 212, 216
Serpent's Mouth, 320
Sertorius, 94
Service tree, 183
Seven Cities, 99, 107, 115, 159
Seville, 226, 231, 237-8, 282, 328, 334, 362
Sforza, Francesco, 62-3
Sforza Ludovico, 38
Sherbro River, 113
Shetland, 140, 190-2, 195-6
Sicily, 20, 47, 58-9, 101, 251
Sierra Leone, 108
Sinclair, Henry, 190-1, 193, 196-8, 204-5
Sixareens, 199
Skalholt, 144
Skraelings, 165, 175, 184
Snorri Sturlusson, 167
Socotra, 20, 58

Southampton, 19, 57, 61, 65
Spinola, Baptista, 86
Spice trade, 16, 20, 135, 216, 255, 263, 285, 303-4, 316
Spitzbergen, 156, 189
St. Amaro, 233
St. Ambrose, 325
St. Augustine, 42
St. Brandan, 193, 212
St. Christopher's, island, 293
St. Elmo's Fire, 288
St. Elmo Cape, 266
St. George's Bank, 18, 30
St. George Fort, 139, 212, 219-20, 223, 279
St. Jerome, 43, 95
St. John's, island, 293, 335
St. Martin's, island, 293
St. Michael's, 272
St. Nicholas, church, 182
—— —— harbor, 259
St. Thomas, church, 192, 194
—— —— fort of, 302-3, 313
—— —— island, 207
St. Vincent, Cape, 12, 56-7, 71-3, 113, 127, 282, 317-19
Statius Sebosus, 115
Stockfish, 140, 149, 192
Stone axes, 291, 329
Stone tower in Pamir, 128
Strabo, 124, 346
Strabus, 325
Sugar trade, 58, 92, 100-2, 208
Sunfish, 337
Sweyn of Denmark, 162
Swords, palm wood, 329

INDEX. 379

T

Tacitus, 126
Tartary, 156-8
Teive, Diogo de, 157
Teneriffe, 208-9, 229, 259, 278
Terebinth, 58
Terra Rossa, 15, 24
Theophilus, 128
Thingore, 164, 168
Thorfinn Karlsefne, 175-83
Thorleif Bjornsson, 149-50
Thorshavn, 140, 193, 205
Thorstein, son of Eric the Red, 174-5
Thorwald, 172, 179, 181
Three Points, Cape, 220
Thule, 5, 43, 122, 123, 126, 131-2, 138-9, 143, 154
Tiburon, Cape, 310
Tides, 138, 188, 205, 282
Tiflis, 20
Tin, 60, 118, 172
Titianus, Itinerary of, 128
Tobacco, 242, 256
Tobazo, Antonio, 85
Torfoeus, 165
Torres, Antonio de, 155
Torres, Luis de, 253
Torriano, 38
Tortuga, 304
Toscanelli, 107, 134-7, 234
Triana, Roderigo de, 239
Trinidad, 320-2
Tristan, Diego, 352
Tropic birds, 102, 232-5
Tunis, 56
Tunnies, 109, 232, 234, 266-7

Turtle, 209, 284, 291, 307-8, 350
Turtledove, 234
Tyre, trade of, 19-20

U

Ufizzi Gallery, Florence, 77-81
Ulmo, Fernand d', 159

V

Valcalda, 17, 28
Valladolid, 364
Vasco da Gama, 87
Vaz, Tristram, 93, 97
Vazo, Antonio, 85
Vega, 298-9, 313, 327, 331
Velasco, Pedro de, 158
Velasquez, Pedro, 157
Venezuela, 324
Venice, 12, 13, 52, 63-4, 345
—— trade of, 57-9, 101-2
Veragua, 43, 339, 345-6, 349
Vespucci, Amerigo, 328
Verde, Cape, 100, 113-15, 208, 220
Verga, Cape, 210
Villa, Pedro de, 268
Villafranca, 280
Vincenti, Martin, 105
Vines, 170, 176, 181, 293, 303
Vinland, 160, 162-5, 167, 175-7, 180, 183-5, 191, 193, 204
Virgin Isles, 293
Visconti, family, 88
Viverro, 50, 52
Volcanoes, 189-94, 209-12, 229

W

Walkendorf, Archbishop, 185

Warwick, the King-maker, 65-70
Watling's Island, 240-2 (*see* Guanahani and San Salvador)
Wells, Isle of, 337
Westmann Isles, 132, 148
Whale, 103, 151, 175, 180, 233, 246
Whiteman's Land, 173, 181
White Sea, 156, 161, 194
Wididale, 168
Wine trade, 92, 101
Witnesses' Islands, 324
Woman's Island, 335
Wool trade, English, 20, 58-60, 149

X
Xaragua, 299, 327, 332, 357

Y
Yams, 216, 254, 292, 309, 339
Yarmouth, 147
Yucatan, 115, 338
Yucca, 254, 292

Z
Zabræ, 129
Zacton, 135
Zarco, 93, 96, 97-9
Zeni, voyages of, 188-93, 195-200, 204

www.ingramcontent.com/pod-product-compliance
Lightning Source LLC
Chambersburg PA
CBHW030400230426
43664CB00007BB/680